Norfolk Record Society
Volume LXIX for 2005

John Buxton (1685–1731), a portrait attributed to Michael Dahl (NWHCM: 1963.268.7). The date is not known but letter no. 74 from John Buxton to Robert Buxton, dated 3 September 1726, refers to the arrival of a portrait of Anne Buxton after a two year wait, with John Buxton's portrait seemingly already in the family's possession (CUL Buxton Papers, 35/60).

JOHN BUXTON
NORFOLK GENTLEMAN
AND ARCHITECT

Letters to his Son

1719–1729

Edited by
ALAN MACKLEY

Norfolk Record Society
Volume LXIX
2005

First published in 2005
by the Norfolk Record Society

ISBN 0 9538298 7 1

Produced by John Saunders Design & Production
Printed by Biddles Ltd. King's Lynn

Contents

Illustrations

Plates

The frontispiece and plates 1–2 are reproduced by kind permission of Norwich Castle Museum and Art Gallery. Plates 3 & 7 are from originals in a private collection. Plate 6 is reproduced by kind permission of the Syndics of Cambridge University Library.

Figures

Preface

The first steps towards the publication of John Buxton's letters were taken by Anthony Paget Baggs. He transcribed some two-thirds of the letters presented in this volume, and drafted notes about the Buxton family. I owe him a considerable debt for his work and also one to the compiler of the catalogue of the Buxton Papers in the Manuscripts Reading Room of Cambridge University Library. Navigating through this large collection has been much easier for me than it was for earlier users of the archive. Thanks are also due to the staffs of the Norfolk Record Office, Norwich Millennium Library, Cambridge University Library, the library of the University of East Anglia, Norwich Castle Museum and Art Gallery, and the Suffolk and Buckinghamshire Record Offices.

David Cubitt's knowledge of Norfolk and Norwich people proved invaluable and the Suffolk Local History Council's excellent network of parish recorders, including Graham Blaxill, Sue Risborough, Brian Seward, Jill Stevens and Wendy Walpole, assisted with questions about the parishes where the Buxtons had connections. Nesta Evans and Chris Reeve answered queries about horse racing and Beccles and Bungay. Andy Nicholson identified people and places in Nottinghamshire. Elizabeth Stratton, Edgar Browning Archivist at Clare College, Cambridge, was able to identify masters, tutors and alumni mentioned in John and Robert Buxton's letters. Sir Thomas Beevor and Hugh Beevor were generous with their advice and time concerning illustrations of John Buxton's houses.

The identification of John and Robert Buxton's books was a challenge and Dr Suzie West provided help with sources. Interpreting the Buxtons' use of Latin and Italian also required specialist assistance. I am indebted to Professor Christopher Harper-Bill for handling John Buxton's sometimes wayward Latin, not helped by my hesitant transcriptions. Dr James Campbell and Professor James Diggle finally established the meaning of a statement supposed to have been made by the Kent country house, Mereworth Castle. Allessandra Mattanza helped with an Italian proverb. Following Robert Buxton to Oxford, I contacted the Museum of the History of Science, housed in a building he visited. Andy Hudson, the librarian, introduced me to anamorphosis and an anamorphoscope of the type seen by Buxton in 1729.

The Norfolk Record Society's General Editor, Professor Richard Wilson, provided encouragement and support and his pertinent questions and editorial pencil have improved this volume. Lastly I thank my wife Ursula for tolerating the presence of the Buxton family in our house for many months. They were demanding guests and, until now with my work finished, would talk only to me.

The letters are published with the permission of the Syndics of Cambridge University Library.

Alan Mackley
Editor
Blythburgh, Suffolk

Abbreviations

Blomefield	F. Blomefield, *An essay towards the topographical history of the county of Norfolk*, continued by C. Parkin, second edition, 11 vols (1805–10)
Burke's and Savills	*Burke's and Savills Guide to Country Houses*, III, East Anglia (1981)
Colvin	H. Colvin, *A Biographical Dictionary of British Architects 1600–1840*, third edition (New Haven and London, 1995)
Cozens-Hardy	B. Cozens-Hardy and E.A. Kent, *The Mayors of Norwich, 1403–1835* (Norwich, 1938)
CUL	Cambridge University Library
d.	pence (12d. = 1s.; 240 d. = £1)
Drabble	*The Oxford Companion to English Literature*, ed. M. Drabble (Oxford, 1985)
Foster	Joseph Foster, *Alumni Oxonienses, 1715–1886* (2 vols. Oxford, 1888)
Hasler	P.W. Hasler, *The History of Parliament, The House of Commons, 1558–1603* (3 vols. 1981)
Henning	B.D. Henning, *The History of Parliament, 1660–1690* (1983)
Ingamells	J. Ingamells, *A Dictionary of British and Irish Travellers in Italy 1701–1800* (New Haven and London, 1997)
NRO	Norfolk Record Office
ODNB	*Oxford Dictionary of National Biography* (Oxford, 2004)
Pevsner	*The Buildings of England:*
	Bedfordshire and the County of Huntingdon and Peterborough (Harmondsworth, 1968)
	and Elizabeth Williamson, *Buckinghamshire* (Harmondsworth, 1994)
	Cambridgeshire (Harmondsworth, 1970)

	and Elizabeth Williamson, *Derbyshire* (Harmondsworth, 1979)
	and Bill Wilson, *Norfolk 1: Norwich and North-East* (Harmondsworth, 1997)
	and Bill Wilson, *Norfolk 2: North-West and South* (Harmondsworth, 1999)
	and Elizabeth Williamson, *Nottinghamshire* (Harmondsworth, 1979)
	and Jennifer Sherwood, *Oxfordshire* (Harmondsworth, 1999)
	Staffordshire (Harmondsworth, 1974)
	and Alexandra Wedgwood, *Warwickshire* (Harmondsworth, 1966)
Rye	W. Rye, *Norfolk Families* (Norwich, 1911–13)
s.	shillings (20s. = £1)
Sedgwick	Romney Sedgwick, *The History of Parliament, The House of Commons, 1715–1754* (2 vols. 1970)
Sloan	A. W. Sloan, Englis*h Medicine in the Seventeenth Century* (Durham, 1996)
SRO	Suffolk Record Office
Thorne	R.G. Thorne, *The History of Parliament, The House of Commons, 1790–1820* (5 vols. 1986)
Venn	John Venn and J.A. Venn, *Alumni Cantabrigienses* (6 vols. Cambridge, 1922–54)

Editorial Practice

Rules of Transcription

Original spelling has been retained, with some departures from modern practice identified to avoid ambiguity. Underlinings have been transcribed as used by the letter writers. '&ca' has been transcribed '&c.' Punctuation has been modernised and contractions and abbreviations expanded except where the usage is still current. Abbreviated Christian names have been extended.

Capitalisation has been modernised and used sparingly. Nicknames, pet names and courtesy titles used within the Buxton family and of their acquaintances have been capitalized. Titles, ranks and administrative posts have been capitalized when accompanied by a personal name, and institutions when associated with a place.

For personal and place names, a corrected or modern equivalent has been added in square brackets, at the first occurrence in each letter.

The letter writers used the old calendar with the year ending on Lady Day, 25 March. Dates have been converted to modern practice and expressed at the heads of letters in the form '10 April 1723'. Monetary symbols such as £, s., and d., have been added where necessary to aid clarity.

Symbols and Editorial Conventions

italics	Editorial additions, within the text contained by square brackets.
[word]	Words missing through damage to MS that have been supplied.
[*? word*]	Missing words that cannot be supplied.
* *	Insertions by the letter writer.
< >	Deletions by the letter writer. Insertions and deletions have only been marked when they suggest a change of mind.
[?]	Uncertainty about the transcription of a word.
/…../	Marginal entry or annotation by the letter writer.

Sources

London may be assumed to be the place of publication unless otherwise indicated.

Word definitions, unless otherwise noted, are based upon the *Oxford English Dictionary*, second edition, CD-ROM version 3.01 (Oxford, 2002). Where reference has been made to the *Oxford Dictionary of National Biography*, the on-line 2004 edition has been used. Not all of the sources consulted for Norfolk and Norwich family histories in the preparation of the footnotes have been individually cited. They include original sources such as parish registers, freemen's rolls, wills and monumental inscriptions, and histories of places and institutions. Reference books such as *Burke's Landed Gentry* and *Kelly's Local Directories* have also been used without citation.

Introduction

The Letters

John Buxton (1685–1731) was a south Norfolk landowner with a reputation as a skilful amateur architect. By his early thirties he was securely settled with his wife Anne and a growing family at Channonz Hall in the parish of Tibenham, where the Buxton family had held property for at least two hundred years. The four thousand acres he owned were concentrated in Tibenham and the surrounding parishes, and in Rushford, some twelve miles to the west near the town of Thetford, on the edge of Breckland.

John Buxton's Norfolk was populous and prosperous. Daniel Defoe travelled through it in 1722.[1] He described the south of the county as thronged with great and spacious market towns. Even the villages were so large and full of people that they were equal to market towns in other counties. The countryside prospered alongside Norwich, the second city in England, enjoying the wealth created by its thriving textile industry.

John Buxton had four surviving sons. The letters presented in this volume were written between 1719 and 1729 to his eldest son Robert (1710–1751). The series begins with nine-year-old Robert at school in Harleston, a small market town just twelve miles from Channonz. Robert then spent some years under the same master at a school in the village of Playford, near Ipswich, Suffolk.[2] The correspondence continued when Robert entered Clare Hall in the university of Cambridge. It ends with Robert just down from Cambridge at the age of twenty, a few months before his father's death. Only a few letters survive from the early years but for 1724 there are fourteen, and over twenty for each of the years from 1725 to 1729, suggesting that a letter was written around once a fortnight. Few of Robert Buxton's letters to his father have survived.[3] The published letters are however part of a large collection that includes letters

[1] D. Defoe, *A Tour through the whole Island of Great Britain*, ed., P.N. Furbank, W.R. Owens and A.J. Coulson (New Haven and London, 1991), pp. 23–4.

[2] The first letter written to Playford is no. 17, 21 April 1723, p. 43, below.

[3] An example is letter no. 135, 7 September 1729, p. 154, below.

written by other members of the family to Robert Buxton both at school and at Cambridge. There are also letters written by John Buxton, and by his wife Anne, to each other and to other people. Reference is made to some of these.

The main features of John Buxton's estate, his activities, his interests and enthusiasms, and those of his son, can be established not only from the letters but also from other papers in the Buxton archive. Financial accounts, rentals, journals and book lists, add to our knowledge of the Buxtons' social and economic status, their practical and intellectual interests, their love of books and their delight in architecture and visiting country houses.

The introduction considers first the relationship of the letters to the large collection of surviving Buxton papers. The rise of the family as south Norfolk landowners is then summarised before considering the light thrown by the letters on the relationship between father and son, the nature of Robert's education, and broader aspects of family life in south Norfolk in the 1720s. John Buxton's position as a significant member of the landed community is discussed, with particular reference to his architectural interests and building activity.[4] In conclusion, a brief history of the Buxton family from the death of John Buxton to the sale of its Norfolk estates in 1898 is provided.

The Buxton papers

John Buxton's letters are a small part of the voluminous surviving papers of the Buxtons, a Norfolk gentry family of Channonz Hall, Tibenham, and later of Shadwell, near Thetford. The major part of the collection was presented to Cambridge University Library by Maud Buxton in 1901, following the sale of Shadwell Court.[5] She presented additional papers between 1908 and 1926, and a further box of material was transferred from the Wiltshire Archaeological Society in 1966. The collection now comprises 131 boxes and miscellaneous individual items, extending to about 11,600 documents dating from around 1160 to 1926. There are over 1,200 charters and deeds, half of which date from before 1517. Long runs of court rolls and court books from the early fourteenth century survive, with surveys, rentals and accounts. The personal papers include household, political and administrative material,

[4] This introduction draws upon unpublished notes made by Anthony Paget Baggs when he transcribed some of the letters, and the fine catalogue for the Buxton archive prepared in the 1990s in the Cambridge University Library Department of Manuscripts. G. Wiedermann, 'The Buxton Papers', *Bulletin of the Friends of Cambridge University Library*, 19 (1998), pp. 28–31.

[5] The house, when built by John Buxton, was described as Shadwell Lodge. In its extended nineteenth-century form it became Shadwell Court. The property is now known as Shadwell Park.

with over 3,000 letters. There are about 100 wills and probates, together with the architectural drawings of John Buxton.

Although the Buxton papers were not fully catalogued until the 1990s[6] they have long attracted the attention of historians. The Reverend E.K. Bennet, rector of Brettenham, a parish church on the Buxton estate, acted as family archivist in the 1880s and compiled the first calendars of letters and medieval deeds.[7] Early in the twentieth century, Dr Augustus Jessopp published a report on the collection for the Historical Manuscripts Commission[8], including his transcripts of a selection of letters from the sixteenth and seventeenth centuries. More recent published work based upon the Buxton papers includes a study of agrarian history in south Norfolk, John Buxton's architectural activities, and the decorative painter and portraitist Thomas Bardwell.[9]

The Buxton family

The Buxtons were an old Norfolk family, probably originating from Oulton or Irmingland near Buxton, from which the family name almost certainly derives.[10] John Buxton junior (d. 1522) is the earliest family member to be recorded. Robert Buxton (d. 1528) acquired the manor of Channonz near Tibenham by marriage to Christiana Glemham; his son John (1488–1572) built Channonz Hall during the 1560s. It was the Buxton family home until

[6] The catalogue is available on-line at http://www.lib.cam.ac.uk/MSS/Buxton/

[7] Bennet's particular interest was Rushford College. He published 'Notes on the original statutes of the College of St John the Evangelist of Rushford, Co. Norfolk, founded by Edmund Gonville, A.D. 1342', *Norfolk Archaeology*, 10 (1884–7), pp. 50–64, and 'The College of St John the Evangelist of Rushford, Co. Norfolk', *Norfolk Archaeology*, 10 (1884–7), pp. 277–382.

[8] Dr Augustus Jessopp (1823–1914), schoolmaster and historian, was headmaster of King Edward VI's School, Norwich, from 1859 to 1879. He retired to become rector of Scarning (Norfolk). A. Jessop, 'The Manuscripts of Miss Buxton at Shadwell Court, Norfolk', Historical Manuscripts Commission *Various Collections*, 2 (1903), pp. xix-xxiii and 227–88.

[9] A.J. Davison, 'Some aspects of the agrarian history of Hargham and Snetterton as revealed in the Buxton MSS', *Norfolk Archaeology*, 35 (1970–73), pp. 335–55; M. Girouard, 'Shadwell Park, Norfolk. The home of Sir John and Lady Musker', *Country Life*, 2 July 1964, pp. 18–21 ('Part I') and 9 July 1964, pp. 98–102 ('Part II') and 'Shadwell Park, Norfolk' in *The Victorian Country House* (New Haven and London, 1979), pp. 194–204; A.P. Baggs, 'Channons Hall', *Norfolk Archaeology*, 34 (1966–9), pp. 9–13; E.J. Rose, 'The Aslacton painting of Channonz Hall, Tibenham, and an early cartographic illustration', *Norfolk Archaeology*, 40 (1987–89), pp. 109–13; M. Kirby Talley, 'Thomas Bardwell of Bungay, artist and author, 1704–1767, with a checklist of works', *Walpole Society*, 46 (1976–8), pp. 91–163.

[10] The Buxton family tree is shown in Figure 1.

replaced in the eighteenth century by Shadwell Lodge, built by John Buxton, the writer of these letters.[11]

The family prospered through careful land management and judicious marriages. Their rise to prominence in Norfolk landed society followed Robert Buxton's (*c.* 1533–1607) appointment as surveyor and lawyer to Thomas Howard, fourth Duke of Norfolk, from 1559 until the duke's death in 1572. He then served the duke's son Philip, Earl of Arundel in the same capacity and astutely profited from the political downfall of the earl and his attainder, being appointed one of the government's surveyor generals of the Howard lands in Norfolk and Suffolk. He was rewarded first with the lease of Rushford College (1580) and then obtained a license to purchase the property in 1599. Robert Buxton was active in both local and national politics: he was mayor of Thetford in 1588 and 1597, a justice of the peace in Norfolk in 1590–7 and 1604–7; and M.P. for constituencies in Sussex under Howard patronage at various times from the 1550s to the 1580s.

Robert's great-grandson John (1608–60) led the family during the political turmoil of the seventeenth century, facing civil war and, as one identified with the royalist cause, particular problems during the Interregnum. John continued the family tradition of legal training (he was admitted to Gray's Inn in 1626) and was a notable patron of the theatre and collector of books.[12] But as an important member of the Norfolk gentry he was inevitably drawn into political conflict. He was a lieutenant colonel in the county militia and although involved in mustering troops and military exercises, yet does not seem to have taken part in any civil war campaigns. He became high sheriff of Norfolk in May 1638. His obligation to collect ship money exposed him to the prospect of being called before a committee to account for his actions when the Long Parliament of 1640 declared the collection of the tax illegal. No action ensued but he could not avoid some harassment by the army in the 1640s and, in 1656, when he was elected M.P. for Norfolk, he was barred as a royalist from taking up his seat. Robert Buxton died in 1660 just one month before the Commonwealth collapsed and Charles II made his entry into London.

Robert Buxton was succeeded by his son Robert (1633–62) who died in his twenties, surviving his father by only two years. The following generations

[11] John and Robert alternatively recur as the names of the heads of the Buxton family.

[12] This is when the Buxton library was established. Details of this, and John Buxton's expenditure during his months as a student at Gray's Inn, and the early years of his marriage, including the birth of his first child and the refitting of Channonz Hall, are discussed in D. McKitterick, '"Ovid with a Littleton": the cost of English books in the seventeenth century', *Transactions of the Cambridge Bibliographical Society*, XI:2 (1997), pp. 184–234.

were also short-lived. John Buxton (1659–82) was only three when his father died and, like him, he was not to live long, being only 23 when he died at Orleans while on a continental tour. His brother Robert (1659–91) continued the family line. He married Elizabeth Gooch (1664–1730), 'Grandmother Gooch' of the letters, daughter of Leonard Gooch of Earsham (d. 1686), a property that would devolve to their son John (1685–1731) through his mother. Other Gooch connections were important to John. His aunt Barbara Gooch married Sir Edward Ward Bt (1684–1719) of Bixley. Bixley and Earsham were both to provide John Buxton with an opportunity to deploy his skill as an amateur architect. But his most important connection came through Leonard Gooch's brother Clement whose daughter Anne (1691–1741) he was to marry.

John Buxton was born at Wenhaston in east Suffolk[13] on 15 September 1685. The Buxtons had relatives in the area. Isabella Buxton (1628–64) had married into the Acton family of Bramfield in the mid seventeenth century, and her brother John (*c.* 1640–1714) established a branch of the family at South Elmham, St Margaret. John Buxton's father maintained the Buxton family heads' melancholy tradition of dying young, at the age of 32, when John was only six. Yet, unlike many contemporaries, the Buxtons survived in the male line through the testing years of high mortality from around the mid seventeenth century to 1730. Nevertheless, John Buxton's frequent apprehension for the health of his family that is such a feature of the letters is understandable.[14]

Only fragmentary information has survived concerning John Buxton's early years. His mother's account book records his school expenses in Bury St Edmunds (Suffolk) in the year of his father's death: half a year's board cost £8 12s. 6d. with dancing and writing extra. Four years later, when he was ten, he was at a Mr Turner's school in Fressingfield, also in Suffolk. Boarding for three-quarters of the year cost £9 and schooling £2 4s. 6d. with no extras noted. Buxton later recalled an aspect of his schooldays in a letter to twelve-year-old Robert in 1722: 'The pleasure of breaking up school I remember used to be very great when I was your age'.[15]

John Buxton entered Clare Hall, Cambridge, in May 1703. It is not known whether he graduated but in one of his letters there is an indication that he left to attend Gray's Inn.[16] In 1704 he inherited a small estate at Earsham[17] from

[13] Wenhaston: a village near the market town of Halesworth, 11 miles south-east of Bungay. John Buxton's birthplace is given in the Clare Hall index of alumni.

[14] See p. 16, below.

[15] Letter no. 15, 4 December 1722, p. 41 below.

[16] Buxton does not appear as a graduate in either the Clare Hall index of alumni or Venn. See letter no. 112, 6 March 1728, p. 128, below.

[17] Earsham: a south Norfolk village and parish close to the county boundary, on the river Waveney one mile west of Bungay.

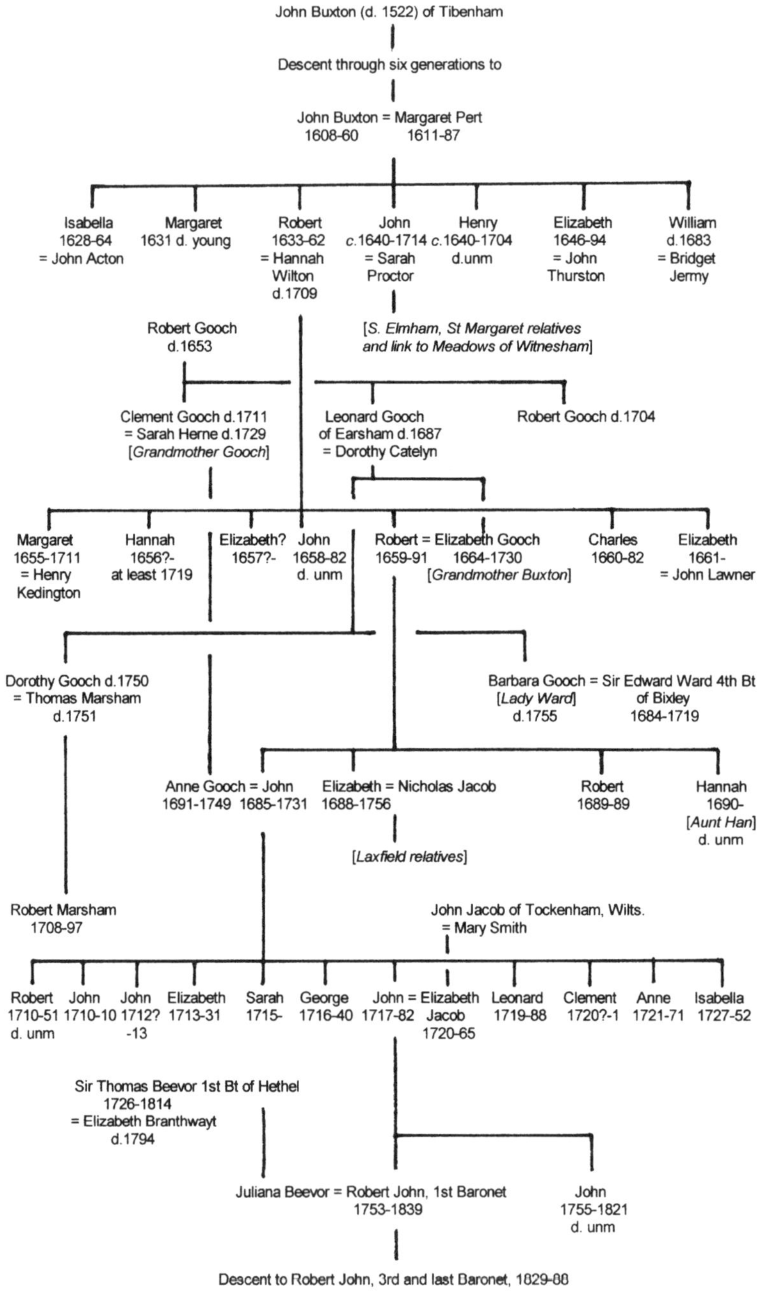

FIGURE 1. The Buxton family tree and its connections with the Gooch family.

his childless uncle, Robert Gooch.[18] Five years later, when 24, he married within the south Norfolk gentry community, to a cousin on his mother's side, eighteen-year-old Anne, the daughter of Clement Gooch of Earsham and Sarah Herne. In the same year he attended the sale of the contents of the Paston property, Oxnead Hall, and spent over £200 on pictures and furniture.[19]

Newly married, John Buxton calculated his wealth in 1710.[20] His annual rental income had been £1,007 before his marriage and was now £1,183. Valuing his land at 20 years purchase and taking into account his wife's marriage portion of £3,000, and a further £1,000 due at her father's death, less £3,000 paid to his sister, John Buxton was worth £26,660. A survey by John Buckenham in 1719 showed that Buxton's estate extended to 4,482 acres.[21] Although his rental income reflected that much of his estate was either marginal breckland around Rushford, or heavy south Norfolk clayland in the Tibenham area, John Buxton was clearly a member of the greater gentry, both by income and landholding.[22]

John Buxton's family was not then living at Channonz, the house being occupied by his mother. He was probably residing at Topcroft, where his first children were born.[23] Certainly, John Buxton's family eventually settled at

[18] CUL Buxton Papers, 97/16, Will dated 1695 of Robert Gooch of Earsham, probate granted in 1704. Four farms in Earsham that Robert had inherited from Leonard Gooch went directly to John Buxton. The manor of Dubballs in Earsham, with a house and farm, was left to Robert's brother Clement (he was living in the house and rented the farm) for his life. On his death the property went to John Buxton. John Buxton's patrimony was managed in conjunction with his mother. An agreement to lease Buxton land in Rushford to Thomas Slapp in 1705 is signed by John Buxton of Channonz and Elizabeth Buxton of Rushford (where she occupied a house at times during the period of the letters). CUL Buxton Papers, 122/34.

[19] Oxnead Hall, the Paston seat, was a sixteenth-century house extended by Sir William Paston (d. 1663) when the fortunes of the family were at their zenith. R.W. Ketton-Cremer, *Norfolk Portraits* (1944), pp. 17–40. The sale was forced by the vast debts of William Paston, second Earl of Yarmouth, who died, the last of his line, on Christmas Day, 1732. Buxton bought portraits and furniture, probably not just for himself, given that his purchases included 82 pictures and 54 chairs. Ketton-Cremer, in *Norfolk Portraits*, pp. 22–57 and *Norfolk Assembly* (1957), pp. 218–9, discusses Buxton's acquisitions after the break-up of the Paston estate following the earl of Yarmouth's death.

[20] See Appendix B.

[21] The largest single holding was 2,461 acres in Rushford, followed by 752 acres in Tibenham, 277 acres in Bunwell and 184 in Thuxton. CUL Buxton Papers, 96/49.

[22] The statistician Gregory King's (1648–1712) *Natural and Political Observations upon the State and Condition of England, 1696* (not published in full until 1801) provides the analysis of gentry landholdings and income closest in time to John Buxton. King's work is discussed by G.E. Mingay, *English Landed Society in the Eighteenth Century* (1963), p. 22.

[23] Twins John and Robert, born in 1710, of whom only Robert survived. An earlier generation

Earsham (a son, John, was born there in 1717) where he built a new house around 1712[24] establishing a reputation as 'A fine genius very curious in such designs, which he shewed also in the very neat house he built at Earsham'. He also provided a design for the rebuilding of Bixley Hall, Sir Edward Ward's house, paid for, it was suggested at the time, with the marriage portion of his wife, Barbara Gooch.[25]

Given only occasional references to servants in the letters it is not possible to judge the size or composition of John Buxton's household. Neither he nor his wife used this term. They wrote of 'the family' as embracing not only parents and children and relatives but also the servants living under their roof.[26] It was therefore a particular affront to John Buxton for him to find an addition to the 'family' when he returned to Channonz after visiting Robert in Suffolk in July 1726:

> Don't you think I was much surprized when I last returned from you to find the addition to the family here.[27] Their foolish management is no less to be blamed than their vice. I have determined for example sake that Richard shall leave my service, my Lady Ward's man comes in his room.

Anne Buxton included her cooks and maids in her 'family' when she wrote to Robert:

> My family still continue in great disorder; & one of my new cookes came a Sunday so ill that I was forced to send her home againe; & now my maid Bab have heared of a place & is a going.[28]

of Buxtons had moved to Topcroft Hall, owned by the family of Hannah Wilton, the widow of Robert Buxton (John Buxton's great uncle), after his death in 1662.

24 John Buxton signed an agreement on 6 June 1712 with John Rackham of Bungay, for 'carpenters work of a capital mansion ... now erecting at Earsham'. Rackham was still working there in 1713 (on a dove-house) and received payments through to October 1714. CUL Buxton Papers, 122/42. See p. 23, below.

25 James Hargrave Harrison, *Postwick and relatives, written in the early part of the eighteenth century*, ed. Thomas Harrison (Great Yarmouth, 1858), p. 17. The text is dated 1735–6. Sir Edward Ward died in 1719.

26 The 'language of kinship' is discussed by Naomi Tadmor in *Family and Friends in Eighteenth-Century England*, (Cambridge, 2001).

27 Apparently a reference to an illegitimate birth resulting from a liaison between Buxton servants. Letter no. 70, 26 July 1726, p. 90, below.

28 Letter from Anne Buxton to Robert Buxton, addendum to letter no. 100, 4 October 1727, p. 117, below.

Only fragmentary information survives about John Buxton's public activity up to 1719. He held militia commissions as a captain in 1713 and major in 1715 in the White Regiment of Foot raised in Earsham Hundred, and he was nominated a deputy lieutenant of the county in 1731.[29] He was a justice of the peace but there is no evidence of any further involvement in public affairs. He concentrated upon estate matters and his growing family. Earsham was sold in 1720 to Colonel Windham[30]; other property was inherited and bought. Although the composition of his estate changed, his annual rent roll in 1729 was £1,173 10s., little different from its proceeds in 1710.

John Buxton never went on a continental Grand Tour, then such a fashionable part of a gentleman's education. Yet, with a growing interest in architecture, he made an extended journey through England in May 1720, when he visited many country houses as far north as Lancashire and Yorkshire. The brief journal he kept is reproduced as Appendix E. Other journeys, for example to Bath, may have been occasioned by concerns about his health.

Travel provided many opportunities for looking at buildings. From London in 1717 John Buxton wrote: 'I have hitherto diverted myself with seeing the fine buildings about the town built since I lived here and am amazed wherever I turn myself'.[31] With a fierce pride in his native county, his feet were nevertheless always firmly upon the ground: 'I have beheld the court without one wish to dwell there, nor did the view of Sir Richard Child's magnificent house and gardens raise on envious thought ... this afternoon was spent at Greenwich where I saw the finest painted ceiling in England'.[32] Three weeks later he was in Bristol but not impressed:

[29] CUL Buxton Papers, 99/9–14.

[30] Colonel William Windham (1673–1730) of Earsham, was a younger brother of Ashe Windham of Felbrigg. Educated at Eton, he pursued a military career, losing a leg at the battle of Blenheim (1704). Married to Anne Tyrell, he settled first in Essex. An active speculator during the South Sea Bubble, he seems to have avoided the losses made by other members of the Windham family and was able to buy the Earsham Hall estate from John Buxton. Ketton-Cremer, *Norfolk Portraits*, p. 70 and *Felbrigg, the Story of a House* (1962), pp. 78, 80, 94 and 100.

[31] CUL Buxton Papers, 105/5, letter from John Buxton to Anne Buxton at Earsham, dated London 28 June 1717.

[32] CUL Buxton Papers, 105/6, letter from John Buxton to Anne Buxton at Earsham, dated London 4 July 1717. The financier Sir Richard Childe's (cr. Viscount Castlemaine 1718 and Earl Tylney 1733, d. 1750) Wanstead House (Essex), designed by Colen Campbell (1676–1729), was the first great Whig palace and built *c.* 1714–20. The house was demolished in 1824. C. Hussey, *English Country Houses. Early Georgian 1715–1760* (1955), p. 16; Colvin, p. 211. The Painted Hall of Greenwich Hospital was executed by Sir James Thornhill (1675–1734) in 1707–14, its baroque interior regarded as his masterpiece. G.Worsley, *Classical Architecture in England. The Heroic Age* (New Haven and London, 1995), p. 72.

> I went yesterday to Bristol, a place I had never seen before and returned [*to Bath*] this morning. It did not answer expectation, though it is reckoned here the second town in England. I think Norwich twice as large and ten times a finer town. The roads exceeding bad so that wherever I go I like my own county better than ever.[33]

But there were always grand houses to see:

> I went out at seaven this morning to Badminton, a seat of the duke of Beaufort and am just now returned at eight. It is 14 miles from this place but well worth the trouble, having the finest park I ever saw, though nothing extraordinary in the house.[34]

But the press of company in Bath during the season was not to John Buxton's taste. He wrote home in August 1717:

> This place ... is as full of company as possible. The church, the assembly, the bath and raffling shops are monstrously crowded with hoop petty coats and the streets being very narrow are scarce wide enough for some extravagant ones. I hope our country will escape this excess of this fashion which some say is about going out. I'm sure is very inconvenient in all publick places, but the ladies must be pleased.[35]

Lest his wife should think that his head had been turned by fashionable company in Bath, John Buxton reassured her with especial charm for someone married for eight years:

33 CUL Buxton Papers, 105/10, letter from John Buxton to Anne Buxton at Earsham, dated Bath 27 July 1717. The population of Norwich had probably reached 30,000 by 1700, making it easily England's largest inland town and, after London, its second city. This position was however under threat with the growth of Bristol founded upon Atlantic trade. By 1750 Bristol's population was larger than Norwich's. P.J. Corfield, 'From Second City to Regional Capital' in, C. Rawcliffe and R. Wilson, eds, *Norwich since 1550* (2004), pp. 142 and 158.

34 Badminton House was extensively remodelled by Henry Somerset (1629–1700) the first duke of Beaufort, between 1664 and 1691. John Buxton was not impressed by the interior although leading craftsmen of the Royal Works had been employed, but changes to the interior planned by Henry Somerset (1684–1714) the second duke, had not been started at the time of his death. The park was substantially extended before 1700, with the house at the hub of a great wheel of radiating avenues. N. Kingsley, *The Country Houses of Gloucestershire, II, 1660–1830* (Chichester, 1992), pp. 54–61.

35 CUL Buxton Papers, 105/18, letter from John Buxton to Anne Buxton at Earsham, dated Bath 27 August 1717.

> Nor have I seen any woman so fine or beautiful that I could choose to spend my days half so soon as with my dear wife who have made me more happy than I know any one in the married life or out of it.[36]

John Buxton and his children

By 1719 when this series of letters begins, the Buxtons were living at Channonz Hall. There were then six children. A second John had died as an infant around 1712, but the surviving Robert had two younger sisters, Elizabeth (b. 1713) and Sarah (b. 1715), and three younger brothers: George (b. 1716), John (b. 1717) and through whom the Buxton line was eventually to descend, and Leonard (b. 1719). There were more children to come: Clement, who died as an infant in 1721, Anne (b. 1721) and Isabella (b. 1727). All feature in John Buxton's letters.

In writing to Robert, John Buxton sought to instruct and exhort, defining his expectations for his son in terms of morality and duty. In sending news and gossip not only of the immediate family but also the extended network of cousins in Norfolk and Suffolk, and of friends and neighbours, John Buxton provided a framework within which his son's relationships could develop. He also offered reassurance that Robert was not forgotten during his absence at school. Robert was not shielded from the unpleasant realities of the early-eighteenth-century prevalence of sickness and death, even the suffering of those closest to him. John Buxton dealt with contemporary fears of disease with a frankness that suggests that omissions from his letters provide real insights into his own character and interests, and that he did not consciously withhold sensitive information, or any that he thought would not interest his son. John Buxton's scant coverage of politics is therefore indicative of only a moderate interest in the subject. While some discussion of estate management and money might be expected, its absence suggests a lack of concern about them that came from a period of stability in both matters. A significant omission is any reference to church attendance or formal worship. Morality clearly mattered to John Buxton, churchgoing seemingly did not.

Above all, John Buxton's letters are a medium through which he could share his great enthusiasms with his growing son. Frequent references to books and architecture include responses to Robert's own significant contributions to the exchange. Robert's letters have not survived but they obviously contained more than just formal reactions to his father's interests.[37]

[36] CUL Buxton Papers, 105/19, letter from John Buxton to Anne Buxton at Earsham, dated Bath 31 August 1717.

[37] Letter writing in this period is discussed by Rebecca Earle, 'Letters, writers and the

John Buxton was a loving father who took delight in all his children. His sons at school were not forgotten, as this collection of letters shows. And not only did Robert (and presumably George and John) receive frequent letters from their father, their mother also wrote to them. They also heard from other members of the family. Robert received letters from his grandmothers Buxton and Gooch, and from his aunts Elizabeth, Dorothy and Hannah, who sent him some lemon cakes 'which you used to like'.[38] His sisters Elizabeth and Sarah wrote in charming childlike hands at the age of ten. He also heard from his brothers and from his Marsham cousins. In this way the extended family maintained its links and each member, especially it seems the female members, remained well informed about the activities of the others.

Writers could not be certain that their letters would arrive safely. John Buxton expressed annoyance that 'the posts and carriers are very careless'.[39] He was especially scathing about the attitude to prepaid mail. He wrote to his wife:

> The letters are very apt to miscarry by the rogery of the post when you pay for them at the place they are put in at. All letters are to be paid for at the place they are sent to, for otherwise when you pay at Ipswich and writ upon the letters 'post paid' the post will pocket the money and throw away the letter. Some letters from Diss have been found in the road that disposed of by the posts and this is one of the reasons so many of ours have been lost.[40]

Anxious that the news of his grandmother Gooch's death should reach Robert quickly – he was then visiting his Marsham cousins at Stratton Strawless – John Buxton duplicated his letter, sending one by the Buckenham post and the other for collection at Mr Croshold's in Norwich.[41]

In his letters to Robert, an observant and caring John Buxton recorded the development, play, and the individual characters of all his children. We cannot know how much John Buxton's approach was influenced by his own childhood. He could hardly have known his father and he was sent away to

historian', and Susan Whyman, '"Paper visits": the post-Restoration letter as seen through the Verney family archive', in Rebecca Earle, ed., *Epistolary Selves: letters and letter-writers, 1600–1945* (Aldershot, 1999), pp. 1–36.

38 CUL Buxton Papers, 104/11. Letter from Hannah Buxton to Robert Buxton, late 1722 or early 1723.

39 Letter no. 59, 17 February 1726, p. 80, below.

40 CUL Buxton Papers, 105/84. Letter from John Buxton to Anne Buxton addressed to Mr D'Oyly's house at Playford, 2 April 1729.

41 Letter no. 149, 2 December 1729, p. 167, below.

school, as his own sons were, at an early age. At home there was his mother and two younger sisters but no brothers. His Buxton uncles died before he was born. If he had a male mentor we do not know who he was.

John Buxton wrote with pleasure about the activities he shared with his children. In October 1724 he recorded that George and John were helping to plant acorns and that their sisters (then aged eleven, nine and three) would also be joining in.[42] After the birth of Isabella in 1727 he wrote:

> Since your mother's being in bed your little sister Sarah has been both nurse & surgeon & is very expert. Lenny [*he was eight*] continues his part & is very dextrous at the candle. Betty's part is now with your mother & performs it with great assiduity & care. It is pleasant to see them give me such hopes of their being of some use in the world, a thing the ladies of this age do little think of.[43]

The tiny Isabella also drew approving comment from her father. In 1729, when she was two, she clearly charmed not only John Buxton:

> Isabell now comes into my chamber, & would fain write, she talks a great deal, lives all day with her grandmother Buxton & I never saw my sister so fond or oblidging to any child in my life, but Isabella has peculiar charms, & people can't help being delighted with her.[44]

With the older boys at school, the remaining family sometimes travelled together to visit friends and relations, for example to Laxfield some twenty miles distant. Mother and daughters even attended Bungay horseraces together in 1725.[45] John Buxton reported this to Robert without expressing approval or disapproval, but it is noteworthy that he forbad Robert and George to go to the races in Ipswich in 1726 because he did not think that it was a suitable event for them to attend.[46] Mother and daughters made a much longer journey to Doddershall in Buckinghamshire in 1729, in the company of Robert just down from Cambridge, to stay with a distant cousin, Mrs Lettice Pigott.[47]

Such journeys in the pre-turnpike period were not undertaken lightly. The

42 Letter no. 33, 27 October 1724, p. 57, below.
43 Letter no. 82, 6 March 1727, p. 101, below.
44 Letter no. 140, 29 September 1729, p. 159, below.
45 Letter no. 43, 11 July 1725, p. 67, below.
46 Letter no. 66, 5 June 1726, p. 87, below.
47 Letter no. 136, 14 September 1729, p. 155, below.

letters suggest that the condition of the roads was always a concern, even in summer. From June to August in 1725 John Buxton described the Suffolk roads as being too bad to travel on: his mother was prevented from making the journey from Laxfield to Channonz.[48] By November of that year the roads were worse than he had ever known them.[49] Cross-country journeys posed additional problems when worries about the weather were compounded by ignorance of the routes themselves. In 1729 John Buxton advised his wife to return home from Buckinghamshire via London because 'wet weather must have made the cross roads impracticable'.[50] Anne Buxton was also apprehensive that the roads would have been damaged by heavy traffic around Stourbridge fair near Cambridge.[51] Four days were allowed for the London-Norfolk leg of the journey, the travellers making no more than twenty-five miles a day.

Examples of a close family cohesion should not obscure the fact that John Buxton clearly distinguished between his sons in respect of his hopes for them and the education that he therefore thought appropriate. He also had no doubt that women had a particular role to play in life, if at times he seems to regret that they might not receive the education that would allow them to fully realise their potential. We have seen above his comment about his own daughters that: 'It is pleasant to see them give me such hopes of their being of some use in the world, a thing the ladies of this age do little think of.' John Buxton's ideal woman was epitomised by Eve in John Milton's *Paradise Lost*: 'For nothing lovelier can be found in woman than to study household good, and good works in her husband to promote.' And yet he wrote of the young Lady Selina Shirley, who was about to embark upon a journey to France:

> This young lady talks of crossing the sea & of all the fatigues & hazards of travell with great ease & indifference & makes as little of it as some people do of a Norwich journey. She has a fine temper of mind and body; what a fine thing would a right education have made her.[52]

This is a more attractive attitude to us than the blunt reminder given to Robert Buxton to write to his aunt Lady Ward: 'I fancy it would oblidge your

[48] Letters no. 41, 16 June 1725, and nos. 43–5, 11 July and 1and 11 August, 1725, pp. 64–70, below.

[49] Letter no. 47, 1 November 1725, p. 71, below.

[50] Letter no. 140, 29 September 1729, p. 159, below.

[51] CUL Buxton Papers, 105/86. Letter from Anne Buxton to John Buxton, Doddershall, 28 September 1729. Stourbridge fair , described by Defoe as not simply the greatest in the whole nation but the world, was held at Chesterton, near Cambridge. Defoe, *Tour*, pp. 37–8.

[52] Letter no. 47, 1 November 1725, p. 71, below.

Aunt Ward to send her the remarkables of the day, the king passes at Cambridge: a short account of such things as you think women can understand or be pleased with'.[53]

John Buxton's objective for his eldest son's education was stated in the first letter in this series. Robert was to be instructed in those things that are necessary for a gentleman to know. His collection of books, listed when he was thirteen years old and enlarged during his school and university years, is impressive and revealing.[54] The bible and the book of common prayer are listed, with a number of theological commentaries. There are textbooks covering Latin and Greek, and the modern languages French and Italian. Classical literature is strongly represented, with the French works of Molière and Racine, and those of John Milton. There are history, geography and mathematics books, and accounts of travel. The works of Erasmus, Rousseau, Bacon and Locke are present. There are several volumes of instructions to young men, and books about human anatomy and health. There is a single novel: Congreve's *Incognita; or, Love & Duty Reconciled.* The range is broad and demanding with a classical emphasis tempered by modern works. Robert was expected to be informed about the world and to develop the capacity for critical enquiry and the application of reason, to become a man of the Enlightenment.

A different emphasis was chosen for John junior. He was sent to the Free Grammar School in Bury St Edmunds, where John Buxton himself had been educated. The father wrote to Robert:

> Not that I prefer that to the place you are in, only the views I have in life for him being different I have judged it more proper for him to be brought up at a publick school & in the more common method. Besides, another reason which weighed very much with me, that if George & he were at the same place one of them might have been discouraged as I found by the little time they were together.[55]

George and John were judged to have different levels of ability, or at least application. George joined Robert for a classical education at Playford, yet ironically it was John who would become head of the family following the deaths of both of his older brothers.

[53] Letter no. 117, 19 April 1728, p. 136, below.

[54] See Appendix A, J. Black, *Eighteenth-century Britain, 1688–1783* (Basingstoke, 2001), p. 13, discusses the composition of private libraries of this period.

[55] Letter no. 60, 21 February 1726, p. 80, below.

Health

Concern about health and sickness, and reports of deaths, are a constant theme in the letters. John Buxton's hypochondria was justified. He needed no reminding of the early deaths of his father and grandfather, and the loss of infant children. Moreover, his own health was poor. His letters refer to periods of ill health, and an open sore that refused to heal. A letter to Robert Buxton from the reverend Dr William Herring in early 1727 illustrates the anxiety that John Buxton's family and friends felt:

> I was very glad to find so good an account of your major's indisposition in your kind letter. I hope he will meet with no delay in the recovery of his health and quickly free you from the anxiety I am sure you have laboured under.[56]

In recording the melancholy toll of death among his family, friends and acquaintances, John Buxton reflected his experience of what historians were later to recognize as one of the most significant mortality crises since the mid sixteenth century. In the years from 1727 to 1730 the annual death rates in England were from 35 to 40 per cent above the trend average, with some of the highest rates in the whole period until the end of the nineteenth century.[57] None of the bad news about sickness and death seems to have been concealed from the young Robert whose own health gave cause for continual concern. It was uppermost in the mind of his eleven-year-old sister Elizabeth when she won an opportunity to make a wish in a family game:

> The contest about the wish in the lot of the merry thought fell between Betty & Sarah. Betty pulled the longest bone & when I asked her what she wished for she said it was that you might have your health. I kissed her for her kindness to you & shall always love her the better.[58]

The dire consequences of catching a cold or fever, and the prevalence of the ague, were well recognized. John Buxton regarded Tibenham as a particularly unhealthy place in winter, fuelling, as we shall see, his desire to move to Shadwell in those months. In November 1726, with Sarah suffering from a

[56] CUL Buxton Papers, 35/66, letter from William Herring D.D. to Robert Buxton, 16 January 1727.

[57] E.A. Wrigley and R.S. Schofield, *The Population History of England 1541–1871* (Cambridge, 1989), p. 333, table 8.11 and p. 682, fig. A10.12.

[58] Letter no. 29, 26 August 1724, p. 53, below.

fever, John Buxton entertained Sir Robert Kemp and his family with some of his excellent beef, 'the best I ever eat', adding wryly that 'this advantage at least our dirty country gives us'.[59]

Smallpox was especially feared. What had been an endemic but relatively mild feverish complaint, appeared in a more virulent form in the sixteenth century. Death rates rose through the seventeenth century with periodic epidemics, especially in crowded towns. Smallpox became the most common and lethal disease of young children in the early eighteenth century.[60] Isolation was the only defence and places known to have outbreaks were avoided. Robert was cautioned to avoid Ipswich and Oxford in 1729 because of smallpox in those locations. In the same year the children of several of John Buxton's friends, and six servants of Charles Slapp, his tenant at Rushford, caught the disease. It was rife in Norwich.[61] John Buxton was aware of inoculation as a preventative measure against smallpox, although, because smallpox itself was injected, the procedure was attendant with danger. He wrote from London to his wife in 1722:

> The young princesses who were lately inoculated for the smallpox are in a fair way to do well. Though Lord Sunderland's only son by the last lady dyed of them by the same experiment, this method of getting the smallpox well over is much approved on the several hundreds have allready used it with success.[62]

John Buxton regularly consulted the leading physicians of his day: Sir Benjamin Wrench in Norwich,[63] and, when visiting Bath, he saw Dr George

[59] Letter no. 77, 22 November 1726, p. 96, below.

[60] F.F. Cartwright, *A Social History of Medicine* (1977), pp. 77–8. A new variety *variola major* appeared from the east and changed the character of European smallpox.

[61] Letters nos 136, 140 and 146, 14 and 29 September, and 20 November 1729, pp. 155, 159 and 165, below.

[62] CUL Buxton Papers, 105/36, letter from John Buxton to Anne Buxton, 26 April 1722. This new procedure was introduced following the return to Britain of Lady Mary Wortley Montagu, wife of the British ambassador in Constantinople, who had her infant son inoculated there. During a severe epidemic in London she then had her five-year-old daughter inoculated. Royal permission was given for a trial on prisoners facing execution in Newgate prison, and then for a second trial involving eleven children from charity schools. Given the evidence of the successful reduction of the virulence of a smallpox infection, King George I commanded that two of his grandchildren should be inoculated. Strictly speaking this procedure is variolation, the term inoculation referring to Edward Jenner's (1749–1823) demonstration of the successful and safer use of cowpox virus, published in 1796. Cartwright, pp. 80–1.

[63] Sir Benjamin Wrench (*c.* 1662–1746), was the son of John Wrench (1624–1697), sheriff of Norwich 1669 and mayor 1688, and his second wife Anne (d.1685), the daughter of John Rayley, mayor in 1649. Benjamin Wrench was a celebrated Norwich physician, knighted in 1720, and

Cheyne, passing on to Robert his advice about the efficacy of flesh broth for the sick.[64] But the value of the advice the doctors could give was constrained by their lack of knowledge of the causes of disease and their reliance upon traditional remedies that ranged from the possibly beneficial to the probably dangerous. Sir Benjamin Wrench favoured sea bathing and Robert at Playford, within easy reach of the estuary of the river Orwell, was well placed to take his advice. Purging with rhubarb and other plant extracts was common. The use of Peruvian bark, containing the active principle of quinine, could be of use against ague.[65] But frequent recourse to bleeding for a wide range of ailments, even for infants, was of doubtful benefit.[66] Bleeding was recommended to Robert on several occasions, for example in the winter of 1725 in order to manage colds and coughs (to be followed by a purgative dose of rhubarb), and eleven-year-old Sarah was bled in the following year for a bout of fever.[67]

consulted by many of the leading families in the county. He married three times, first in 1690/1 to Rebecca Rayley, who died 1736/7. Then, in his seventy-first year, stimulating ribald jests from his contemporaries, he married Sarah Littel of Norwich. After her death in 1739/40 he married yet again, to a Norwich widow Mrs Laton. Wrench's house was on the south side of Lobster Lane, an extension of Pottergate. It later became the New Lobster inn, then a corn hall and is now occupied by Jarrold's department store. R.W. Ketton-Cremer, *Country Neighbourhood* (1951), pp. 64–5 and 212. A portrait of Wrench in 1746 by John Theodore Heins (1697–1756) is in the Norwich civic collection. Andrew Moore and Charlotte Crawley, *Family and Friends. A Regional Survey of British Portraiture* (1992), pp. 47–48 and 207.

[64] Letters no. 19, 11 August 1723, and no. 33, 27 October 1724, pp. 45 and 57, below. George Cheyne M.D. (1671/2–1743), physician, was born and educated in Scotland, moved to London and was elected a fellow of the Royal Society in 1702. From about 1715 he developed his medical practice, spending part of each year in Bath. He published mathematical, philosophical and medical works. He served especially the aristocracy and landed classes who suffered from diseases of over-indulgence, addressing them through a series of self-help texts emphasising that health was the responsibility of the individual and that failure to maintain one's health was a sin. A. Guerrini, 'George Cheyne (1671/2–1743)', *ODNB.*

[65] 'Peruvian Bark': the powdered bark of the cinchona tree introduced into Europe by Jesuit missionaries, reached England about 1665. Its active constituent was quinine, an effective treatment for ague (malaria). The high cost of this remedy led to experimentation with other barks, including that of the walnut tree. Sloan, p.147.

[66] When disease was generally believed to be due to imbalance of the humours of the body, most patients would expect to have some blood withdrawn as part of the treatment for a wide range of ailments. Blood-letting was usually performed by a surgeon and in this case by venesection, a vein being incised with a sharp knife and the blood collected in a convenient receptacle. The use of leeches became more popular as the eighteenth century progressed. Sloan, pp. 59–60. The Norfolk cleric Edmund Pyle wrote that infants were bled when only a few days old and that a visitor, Miss Greenwood, was 'lam'd with bleeding and her arm is quite wither'd now'. E. Pyle, *Memoirs of a Royal Chaplain (1729–1763): the correspondence of Edmund Pyle D.D. with Samuel Kerrich*, ed. A. Hartshorne (1905), pp. 45 and 102.

[67] Letters nos 59 and 77, 17 February and 22 November 1726, pp. 80 and 96, below.

Books

John Buxton loved books and his letters to Robert are filled with comments about them and recommendations for reading. He read Latin, Greek, French and Italian and his chosen books were as likely to have been published on the continent of Europe as in Britain. Parcels of books were sent from Channonz to Playford and Cambridge. The earliest reference to the purchase of books for Robert, then thirteen years old, concerns a ten-volume illustrated set of books by Bernard de Montfaucon (1655–1741), about the monuments of antiquity, published in Paris.[68]

John Buxton had his literary favourites: 'you have a great deal of pleasure I make no doubt', he wrote in 1728, 'in reading Milton, and you will find no abatement upon doing it often, he is all over wonderful, the part you mention is truly sublime'.[69] He also read Jonathon Swift with delight but was dismissive of the work of George Farquhar.[70]

The books listed in Appendix A are clearly Robert's, with many newly bought textbooks among more general works. The two subjects closest to John Buxton's interests are missing: architecture and gardening. These would be expected to feature in his own library at Channonz but no details about it have survived. However, it is clear that John Buxton was an avid reader of periodicals containing details of forthcoming publications. He wrote to Robert about new books and discussed them with him soon after they had been bought. His comments about John Gay's play, *The Beggar's Opera*, and the public debate stimulated by its performance in 1728, were conveyed to Robert not long after the play's opening.[71] Books were bought in Norwich, Ipswich, Cambridge and London. John Buxton never begrudged the expense: 'I shall never think your mony ill layed out when it is done with any view towards your improvement'.[72] Robert's interests can be judged from his father's reactions to his letters and it seems that he was successful in transmitting his enthusiasms to his son.

[68] Bernard de Montfaucon (1655–1741), *L'antiquité expliquée et représentée en figures* (Paris, 1719). A supplement was published in 1724.

[69] Letter no. 122, 7 July 1728, p. 140, below.

[70] Letter no. 79, 13 December 1726, p. 98, below.

[71] Letter no. 116, 15 April 1728, p. 135, below.

[72] Letter No. 114, 1 April 1728, p. 131, below.

Social and political life

The extent to which John Buxton's life was focused upon south Norfolk is revealed by Figure 2 which shows the geographical concentration of the places mentioned in his letters. In writing to a son it is not surprising that Buxton cousins at Laxfield and South Elmham, St Margaret in Suffolk, the Marshams at Stratton Strawless, and the Wards at Bixley and in Norwich, are mentioned frequently. But John Buxton's social connections were also to be found in south Norfolk. The Branthwayts of Hethel were particularly close, with Arthur Branthwayt being John Buxton's travelling companion to London and Bath in 1723.

Although the government leaders of the day, Viscount Townshend and Sir Robert Walpole, both came from great Norfolk families, political matters do not feature prominently in the letters. John Buxton waited upon both Sir Robert and Lord Townshend when he was in London. They were both out.[73] He did however dine with Sir Robert's brother Horatio in London and Bath.[74] John Buxton informed Robert about the selection of candidates for Norwich and the county in 1728 but his interest was muted. 'Abundance of people have been talked of for candidates for the county, among others Mr Woodhouse[75] if his father will not stand' he wrote, continuing: 'I do not much trouble my self about it though should like to see our selves represented by gentlemen of worth'.[76] After the election John Buxton paraded with fellow gentleman to support the successful county Whig Sir Edmund Bacon[77] and described for Robert the impressive assembly of upwards of 1,200 men outside Norwich who rode with their new member into the city.[78]

[73] CUL Buxton Papers, 105/6, letter from John Buxton to Anne Buxton, from London 4 July 1717. Sir Robert Walpole of Houghton, created Earl of Orford in 1742 (1676–1745), politician and prime minister 1721–42. Charles, second Viscount Townshend of Raynham (1675–1738), politician, was dismissed in 1717 and Walpole also resigned. Townshend returned to office in 1720, becoming Secretary of State in 1721, finally retiring in 1730. His interest in agricultural improvement earned him the nickname 'Turnip Townshend'.

[74] CUL Buxton Papers, 105/16, letter from John Buxton to Anne Buxton, from Bath 21 August 1717. Horatio Walpole (1678–1757) was created first Baron Walpole of Wolterton in 1756.

[75] The Tory William Wodehouse (?1706–37) of Kimberley Hall, son of Sir John Wodehouse, fourth baronet (1669–1754) was M.P. for Norfolk from 1734 until his death. He was succeeded by his younger brother Armine (*c.* 1714–77), later fifth baronet, who represented Norfolk from 1737 to 1768.

[76] Letter no. 119, 3 June 1728, p. 138, below.

[77] Sir Edmund Bacon of Gillingham, fifth baronet (d. 1734).

[78] Letter no. 122, 7 July 1728, p. 140, below.

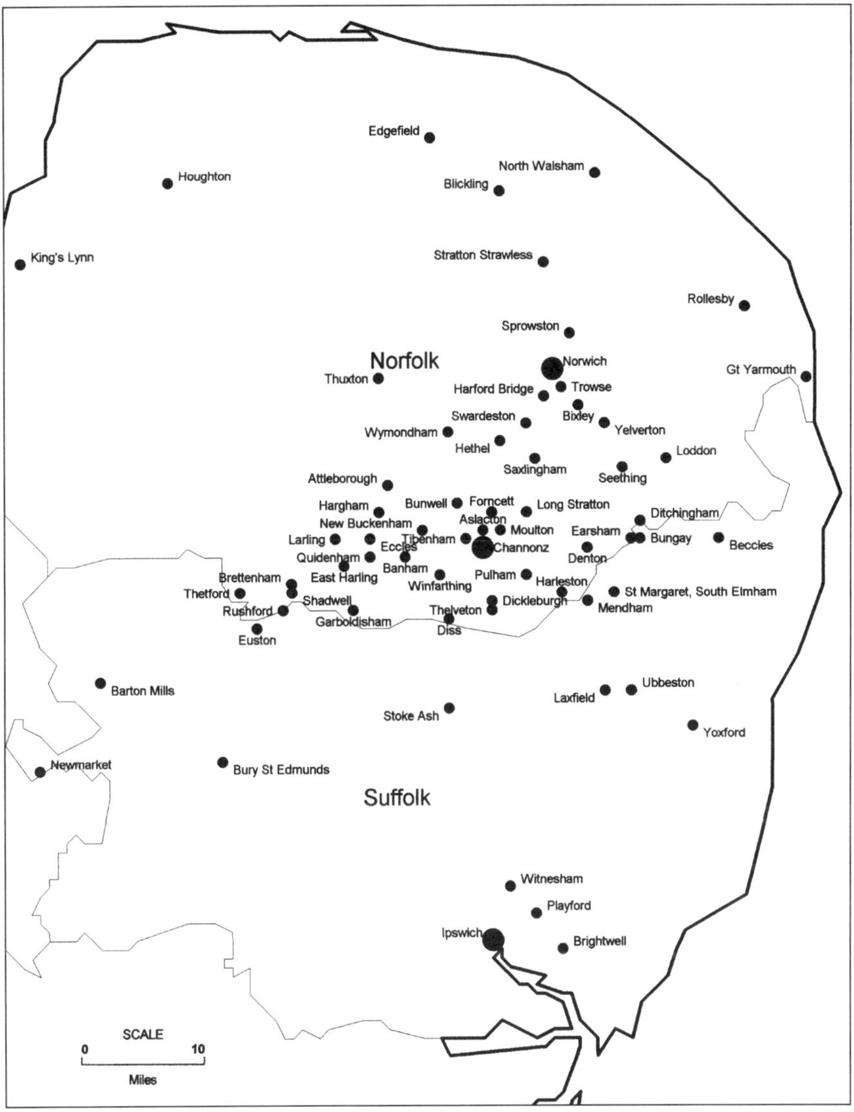

FIGURE 2. Map of places mentioned in the letters

John Buxton's limited coverage of political issues is an example of the interest of his letters not only for what they contain but also for what they leave out. There is little about estate management. Another significant omission is religion. John Buxton was not a deeply religious man. His letters contain many conventional pieties and references to God but there is not one mention of attendance at church in Norfolk (beyond christenings and funerals), or inquiry about Robert's practice at school or university. Buxton certainly moralizes: he abhors drunkenness, and immorality on the part of servants led to their dismissal. He allied himself to the puritan condemnation of *The Beggar's Opera*, for its depiction of low life on the stage rather than for its thinly veiled depiction of leading politicians of the day. But he was a moderate man without passion for either religion or politics.

As a justice of the peace, John Buxton attended sessions, and he enjoyed the theatre. But he does not seem to have been a sporting man. His comments about horse racing at Bungay and Ipswich are equivocal, and he left shooting to others. Nevertheless, he could recognise the legitimacy of his children's interests. George, then fourteen years old, wrote to his father from school at Playford, seeking permission to have a gun. John Buxton was not happy about it. He wrote back:

> Not that I would have you to be ever at your book. There is a time for play and divertion as well as study ... I think the using guns among schoolboys is a dangerous pastime and may be attended with such consequences to yourself or to others that I can by no means allow of it and should be concerned if any one els while they are schoolboys are allowed. It is what your brother [*Robert*] never was nor any one while he stayed at Mr D'Oyly's.[79]

However, John Buxton tempered his denial of George's wishes with some constructive encouragement. The letter continued:

> When you come home this divertion will be the newer and more agreeable and to make it the more so I have bought for you at London a new flying gun of the best make in England, of a size proper for your use, which cost me 3 guineas ... so you see I was not unmindfull of procuring things for your pleasure.

Architecture and building

In addition to a passion for books, architecture was the other great interest that John Buxton encouraged in his son. Where John Buxton learned his architecture is not known. A gentleman of his day could hardly have escaped the excitement about the subject in the post-Restoration period and the growing number of examples of the application of classical principles of

[79] CUL Buxton Papers, 105/94, Letter from John Buxton to George Buxton at Playford, 20 October 1730.

design.[80] The earliest surviving evidence of John Buxton's skill as a designer and builder is Earsham Hall, built when he was in his late twenties. Bixley Hall, a similar house designed for Sir Edward Ward Bt, is of about the same date.[81] He made a tour through England in May 1720 when he visited many country houses.[82] The two architects with whom he had contact during the period of the letters were both younger men. Edward Lovett Pearce (d. 1733) – a distant cousin – was about fifteen years his junior.[83] James Burrough (1691–1764), half a dozen years younger than Buxton, had been educated at the same Bury St Edmunds school.[84] Robert Buxton passed on to his father some comments Burrough had made about the design for Shadwell but neither of these architects could have inspired Buxton's original interest in the subject.

If the early background to John Buxton's architectural activity is not known, there is no doubt about the enthusiasm with which he described to

80 Sir John Vanbrugh's letter to the earl of Manchester in 1708 in which he exclaimed 'All the World are running Mad after Building, as far as they can reach' exemplifies the excitement generated at the time by new buildings. G. Webb, ed., *The Complete Works of Sir John Vanbrugh*, iv (1928), p. 25.

81 Earsham Hall was a seven by five bay house with three storeys and a parapet below a top storey. The house was extended later in the eighteenth century and in the nineteenth century. It survives today. Burke's and Savills, p. 107; Pevsner, *Norfolk 2*, pp. 315–6. A house had been built at Bixley in the sixteenth century by Edward Ward of Postwick. Its early-eighteenth-century replacement was a seven by seven bay house of two storeys and an attic storey over a basement. The builder's great-grandson, Sir Edward Ward, the eighth baronet, died *c.* 1770 without issue and the property passed through his aunt Susan (d. 1771, daughter of the fifth baronet) to her husband Neil Primrose, Earl of Rosebery. The estate was sold in 1884 to the Colman family and the house demolished early in the twentieth century having been unoccupied for many years. B. Cozens-Hardy, 'Some Norfolk Halls', *Norfolk Archaeology*, 32 (1961), p. 169; Burke's and Savills, p. 89. See Plates 4 and 5.

82 Appendix E.

83 Edward Lovett Pearce (? – 1733) was the son of General Edward Pearce and his wife Frances, daughter of Christopher Lovett, a Dublin merchant. The family had property at Whitlingham (Norfolk). Pearce studied architecture in Italy 1723–4 and although his architectural career was brief, by 1731 he had become the leading Palladian architect of his day in Ireland. In Norfolk, in addition to advising John Buxton, he surveyed Heydon Hall, the Earle family's seat. He was knighted in 1732 and died while still in his thirties. Pearce was a cousin of Sir John Vanbrugh. Colvin, pp. 745–6; E. McParland, *Public Architecture in Ireland, 1680–1760* (New Haven and London, 2001), pp. 11, 177–9 and 185.

84 James Burrough (1691–1764), later Sir James, the son of a Bury St Edmunds physician, was educated at the Free Grammar School in Bury and took his M.A. at Gonville and Caius College, Cambridge in 1716. In parallel with an academic career he established a considerable reputation as an amateur architect. Most of his executed works were in Cambridge, including a new chapel for Clare Hall (1763–9). He also designed the interior of Norwich Assembly Rooms in 1754. Colvin, pp. 193–4.

Robert first his repair and modernisation of Channonz Hall, then the design and building of Shadwell Lodge, and, throughout the period, the building activities of his contemporaries in Norfolk and farther afield. Colonel Harbord's new house attracted his eye.[85] He noted changes at his Branthwayt friends' house at Hethel, commenting that it 'can never be made what one woud call a good one'.[86] Buxton's awareness of fashionable building elsewhere is demonstrated by his comments on Mereworth Castle in Kent, newly built for Colonel Fane.[87]

Robert was encouraged to study buildings whenever he had the opportunity. When preparations were being made in 1729 for Anne Buxton with her older daughters and Robert to visit Mrs Pigott at Doddershall (Buckinghamshire), John Buxton advised his son:

> It would not be amis if you carry about with you a little sketch book in octo or 4to doubled, to put plans of houses you think worth noting. If you make one of Dodershall it will give me a better idea of the plan than any description, in which you may note the plan of gardens, offices, park &c. with the bearing.[88]

Robert Buxton may have made a plan of Doddershall. He certainly made detailed notes during his journey, beginning on the very first day with a meticulous observation that would have delighted the practical builder in his father: 'Came on to Barton Mills to lodge. Observed at the inn there a neat sort of pavement in the yard, of little round stones gathered in the field at 2d. per bushel and laid by a man at Mildenhal[*l*] for 1s. 6d. per day'.[89]

The first reference to the repair and modernisation of Channonz Hall dates from 1723. The house had been built in 1569.[90] In July 1723 John Buxton reported that his work on the courtyard walls was almost finished but that work inside the house went on slowly. Robert's status as eldest son is implicit in the form of his father's address to the thirteen-year-old: 'I shall go on with the greater pleasure in whatever I undertake having your advantage always in my view'.[91] A year later the internal rooms were all painted but the staircase

85 Letter no. 24, 10 June 1724, p. 48, below.

86 Letter no. 78, 30 November 1726, p. 97, below.

87 Letter no. 43, 11 July 1725, p. 67, below.

88 Letter no. 133, 2 September 1729, p. 152, below.

89 Appendix F.

90 Baggs, 'Channons Hall', pp. 9–13. A later painting of Channonz, possibly from about 1726 and therefore representing the building as modernised by John Buxton, survives on panelling in a house in Aslacton. Rose, 'Aslacton painting', pp. 109–13.

91 Letter no. 18, 22 July 1723, p. 44, below.

was not plastered and the work was progressing 'slow beyond my patience'.[92] Work seems to have been finished by the end of 1724. The house had been modernised and made more convenient: the drawing room chimney, for example, had been taken down to roof level and rebuilt with a narrower flue to prevent the fire smoking. John Buxton recognised that he was a difficult man to please: 'The blue room is finished & the alteration to every ones liking as well as my own, which is somewhat unusual'.[93] He dealt sympathetically with the external fabric and wrote:

> The windows are all finished in the front of the house & the capitals or tops of the pillars at the corners all repaired & now stand in the same form they were first built in, the fanes only left out.[94] The out side of the house is now entirely finished & seems so sound & firm to bid fair to remain two centurys more <if some> if no extraordinary accident happens to it.

John Buxton's hopes for the durability of Channonz were optimistic. The house survived for a little over 60 years. Two of its three wings were pulled down when the family completed its removal to Shadwell Lodge in 1786.[95]

Building at Shadwell

Within a few months of completing the Channonz project, John Buxton, depressed by the thought of having to spend another winter on the bleak, cold, south Norfolk clays at Tibenham, raised the question of building at Shadwell. 'This dismal season', he wrote in February 1725, 'has made me come to a resolution of doing something at Shadwell'.[96] The Buxtons had owned land in the parish of Rushford, of which Shadwell was a hamlet, since the sixteenth century. Although only twelve miles from Channonz, in the direction of Thetford, the family were occasional residents there and were aware of advantages the location offered: a much drier site and a more attractive undulating landscape. Nevertheless, for John Buxton to contemplate a move, having just repaired his main house, was rather surprising. However, at this stage, it is clear that he wanted a winter retreat.

[92] Letter no. 24, 10 June 1724, p. 48, below.

[93] Letter no. 27, 5 August 1724, p. 51, below.

[94] Fane: a flag, banner or pennant, or weather vane. *OED*. The painting of Channonz Hall (Plate 3) shows such devices topping the corner pillars, the centres of the gables and the tops of the dormer windows of the house.

[95] Baggs, 'Channons Hall'.

[96] Letter no. 60, 21 February 1726, p. 80, below.

The choice of the site, and the design of the house, were to occupy John Buxton's mind for the next year. His letters to Robert reveal the criteria he thought most important for achieving a good result, addressing the young Robert as an adult, seeking his son's comments upon his plans, and treating his reactions with respect, always striving to achieve a common purpose for the scheme. The availability of water; the nature of the air, soil and, above all, prospect; concerned him. Within the house privacy, communication and noise were all considered. The prospects commanded by the rooms were important. Whereas the view of a yard would be acceptable from a room when in use by John Buxton, if it doubled as a room for entertaining company, the prospect would not be so agreeable.[97]

We have seen that John Buxton knew that he was a difficult man to please. Nevertheless, he recognised the importance of reaching conclusions, for although 'we cannot have everything in a scituation we ought to take that with most advantages'[98], he also wrote 'we must not always be fluctuating for then there coud be no action at all'.[99] But perhaps the very fertility of John Buxton's architectural brain encouraged indecisiveness. On 21 December 1725, in the depths of another testing Tibenham winter, he wrote:

> The season continues very unpleasant which with a little cold I have lately taken keeps me within doors. The return of the sun will bring us health and fair weather: two blessings that makes a heaven on earth. However, I have not been idle. Really, I have never studied so hard in my life as I have lately done in scheming about Shadwell. I have built forty houses there which were no sooner finished and thoroughly examined than immediately pulled down and soon after a new one erected. I built one this morning out of the materials of the old ones which at present I think without a fault.[100]

Many different designs for Shadwell survive as plans sketched by John Buxton on scraps of paper, especially on the backs of old letters he had received. An example is reproduced as Plate 6.

The foundations for Shadwell Lodge were dug in March 1727. John Buxton was satisfied with the progress of building during the next few months, spending seven or eight hours every day at the site. Such close attention was needed partly because of a lack of confidence in his surveyor: '[I] find much occation to be there, not knowing how to depend upon the surveyor, who is often

97 Letter no. 77, 22 November 1726, p. 96, below.
98 Letter no. 79, 13 December 1726, p. 98, below.
99 Letter no. 48, 24 November 1725, p. 72, below.
100 Letter no. 55, 21 December 1725, p. 76, below.

absent & as often when there liable to blunder'.[101] In the same vein he wrote to his wife: 'I am so much wanted I find among my workmen and I cannot fix any time to say when I can leave them not having that assistance I expected from my undertaker but he does his best, I believe, but too oft absent to marshall works well enough still but his memory and head quite shattered.'[102] The first floor was completed in July and plasterers and joiners were at work. A year later, in November 1729, the decorative painter Thomas Bardwell was at work in the hall, but there was still glazing to do and the chimneypieces had not been fitted. However, John Buxton's wife travelled to Shadwell in that month with goods for the house and began preparations to make it habitable.[103] John Buxton expressed the hope that within a week the house would be fit to lodge in.

There are no references in the letters to financial matters, whether estate income and expenditure, or the cost of building at Shadwell. However, some fragmentary building accounts have survived.[104] An undated account based on the measurement of the bricklayer's work from the foundations to the fourth [*attic*] floor came to £112 13s. 4d. The bricklayer received 2s. in the pound in lieu of small beer. A building account book was opened on 5 February 1725 and the first entry made on 9 February. Deals and wainscot boards were bought at King's Lynn, transported to Thetford by water, and then carted by an estate tenant to Shadwell. Oak was found on the estate. Brick was made close to the building site. Two hundred and seventy thousand bricks were fired at a cost of 7s. per 1,000 plus certain other charges. In a later brickmaking agreement of 1 August 1730, the price was 8s. per 1,000, with horse and water carts, moulds, barrows and straw provided. A summary of the recorded expenditure between 1725 and early 1730 is given in Table 1 below.

It is unlikely that all tradesmen's bills, for example carpentry, joinery or plastering, are included under the miscellaneous heading. However, with an allowance for such additional costs, and the inclusion of the bricklayer's account, it appears that the cost of the case of Shadwell Lodge was probably some £500 and the finished house not more than £1,000. With spending

[101] Letter no. 87, 1 May 1727, p. 104, below.

[102] CUL Buxton Papers, 105/77, letter from John Buxton to Anne Buxton, no date but catalogued '*c.* 1728'. The name of the 'undertaker' is not given but on other occasions Buxton referred to John Buckenham as his surveyor and, during the building work at Channonz Hall, sent Anne Buxton instructions to pass on to him. CUL Buxton Papers, 105/47, letter from John Buxton to Anne Buxton, from Bath dated 14 September 1723.

[103] Letters nos. 145–6, 18 and 20 November 1729, pp. 164–5, below.

[104] CUL Buxton Papers, 96/51, 'The Particulars of Shadwell Lodge.' and 124/3, 'Shadwell Building Accounts.'

TABLE 1 *Shadwell Building Accounts*

	£	s	d
Deals, wainscot boards and scaffolding	150	00	00
Carriage and expenses	14	07	00
Sawyers	3	07	06
Brick	124	06	08
Lime	3	16	04
Miscellaneous	88	07	01
Total	384	04	07

spread over five to six years (although not evenly), John Buxton spent up to twenty per cent of his gross income on building during this period.[105]

For this sum John Buxton obtained a fashionable house with a 58 x 45 feet plan, a three-bay symmetrical main front, and three storeys plus an attic lit by dormer windows. The house depicted in a surviving watercolour is unadorned[106] although drawings in John Buxton's collection include a house of similar size with more elaborate architectural details, including a roof parapet with decorative urns, and a pediment topped with a central finial.[107]

John Buxton's death

John Buxton had little time to enjoy his new house. He died in 1731. His grieving widow wrote of her 'inexpressible loss' to her cousin Lady Ward:

> I will try to put pen to paper though my eyes flow too full with tears to be able to say much of what my heart will ever be full of. But it is very hard for frail flesh and blood to submit as we ought. ... The greatest thing I have now is to endeavour to do is to make myself as fit as I can to take the best care of my dear children who have lost so good a father ... my thanks to my

105 Building costs are discussed in R. Wilson and A. Mackley, *Creating Paradise. The Building of the English Country House, 1660–1880* (2000), pp. 233–95. L. Stone and J.C.F. Stone, *An Open Elite? England, 1540–1880* (Oxford, 1984), pp. 349–96 and Appendix 2, concluded that a medium-sized country house cost £40 per square of 100 square feet of living space in the 1750s. On this basis the 26 squares of Shadwell could have cost £1,040. Such estimates are very dependent upon the standard of finish. William and John Halfpenny, Robert Morris and T. Lightoler, *The Modern Builder's Assistant* (1757), give a range of costs per square from £40 to £200.

106 Plate 7.

107 CUL Buxton Papers, 29/30a.

> good God in sparing me the life of my son [*Robert*] who is so great a blessing to me.[108]

Twelve-year-old Leonard wrote to his mother from Rendlesham (Suffolk), in an immature hand between lines lightly pencilled on a blank sheet of paper, of his father's 'impartial and equally indulgent love' of all his children. Fifteen-year-old George added a note at the end of the letter: 'I hope dear Madam you will excuse my writing for I can't see and have no candle'.[109] George was to die nine years later, before his mother, in 1740.

John Buxton's last will, dated 16 June 1731, made his son Robert sole executor.[110] Robert inherited all the cash and South Sea stock and annuities, plate, jewels, books, furniture, pictures, household goods at Channonz, Rushford [*Shadwell*] and elsewhere, and cattle. Anne Buxton had the use of furniture at Shadwell for her life which, on her death, was to revert to Robert. John Buxton wrote that he would make no particular provision for his younger children because they were 'reasonably provided for', adding that he would leave room for their mother's kindness to make whatever additions to their fortunes were within her power. Nevertheless, he provided for a payment of £1,000 to Isabella, and £500 to George, when they reached the age of twenty-one. Sarah was given £200 and Anne his wife £100. John Kerridge, his clerk, received £50, and his bailiff Robert Phillips £10. John Buxton remembered his close friends Dr William Herring and Miles Branthwayt with 20s. rings; there were also small legacies for relatives, his pall-bearers, and the poor of Tibenham and Rushford. Since John Buxton provided for the possibility that his executor could not find the wherewithal to pay his debts and legacies, the sum available in cash and investments could not have been great. If necessary, the Loddon estate was to be sold to raise the money.

An inventory of John Buxton's effects at Shadwell valued them at £737 8s. 6d.[111] His beloved books were worth a mere £30, a value dwarfed by the £88 4s. assessment of the contents of his wine cellar, his plate at over £158, and his horses at £164. In the same document there is an inventory for Channonz. It is possibly incomplete although it does refer to the main rooms and numerous chambers: the effects there were valued at only £57 3s. 6d.

108 CUL Buxton Papers, 105/100, letter from Anne Buxton to Lady Barbara Ward, no date.

109 CUL Buxton Papers, 107/6, letter from Leonard and George Buxton to Anne Buxton, dated 9 November 1731. John Buxton, then fourteen years old, wrote his mother a letter dated 28 November 1731 from his school in Bury St Edmunds. CUL Buxton Papers, 107/7

110 CUL Buxton Papers, 43/7a, True copy of his father's will made by Robert Buxton, and 43/7b, Probate of the will, 1732.

111 CUL Buxton Papers, 37/9, 'Inventory of the effects of the late John Buxton Esquire'.

The later Buxtons

Robert Buxton never married, dying in 1751 only forty-one years old. His health had deteriorated through the 1740s and William Herring, in a letter to John Buxton in 1742, doubted that he would ever get better: 'Your poor brother's case is indeed deplorable and made more so by there being so little hope of his recovery'.[112] The family clearly anticipated the possibility that he would never produce children to carry on the Buxton line for they took legal advice, probably in the 1740s, to determine how settlements of £2,000 could be secured for each of John Buxton's four younger children.[113] Written apparently after the death of George Buxton, the legal opinion was clear on the dependence of the younger children's settlements on John junior's success in finding a rich wife. The advice was succinct:

> It will be highly expedient, if not absolutely necessary, that Mr John Buxton should marry a lady with at least £10,000: without which fortune it will be scarce prudent in him to marry at all.

John's position would also depend upon Robert Buxton agreeing to secure to his younger brother the reversion of estates he then possessed, and for their mother Anne (who was to die in 1749) to release to John estates she held for life. If such conditions were met, the lawyers thought that 'Mr John Buxton may reasonably expect to marry an agreeable lady with the above-mentioned fortune'.[114]

John Buxton's marriage to Elizabeth Jacob added Wiltshire property to the Buxtons' Norfolk estate. Now settled at Shadwell, he developed the park around the house built by his father, planted many trees and constructed a lake in the 1750s. He was more active in county politics than his father had been, allying himself with William Fellowes in 1754 to contest, unsuccessfully, the county seats for the Tory cause. He was succeeded in 1782 by his son Robert John (1753–1839). Robert John married Elizabeth Beevor in 1777, apparently without his father's consent. For this and perhaps other reasons father and son were estranged. Robert John and his wife remained on a

112 CUL Buxton Papers, 108/29, Letter from William Herring to John Buxton, Kensington, 27 September 1742.

113 CUL Buxton Papers, 37/58, 'Legal advice re settlement on John Buxton's four younger children'. The document is catalogued as 'about 1730' but a date in the 1740s after the death of George seems more likely. One implication of the advice is that Robert Buxton was not expected to marry.

114 John married, about 1752, Elizabeth (1720–1765), daughter of John Jacob of Tockenham (Wiltshire) and his wife Mary. Their son Robert (1753–1839) was created a baronet in 1800.

Wiltshire estate of his mother's family until his father's death. Robert John was an active parliamentarian, sitting for Thetford, 1790–6, and Great Bledwyn (Wiltshire), 1797–1806.[115] He campaigned for the abolition of slavery and advocated prison reform. In the inflationary years of the French Wars he expressed concern for the welfare of the poor, although he supported the landed interest when opposing measures such as the regulation of labourers' wages, and the sale of corn in public markets, which would have benefited the poor. Robert John received a baronetcy in November 1800.

Robert John's son John Jacob (1788–1842), the second baronet, waited many years for his inheritance, being fifty when his father died. He was educated at Harrow and admitted to Trinity College, Cambridge in 1805. He sat, as his father had done, as M.P. for Great Bledwyn (1818–32)[116] and in Norfolk he was deputy lieutenant and high sheriff in 1841. Shadwell Lodge was by then both too small and too old-fashioned and Sir John Jacob engaged the architect Edward Blore (1787–1879) to extend the house in neo-Elizabethan style.[117] But he had only three years in which to enjoy his inheritance before he died in 1842.[118] He was succeeded by his son Robert Jacob (1829–88) the third and last baronet. During his minority the rebuilding of Shadwell was supervised and completed by his formidable mother, who until her death in 1884 at the age of eighty-one, lived with her son at Shadwell. In the first five years after his succession Robert Jacob and his mother made changes to the park and greatly enlarged the eighteenth-century lake. They rebuilt nearby Brettenham parish church in 1852, restored the old buildings of Rushford College in 1855 to provide a vicarage, and built a bridge across an adjoining ford.[119] The architect for this work was Samuel Sanders Teulon (1812–73) who was then engaged to make substantial gothic additions to Blore's recently extended Shadwell, creating from 1856 to 1860, in Mark Girouard's words, 'a dazzling display of Victorian fireworks'.

Educated in Norwich and at Christ Church, Oxford, Sir Robert Jacob was a captain in the Norfolk Rifle Volunteer Corps (1860), high sheriff of Norfolk (1870) and M.P. for South Norfolk (1871–85). In 1865 he married Mary Augusta Harriet (1846?-1913), daughter of John Johnstone of Alva, but they had no sons. Sir Robert Jacob was succeeded by his daughter Maud Isabel

[115] Thorne, p. 350.

[116] Thorne, p. 349.

[117] M. Girouard, 'Shadwell Park, Norfolk' in *The Victorian Country House* (New Haven and London, 1979), pp. 194–204.

[118] He married in 1825, Elizabeth (1803–1884), daughter of Sir Montague Cholmeley and Elizabeth Harrison.

[119] Pevsner, *Norfolk 2*, p. 622.

Buxton (1866–1949). Hers was a troubled inheritance. By the 1870s the Buxtons' Norfolk acreage had increased to 9,309, with, in addition, 801 acres in Wiltshire inherited from the Jacob family, and 80 acres in Suffolk.[120] But, like many large landowners, the Buxtons were ill-prepared for the agricultural depression of the late nineteenth century and the collapse of rents. The concentration of the Buxton property on the light Breckland soils in south-west Norfolk that John Buxton had found a more attractive location for a family house than the wet clays of Tibenham was now to contribute to the family's undoing. Overall, their 10,190 acres generated a modest £7,260 per annum, the annual return from a Norfolk acre being only one quarter of that from the Wiltshire property. The Shadwell estate was one of the many casualties of that period.[121] The estate was sold in 1898 to Mr John Musker, who had made his fortune as co-founder of the Home and Colonial grocery chain. The surviving Buxtons retreated to Wiltshire.[122]

Conclusion

John Buxton was the antithesis of Henry Fielding's Squire Western, that caricature of the uncouth, drink-swilling, fox-hunting, country landowner.[123] 'Booted, bloated and bigoted Squire Westerns were real enough'; Lady Mary Wortley Montagu wrote of them as spending their mornings with their hounds and their nights with as beastly companions, drinking prodigious quantities of liquor. Horace Walpole, who was in a position to know, reckoned their Norfolk counterparts were 'mountains of roast beef'. John Buxton did not fit this stereotype.[124] He had the intellectual interests of a man of the Enlightenment. He was a true country gentleman, without either the political or other involvements to take him away from his south-Norfolk base. Possessing 'a fine genius, very curious in [*architectural*] designs', he was a loving husband and a good father. John Buxton did not live to enjoy his creation at Shadwell and he was spared the knowledge that his two eldest surviving sons would die before securing the family succession. But his letters are a reminder that the early-eighteenth-century country squire could be a man of deep learning, wide interests and great affection.

120 J. Bateman, *The Great Landowners of Great Britain and Ireland* (London, 4th edn 1883), p. 70.

121 P. Barnes, *Norfolk Landowners since 1880* (Norwich, 1993).

122 John Musker's partner was Julius Drewe, who employed Edwin Lutyens to build him Castle Drogo (Devon). J. Brown, *Lutyens and the Edwardians. An English Architect and his Clients* (London, 1996), pp. 231–9.

123 Henry Fielding (1707–54), *The History of Tom Jones* (1749).

124 Roy Porter, *English Society in the Eighteenth Century* (Harmondsworth, 1990), p. 67.

PLATE 1. Anne Buxton née Gooch (1691–1749), a portrait attributed to Michael Dahl (NWHCM: 1963.268.8). Letter no. 74 dated 3 September 1726 from John Buxton to Robert Buxton refers to the arrival of a portrait of Anne Buxton after a two year wait (CUL Buxton Papers, 35/60).

PLATE 2. Robert Buxton (1710–1751) by Thomas Bardwell (NWHCM: 1963.268.22). The date is not known. The name of the sitter and the year of his death are painted on the canvas.

PLATE 3. Channonz Hall (Tibenham, Norfolk) by an unknown artist, possibly before John Buxton's alterations in the 1720s.

PLATE 4. Earsham Hall (Norfolk), built by John Buxton for his own occupation in the first decade of the eighteenth century and sold *c.* 1720. This print dated 1778 and published in M.J. Armstrong, *History and Antiquities of the County of Norfolk* 2 (Norwich, 1781), Earsham Hundred, p. 39, shows the house as built by Buxton with a single-storey dining room added in the 1750s.

PLATE 5. Bixley Hall (Norfolk) designed by John Buxton in the early eighteenth century for Sir Edward Ward Bt (1684–1719). This print dated 1781 and published in M.J. Armstrong, *History and Antiquities of the County of Norfolk*, 7 (Norwich, 1781), Henstead Hundred, p. 12, shows the house after it had passed by marriage to Neil Primrose, Earl of Rosebery, in the 1770s.

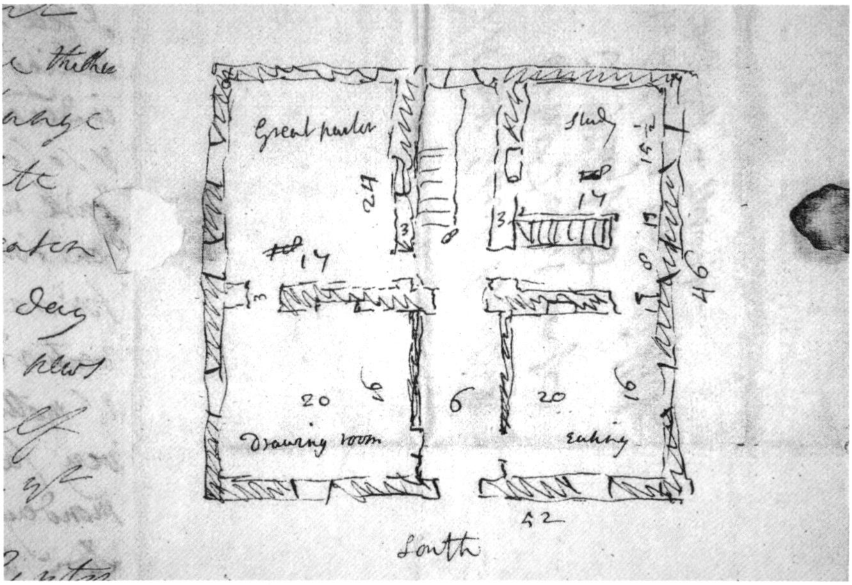

PLATE 6. The development of the design for Shadwell Lodge. A sketch by John Buxton of a plan of a house, included in an undated letter (probably March 1727), no. 81 from John Buxton to Robert Buxton (CUL Buxton Papers, 105/64).

PLATE 7. Shadwell Lodge (Norfolk) by an unknown artist, possibly soon after the completion of the house in 1729.

The Letters

1 John Buxton to Robert Buxton [105/23][1]

No address
Channonz, 4 September 1719

Dear Robert,

I was very glad the weather proved so favourable after you left us here and that you behaved your self so well that Mrs Herne[2] could not help saying a great many handsom things of you to me and whether she is sincere or not, I'm sure she is a very good judge. You oblidge me very much in showing your affection for this place and I could like to have you always with me, if at the same time you could be instructed in those things that are necessary for a gentleman to know. I dare say you will not neglect the oppertunity I have given you but go on to improve your self that I may with the greatest reason as well as with the greatest affection prefer you to the rest of the world.

I am your affectionate
Signed: John Buxton

My service to Mr D'Oyly.[3] George is better.[4]

[1] CUL Buxton Papers, catalogue reference number.

[2] An aunt of John Buxton's wife Anne née Gooch, whose mother was Sarah Herne, referred to as 'Grandmother Gooch' in the letters.

[3] Robert Buxton's schoolmaster, Mr J. D'Oyly. He does not appear in lists of Cambridge and Oxford alumni (Venn and Foster), nor has a link with the D'Oylys of Shotesham Hall been established. A 'Jas. D'Oyly gr[*ammar*]' of Playford was granted a scholastic license on 14 June 1723. E.H. Carter, 'Norfolk and Suffolk Scholastic Licenses Issued 1638–1800' in *The Norwich Subscription Books. A Study of the Subscription Books of the Diocese of Norwich 1637–1800* (1937), p. 190.

[4] Robert Buxton's younger brother born in 1716.

2 John Buxton to Robert Buxton [105/24]

Addressed: To Mr Robert Buxton at Mr D'Oyly's house in Harlston[5]
Ersham,[6] 16 October 1719

Dear Robert,

The joy you give me when I hear you are well and pleased with the place I have put you in is much greater than your affliction which you tell me of, occationed by my not writing and indeed you guess at the true reason that you have not heard from me this great while, for I've been for some time engaged in a good deal of business, and though it makes me forbear sending you letters so often as would. I'm nevertheless always mindfull of you and will by all means I can think of study to promote your true interest as I have hitherto done, and particularly by providing you a master capable of instructing you. And what a happiness is this? What good things will not this produce, when joyned to your resolutions of making a proper use of this kindness and care and your own understanding, and you have as much advantage from both as I could ever wish. I will take care to send you a dictionary and paper as you desire, nor shall anything ever be wanting on my part, so long as you give me testimonies of your duty, to render you a good and happy man.
I am your affectionate father,
Signed: John Buxton

Service to Mr D'Oyly and Mrs D'Oyly. Your brothers and sisters are all well. Mr Herne[7] comes tomorrow.

3 John Buxton to Robert Buxton [105/25]

Addressed: To Mr Robert Buxton at Mr D'Oyly's house in Harlston
Ersham, 27 October 1719

Dear Robert,

Your mother is not at leisure to write so I am to tell you she is very well with the rest of your brothers and sisters but your grandmother and uncle Herne are both ill and not yet removed to their new habitation. I have examined the lottery papers and do not find any of my tickets yet drawn, either blanks or

5 Harleston, a small market town in south Norfolk, on the Suffolk border.

6 Earsham, a south-Norfolk parish near Bungay, where John Buxton built Earsham Hall. See Introduction p. 23.

7 John Buxton's wife's uncle.

prizes. I shall take care to let you know the success of yours when it is drawn but if fortune should not befreind you with a prize, you'll have the satisfaction to remember that a good disposition is of greater value than the twenty thousand pound.

I am your affectionate father,
Signed: John Buxton

My service to your master and to Mrs D'Oyly.

4 John Buxton to Robert Buxton [105/26]

Addressed: To Mr Robert Buxton at Mr D'Oyly's house in Harlston
Ersham, 14 November 1720

Dear Robert,

Last Saturday I bought a bureau for you at Norwich and you will receive it the next by the Harlston carrier. Nor have I been unmindfull of sending the globe but the box I designed to put it in was too small, so you must stay till a larger be made or some safe oppertunity be found of sending it without one. I was extreemely glad to see you so well. I hope no return of your illness will now give you any more trouble. Your mother is very well with all your brothers and sisters and sends you her blessings. Your aunt Buxton is with me but goes tomorrow to Laxfeild [8]. She has enquired much after you, as well as others of your relations, and it is with the greatest satisfaction that I can give them so good an account both of your health and of your inclination to your book. Pray God continue both for your own happiness and mine.

I am your affectionate father,
Signed: John Buxton

Service to your master and to Mr Pitts[9].

[8] Laxfield, a village in north-east Suffolk, the home of Elizabeth Jacob née Buxton, John Buxton's sister.

[9] Possibly an assistant at Mr D'Oyly's school. A candidate is Henry Pitts, admitted to St John's College, Cambridge, in 1679. He was vicar of Roudham, a parish six miles north-east of Thetford, 1701–29. Venn, part I, vol. III, p. 369.

5 John Buxton to Robert Buxton [105/28]

Addressed: To Mr Robert Buxton at Mr D'Oyly's in Harlston
Channonz, 20 May 1721

Dear Robert,

I have the disagreeable news to tell you that your brother Clement[10] dyed yesterday morning. He has been sometime so weak and so ill that I had but fue hopes of his recovery. The rest of your brothers and sisters are well. I hope you will all be so when we meet at Whitsontide. Your horse shall not fail to be ready for you on Thursday next and I do assure you he will bring as welcome a guest as ever came to Channonz.

I am your most affectionate father,
Signed: John Buxton

Your mother sends you her blessing. Give my service to your master.

6 John Buxton to Robert Buxton [105/29]

Addressed: To Mr Robert Buxton at Mr D'Oyly's at Harlston
Channonz, 17 October 1721

Dear Robert,

I very often enquire after you and it is with much pleasure I hear you are well, but much greater it is to know you are dilligent and take care to please your master. This of all things in the world gives me the greatest satisfaction, and even makes me proud when I am told of your good behaviour and that you are desirous to be instructed in such things as will render you both usefull and agreeable, and without the knowledge of them a gentleman makes a most wretched figure, as you I believe have frequently observed in several instances.

This day my servant Bateman removed to Baynard's Hall[11] so I have the whole house to myself, but the part he lived in is not yet fitted up fair for my use. I shall very soon order it to be done and I hope you will eat at Xmas some roast beef out of the old kitchen. The white pidgeons are very well and have drawn another of the same colour to their company. The pheasants are as large as the old ones and come every day into the garden to be fed, not one is yet missing, and last Saturday a young black buck came of himself into my park and seems so well pleased with his reception that I belive he will continue with

[10] Clement was an infant, probably in his first year.

[11] Banyard's was a manor in Bunwell parish, bordering Tibenham to the north.

us. This was a peice of great good fortune and I please myself with the telling it to you who are to be a sharer with me in all the good that befalls me.

I am your affectionate father,

Signed: John Buxton

Present my service to your master. I design waiting on him as soon as I can be at liberty. Your mother, your brothers and sisters are well.

7 John Buxton to Robert Buxton [105/31]

Addressed: To Mr Robert Buxton
Channonz, 29 January 1722

Dear Robert,

I have the greatest pleasure in the world to hear that you are well and at the same time so dilligent to use the oppertunity you have of improving yourself. Mr D'Albiae [?][12] confirms to me this account and I dare say he is not partial, for I am willing to belive every good thing that is said of you, being your most affectionate father,

Signed: John Buxton

You shall have the books as soon as I can get them.

8 John Buxton to Robert Buxton [105/32]

Addressed: To Mr Robert Buxton at Mr D'Oyly's in Harlston
Channonz, 28 February 1722

Dear Robert,

I have sent you the enchiridion and the plays of Racine.[13] Those of Moliere, though I spoke for them at the same time, the bookseller has not procured but I will give orders for them next Saturday, for you shall never want anything in my power while you continue so well and deserve my love.

I am your most affectionate father,

Signed: John Buxton

[12] Not identified.

[13] Enchiridion: a handbook or manual; a concise treatise serving as a guide or for reference. See item 108 in the list of books, Appendix A. Works by Molière and Racine appear in the list as items 13 and 15 respectively.

Your mother and all your brothers and sisters are well but my aunt Herne has been very ill of an ague.[14]

9 John Buxton to Robert Buxton [105/35]

Addressed: To Mr Robert Buxton at Mr D'Oyly's house in Harlston, Norfolk. By Beccles bag.
[*London*] 21 April 1722

Dear Robert,

I am not the less pleased with your letter though I did not answer it immediately. My writing so lately to Mr D'Oyly made me defer this to you which I hope will find you well as it leaves me, for the air and the hours of this place agree with me much better than I expected. It is very agreeable to me to hear you liked your journey to Rushford. You so well behave yourself at school that I shall think myself oblidged to divert you at the time of liberty, and when I do so you have not so much pleasure as myself.

I went the other day to the Charterhouse[15] where I saw old Robin Neve[16] who looks just the same as when in Norfolk. There is a very fine school under the care of good masters. I saw young Mr Tasburgh[17] at the play this night where I often go for I think it the best divertion in the town. I shall expect to hear from you soon and let me know if you want any books and I will get then for you.

I am my dear Robert, your most affectionate father,
Signed: John Buxton

My humble service to your master.

[14] Ague: malaria, a common disease at the time, especially in marshy districts, transmitted by the bite of a mosquito (*Anopheles*). Sloan, p. 51.

[15] The Charterhouse in London was the location of a hospital for pensioners and a boys' school, founded in 1611 by Thomas Sutton (1532–1611), one of the richest men in Jacobean England, who bought the site of the former Carthusian monastery. The school moved to Godalming (Surrey) in 1872.

[16] Probably a member of the Le Neve family of Aslacton, from whom Buxton bought the lordship. Blomefield, V. p. 179.

[17] The Tasburgh family developed a north Suffolk estate from the late fifteenth century, centured upon Flixton Hall from the early seventeenth century. The family suffered financially as Catholics. Their Norfolk seat was Bodney Hall (demolished *c.* 1820), eight miles north of Thetford. The last male heir died in 1736. Young Mr Tasburgh has not been identified. J. Fairclough and M. Hardy, *Thornham and the Waveney Valley* (King's Lynn, 2004), pp. 144–5.

10 John Buxton to Robert Buxton [105/38]

Addressed: To Mrs Buxton at Channonz Hall near New Buckenham, Norfolk.[18] By Attleborough bag.
[*London*] 15 May 1722

Dear Robert,

I take it very kindly your writing in your mother's letter and shall be glad to hear from you every post till I return, which I intend before you go to school. I must know whether you want a new peruke[19]; your hat and stockings I will get for you and either send or bring them down with me. I hope Betty [*Elizabeth*] takes care to oblidge you; George I know is an old freind and Jack and Leonard I dare say are governable.[20] Take care Sarah does not tire you this hot weather with running. I want much to see you together and to tell you all how much I love you.

Your most affectionate father,
Signed: John Buxton

11 John Buxton to Robert Buxton [105/40]

Addressed: To Mr Robert Buxton at Mr D'Oyly's, Harlston
Channonz, 2 July 1722

Dear Robert,

I take the oppertunity of this messenger to tell you how well pleased I am to hear you are well and how much I wish that you may continue so, and I belive the pleasure will not be less on your side to know at the same time that I am perfectly well. I love you with the greatest affection in which I am ever yours,
Signed: John Buxton

[18] The letter to Robert Buxton was written on the same sheet as a letter from John Buxton to his wife. New Buckenham: a parish and village 15 miles south-west of Norwich and four miles west of Channonz.

[19] Peruke: a periwig or wig.

[20] References to Robert Buxton's brothers and sisters. See the Buxton family tree, Figure 1.

12 John Buxton to Robert Buxton [105/41]

Addressed: To Mr Robert Buxton at Mr D'Oyly's in Harlston
Channonz, 29 July 1722

Dear Robert,

If it was a pleasure to you to write me the assurances of your love and duty, you may believe it was no less for me to receive them. You have always been very dear to me ever since you were born and I will own to you my affection has encreased with your years, not only because you are my son, but that also I have discovered many good inclinations in you which give me very good hopes you may one day be a credit and honour to tour family, as well as my comfort and happines. Nothing, dear Robert, shall be wanting on my part to accomplish this or upon all occations to shew you that I am your most affectionate father,

Signed: John Buxton

I saw Mr Sotherton's mother and sister last Saturday at Norwich.[21] They are very well. His uncle Miles has a feaver but is like to do well. Your mother is well and sends love and blessing to you. Jack has a return of his ague.

13 John Buxton to Robert Buxton [105/42]

Addressed: To Mr Robert Buxton at Mr D'Oyly's house in Harlston
Channonz, 24 September 1722

Dear Robert,

I had the greatest satisfaction last Saturday to hear by Mr D'Oyly you had recovered your health after having been as much concerned the time of your illnes. I pray God you may not have any more returns of it, that at the same time you enjoy the happines of being in perfect health. I may have no less happines in seeing you so.

You see I make no scruple to tell you how much I love you without fearing you will make any other use of my fondnes than to believe that whatever I order is as much for your advantage as could be contrived by the kindest father, and indeed I have a great deal of reason for being so. Wherever I go where you are known, people are continually saying things so much to your

[21] Probably members of the Sotherton family of Taverham (Norfolk). The mother of Thomas Sotherton (*c.* 1677-d. by 1747) was Elizabeth, daughter of James Berwick, a Norwich attorney. P. Palgrave-Moore, ed., *Norfolk Genealogy*, 13 (1981), p. 159.

credit, and at the same time that you are so very much like me, that I believe I must through modesty deprive myself of one of the greatest pleasures in the world, least I should be suspected of taking the praise to myself, whilest I appear so well pleased to hear you commended. But however vain I may appear to others who know not the motives and secret springs of my heart, to you I will not only appear but in reallity be your most affectionate father,

Signed: John Buxton

Your freinds here are all well and so are your brothers and sisters. Service to your master.

14 John Buxton to Robert Buxton [105/43]

Addressed: To Mr Robert Buxton at Mr D'Oyly's house in Harlston
Channonz, 20 November 1722

Dear Robert,

I have the satisfaction to tell you your brothers and sisters are now in so fair a way of doing well that I hope the next account you hear will be that they are perfectly recovered. They all have had the chickin pox and those who before never had the measles have now been ill of them. The rest of your freinds here, except your aunt Hannah,[22] are very well. She has had a cold and a little feavorish illnes but is now better.

This is all the news I can write you from this place and I know you will be pleased to hear it from your most affectionate father,

Signed: John Buxton

15 John Buxton to Robert Buxton [105/44]

Addressed: To Mr Robert Buxton at Mr D'Oyly's house in Harlston
Channonz, 4 December 1722

Dear Robert,

I received you letter by Monsieur Cristian[23] and am too much oblidged to you for it, not to let you know it the first oppertunity. The pleasure of break-

[22] Aunt Hannah (1690–?) was John Buxton's unmarried sister.

[23] A Francis Christian (*c.* 1676–1754) was a dancing master in Norwich. In a rented house in the market place he ran, with his wife, a girls' boarding school for dancing, French, music and needlework. T. Fawcett, 'Provincial Dancing Masters: A Postscript', *Norfolk Archaeology*, 35 (1971), p. 195; *Norwich Gazette*, 9 April 1726; Angela Dain, 'An Enlightened and Polite Society' in *Norwich since 1550*, eds. C. Rawcliffe and R. Wilson (2004), p. 211.

ing up school I remember used to be very great to me when I was of your age, but I shall find much greater next Thursday fortnight to see you so well as I hear you now are. If the weather is fair I will send your hobby,[24] otherwise the chariot.

Your mamma is well and all your brothers and sisters who count of your coming home as the greatest pleasure this Xmas is to afford them, and I think it is a complement that your brother George makes you when he says he loves you better than Xmas pye. Your grandmother is not yet gone to Laxfield but designs it very soon with my sister, the smallpox being entirely ceased there.

I take notice that your writing is improved since this last letter which I am very glad to see, for I think it becomes one that is well educated, among other accomplishments, to be able to do that also like a gentleman.

I am, my dear Robert, your most affectionate father,

Signed; John Buxton

Pray give my service to your master.

16 John Buxton to Robert Buxton [105/45]

Addressed: To Mr Robert Buxton at Mr D'Oyly's in Harlston. To be left at Mr Meeks apothecary in Harlston
Channonz, 29 January 1723

Dear Robert,

The weather has been so cold since you left us that I am a little desirous to know how it agreed with you. Your brother George finds he is not proof against the severity of it. He has got a cold and somthing like a rash come out on his face. Your sisters are growing better as well as Jack. Your mother is a little out of order too with a cold as well as myself but we hope to hear yours is quite gon and the satisfaction of that will make us forget our own complaints.

Your mother joyns with me in sending you our blessing and most hearty wishes for your happines. I am your most affectionate father,

Signed: John Buxton

Leonard and Nancy are both well. Your grandmother and aunt send you their service and I mine to your master.

24 Hobby: a small or middle-sized horse, or a pony.

17 John Buxton to Robert Buxton [35/3]

Addressed: To Mr Robert Buxton at Mr D'Oyly's house in Playford[25]
To be left at the post house in Ipswich
Channonz, 21 April 1723

Dear Robert,

I take this oppertunity by Mr Gibbs's[26] servant to make enquiry after your health, and to let you know we are here rather better than when you left us, though neither your brothers nor sisters are quite rid of their coughs. I hope yours is gone; if the change of air has been beneficial I shall not complain of the distance. To morrow I shall be going to Norwich and your mother to Rushford with all your brothers and sisters, where she hopes for the same relief for them you once found there upon the same occation. Indeed, that place is so agreeable both to health and pleasure, that I often wish for better conveniencys of living there, I mean only for a fue months in the winter, for I know no place I like better than this for constant residence, and am extreemly pleased to find you of the same opinion.

I am, dear Robert, your most affectionate father,
Signed: John Buxton

Be perticular in my service to Mr D'Oyly and to my cosen Meadowes and his lady and to Mis[*s*] when you see them.[27]

[25] Playford, a Suffolk parish and village, five miles north-east of Ipswich. This is the first reference to the move of Mr D'Oyly's school from Harleston.

[26] A neighbour of John Buxton's, Charles Gibbs, rector of Tivetshall (Norfolk), two miles south-east of Channonz. Blomefield, I, p.210. He was probably the father of John Gibbs, a contemporary of Robert Buxton's at Cambridge, who was admitted to St Catherine's College in 1727. Venn, part I, vol. II, p. 209.

[27] The Meadowe or Meadows family of Witnesham (Suffolk), a parish and village three miles from Playford. The family was established in the area well before William Meadowe, jointly with his bother Daniel, bought Witnesham Hall from his father-in-law for £1,000 in *c.* 1614. They were connected to the Buxtons of South Elmham, St Margaret, through three marriages. John Meadowe (1657–1716) married *c.* 1679 Bridget Proctor (1655–1737), the daughter and co-heir of Thomas Proctor of Gissing (Norfolk). She was the sister of Sarah who married John Buxton (*c.* 1640–1714). The Meadowe's son John (bap. 13 Jan. 1680–1750) married Margaret, John Buxton's daughter. John Meadowe's sister Elizabeth (d. 1757) married Thomas Buxton (d. 1738), vicar of Syleham (Suffolk), Margaret Buxton's brother. S.M.W. Meadows, *Witnesham and the Meadows family*, unpublished typescript (Long Melford, 1949–50), pp. 139–41. SRO q S Witnesham 9. 'Cosen Meadowes' is therefore John (1680–1750) and 'Miss' his daughter Elizabeth (Betsy). She married John Williams of London where she died of smallpox in 1727. See letter no. 137, p. 156, below.

30 April

This was returned to me on Sunday, Mr Gibbs's son being ill he did not send him to Ipswich. I have received two letters from you for your mother and need not tell you how glad I am to hear you are well. In my next I hope to let you know your brothers and sisters are all so, most of them being now on the mending; I shall go to them on Saturday. If the weather continues warm and your cold quite gon of[*f*], I woud have you try the sea water to bath in.[28] I have made perticular enquiry concerning the effects of it upon a child at Stratton,[29] and am assured it was perfectly cured of as bad an humour as yours two years or more ago, which has never returned since. When you write always say how you are in your health.

18 John Buxton to Robert Buxton [35/4]

Addressed: To Mr Robert Buxton at Mr D'Oyly's in Playford
22 July 1723

Dear Robert,

Your two letters which give so good account of your health have given me also very great satisfaction. I imagine the weather has lately been warm enough for you to repeat the bathing in the sea; I have great expectations from this remedie, and am confirmed in my opinion of it by Dr Wace[30] whom I lately saw at Norwich, and who perticularly enquired of your health. Cozen Meadow is with us still and often remembers you, so does Mis[*s*] Betty. I have little of news for you but only that we all continue well, & this day sennight I left your freinds so at Laxfeild. The court yard walls are almost finished but the work within doors goes on but slowly.[31] I shall go on with the greater pleasure in whatever I undertake having your advantage always in my view.

I am, my dear Robert, your most affectionate father,
Signed: John Buxton

[28] Hydrotherapy, a method of treating diseases with water, is discussed in W.F. Bynum and R. Porter eds, *Companion Encyclopedia of the History of Medicine,* II (1993), pp. 951–5.

[29] John Buxton does not always distinguish between Stratton Strawless, a village seven miles north of Norwich, where the Marsham family lived, and Long Stratton, ten miles south-west of Norwich on the Ipswich road, and four miles north-east of Channonz.

[30] This is probably William Wacey (or Wasey) M.D. (*c.* 1691–1757). He was educated in Norwich and at Caius College, Cambridge. He gained his M.D. in 1723, being physician to Westminster Hospital 1719–33 and to St George's 1733–57. Venn, part I, vol. IV, p. 307.

[31] The remodelling of Channonz.

19 John Buxton to Robert Buxton [35/5]

Addressed: To Mr Robert Buxton at Playford
Channonz, 11 August 1723

Dear Robert,

I have always been pleased to hear from you in your absence, it now gives me greater satisfaction than ever since every account is a new confirmation of your growing more healthfull; I wanted only that to make me the happiest parent in the world. If this new method proves thoroughly succesful I shall think my self still more fortunate, having been the first who encouraged you to use it. I hope now the succeeding years will be free of all pain & sicknes, that you will remember no more of what you have suffered than just enough to make you put a true estimate upon health & believe it of all others the most valuable possession. If you make this use of former illnes as I believe you will, what you have gon thro with has been well worth the enduring. Your experience has early taught you a peice of wisdom that abundance of young men are strangers to, till it is too late for them to reap any advantage by it, & whilest you see the careles ones and the intemperate fading in their prime you may have the satisfaction of preserving your self sound & vigorous in your youth & healthfull even in age. But I've said too much perhaps to one I believe discreet, yet little for a father who knows the dangers of the world, & would if it were possible have you shun them all.

I am going very soon to the Bath[32] where I shall stay about two months; you will sometimes hear from me there & also give me the pleasure of hearing from you. I intend proposing to the taylor to come down to Playford, you shall know his motions when I get to London, which I believe will be on Tuesday sennight,[33] places being taken for me in the coach. I wish you health & an entire conquest over every Latin author you engage with till you have subdued them all & call out for new worlds of Greek to encounter with.

I am, dear Robert, your most affectionate father,
Signed: John Buxton

[32] The healing properties of the springs of Bath were recognised throughout Europe by the thirteenth century. Royal patronage in the seventeenth century enhanced the city's reputation. Bath's rapid growth as a centre for recreation in addition to bathing and drinking the waters began in the early eighteenth century. R. Morriss and K. Hoverd, *The Buildings of Bath* (Stroud, 1993), pp. 6–7.

[33] Sennight: a week hence.

20 John Buxton to Robert Buxton [35/6]

Addressed: To Mr Robert Buxton at Mr D'Oyly's house in Playford near Ipswich, Suffolk
Bath, 9 September 1723

Dear Robert,

I gave directions when I was at London that my taylor should come to you at Playford. I hope he has ere this time been with you, & that you will soon receive your cloaths. I have been very well since I came hither; in about a month I propose leaving it & have thoughts of seeing you as I return to Norfolk. Let me hear how you do when you have received this & direct to me at Bath in Somersetshire.

With service to Mr D'Oyly I end this & am your most affectionate father,
Signed: J[*ohn*] Buxton

I shall write to cozen Meadowe next post.

21 John Buxton to Robert Buxton [35/7]

Addressed: To Mr Robert Buxton at Mr D'Oyly's house in Playford near Ipswich, Suffolk
London, 19 October 1723

Dear Robert,

I did not come to town till last Tuesday though I intended it a week sooner, a fit of the gout which took Mr Branthwayt [34] prevented us. The year is so far gon that I must now make the shortest way home, & see you at Playford some other time. Though I am not to have that pleasure I often have the other of hearing you are well & I hope for the continuance of it. I shall be in Norfolk almost as soon as you'l receive this, designing on Monday to set out. I know not whether it is travelling or the Bath waters that so well agree with me but thank God I find my self perfectly well, & have never had one cold since my leaving the country, nor do I find any inconvenience in the thick and smoaky air of London.

I hope your cloaths are fit & to your liking, but why did not you write to

[34] The Branthwayt (or Branthwait) family owned property at Hethel, seven miles south-west of Norwich, bought by Miles Branthwayt (d. 1612). John Buxton's travelling companion to Bath was Arthur Branthwayt (1687–1724), eldest son and heir of Arthur Branthwayt (d. 1717), barrister at law.

the taylor to let him know they were received. I have bought you three pair of stockings which shall be sent whenever you want them.

I am your most affectionate father,

Signed: John Buxton

Service to Mr D'Oyly. I forgot to say I received another letter from you at Bath writ very well for which I thank you.

22 John Buxton to Robert Buxton [35/8]

Addressed: To Mr Robert Buxton at Playford
Channonz, 27 October 1723

Dear Robert,

My last letter to you was from London by which you were informed of my leaving that place as last Monday. I accordingly set out from thence & had a very pleasant journey, & at the end of it the greatest satisfaction to find your mother & all your brothers & sisters well, as also a good account of your self. They all continue so though your grandmother is not quite recovered but in a very fair way. I have bought for your use the *Antiquitys* of Monfoucon: ten volumes folio the large paper in French & Latin.[35] We shall divert our selves with looking them over when I see you.

With mine & your mother's blessing & best wishes, I am your most affectionate father,

Signed: John Buxton

23 John Buxton to Robert Buxton [105/53]

Addressed: To Mr Robert Buxton at Playford
Saturday 28 March 1724 [*probably*]

Dear Robert,

I had designed myself the pleasure of a journy to Playford upon the most agreeable occation in the world but the ill condition of the roads have discouraged me. However, I will meet you on Monday at Stoke[36] White Horse with

[35] Bernard de Montfaucon (1655–1741), *L'antiquité expliquée et représentée en figures* (Paris, 1719). A supplement was published in 1724.

[36] Stoke Ash, a Suffolk parish and village, six miles south of the county boundary with Norfolk, on the main road from Ipswich to Norwich (now the A140). The White Horse Inn survives today.

the coach to relieve you if you find yourself too much tired. If the morning is but tolerable I will expect you there and your brother in perfect health.

I am your most affectionate father,

Signed; John Buxton

You will come the same way I went with you last, not taking Witnesham[37] in the road, being much about. Service to your master.

24 John Buxton to Robert Buxton [35/10]

Addressed: To Mr Robert Buxton at Mr D'Oyly's house in Playford.
To be left at the Cross Keys [38] in Ipswich, Suffolk
Wednesday, 10 June 1724

Dear Robert,

I have received a letter from you since my return from Laxfeild & your mother has had two, one by Mr Gibbs & one by the post. I also heard of you by Mr Jarmy,[39] & was extreem glad to find the little disorder went of so soon. Your grandmother Buxton is much better but last Wednesday your mother was taken ill with a sort of feaver which affected her stomach, back & bowels. S[*i*]r Benj[*ami*]n [*Wrench*][40] has bled her &c & she is now in the way of recovery though not yet down stairs. Your grandmother Gooch & aunt Herne are at Mr Dalling's [41] for change of air.

Your account of Brightwell[42] is very agreeable, I propose to see that place the next time come in that part of the country. Sunday sennight I was to see Col[*one*]l Harbord & his new building.[43] It is all of white brick, the archi-

[37] Witnesham, a parish and village four miles north-east of Ipswich, the home of the Meadowes family.

[38] An inn in Carr Street, Ipswich. P. Bishop, *The History of Ipswich* (1995), p. 98.

[39] Probably Jermy, of the family of Stansfield near Wymondham.

[40] See note 63, p. 17, above.

[41] Not identified.

[42] Brightwell, a parish and village seven miles east of Ipswich, and five miles from Playford. The attraction for visitors was Brightwell Hall, remodelled in the 1660s by Sir Samuel Barnardiston Bt, deputy governor of the East India Company, who created one of the greatest gardens of the Restoration period in Suffolk. The house was demolished in the eighteenth century. G.L. Gomme, ed., *Topographical History of Staffordshire and* Suffolk (1899), p. 203; T. Williamson, *Suffolk's Gardens and Parks* (Macclesfield and Norwich, 2000), pp. 31–2.

[43] The Harbord family bought the Gunton estate in north-east Norfolk in the first half of the seventeenth century. Colonel Harbord was born Harbord Cropley and changed his name upon inheriting Gunton from his uncle John Harbord who died in 1710 without heirs. Harbord married in 1737 as his second wife Rebecca, daughter of Sir Benjamin Wrench M.D. (see note

traves cornishes & mouldings about the windows of the same, and looks very agreeably. The inside will be large & convenient. It will be covered by September, if this rainy season does not put them back.

The oaks like it very well, never was there a more favourable time, I shall loose very few of them & even the hedge that was I thought past recovery will revive again. The rooms are all painted, but the staircase not plaistered: finishing is slow beyond my patience.[44]

The weather has not for two days been hot enough for you to bath: it must be settled fair before you venture. Your mother will send some phisick time enough, you must take that first and not till a fortnight after go into the sea. Lady Ward has a daughter, your grandmother Gooch stands for it.[45] Your brothers and sisters are well, your mare as fat as the bucks. Old Phanny lost her foal: she was too poor to nurs it. The rest are safe keep their number, the acorns are come up very well in the new grove, and the flocks & herds at present all prosperous. I hope by this time your companions are come to you. Has Georgy got the books he wanted, does he begin to write? [46] Monsieur Xian [*Christian*] speaks extreem well of him.

My love & blessing is with you both from your most affectionate father,
Signed: John Buxton

Your mother sends love & blessing to yourself & Georgy, & says your last letter was a cordial to her.

25 John Buxton to Robert Buxton[35/11]

Addressed: To Mr Robert Buxton at Mr D'Oyly's house in Playford, Suffolk
Channonz, 8 July 1724

Dear Robert,

Last Thurday I came hither from Witnesham & had a very pleasant journey. I

63, p. 17, above), and widow of John Marcon of Norwich. When he died in 1742 the estate was inherited by his nephew William Morden who changed his name to Harbord. Gunton Hall was built for Sir William Harbord in the mid eighteenth century but details of any earlier building there by Colonel Harbord are not known.

[44] The remodelling of Channonz.

[45] The child was the daughter of Sir Edward Ward of Bixley, fifth baronet (d. 1737), and Lady Ward (Susan Randall, d. 1759). Sir Edward had succeeded his father, also Sir Edward, fourth baronet, in 1719. The latter had married Barbara Gooch (d. 1755), the daughter and coheir of Leonard Gooch of Earsham and Dorothy née Catelyn. To stand: to act as godparent or act as sponsor for a child.

[46] Robert's younger brother George (1716–1740), now at Mr D'Oyly's school.

called at Mr Calver's[47] & saw your brothers there who were both well and at play. Your mother grows better as also does your sister Betty [*Elizabeth*], I hope in a little time you will hear they are quite recovered. Lenny & Sarah are perfectly well but your grandmother mends slowly if at all, I shall be very glad to know that your cold is gone of. The weather has lately been unfavourable but I make no doubt of your care. Last Saturday I was with S[*i*]r Ben[*jamin*] Wrench, he says you may take 15 grains of rhubarb in powder & encrease the quantity to 20 as you find it works with you,[48] but this never to be taken near the time either before or after your going into the water, but at 5 or 6 days distance. He also desires you not to remain too long in water.

I saw Mr Sotherton at Norwich, they have not yet fixed him with a master so he is to be for some time at home not much to his advantage. Last Wednesday old Mr Neve of Aslacton[49] was buried there, he has for some time lived at Loddon[50] but finding himself ill he came in a chariot to Aslacton & dyed in three or four days after. Your mare is very well & put to grass, the deer are increased to six or seaven more besides the spotted one from Witnesham, which goes into the park with the rest though it comes twice a day to be fed with milk. The small pox is now so much abated in Norwich that the more timorous make no scruple of going thither.

Let me hear from you pretty frequently no matter how short, but write as your time or inclination allows, for it is much the greatest pleasure to me in the world to know you are well.

I am your most affectionate father,
Signed: John Buxton

My humble service to your master. Betty, Sarah & Lenny send theirs to you with their love. George & Jack would have done the same, but in their absence I engage for them that they will love & serve you. I hope all the things you desired are sent; you are not to take the rhubarb but when your cold is gon & then not ofter than once in a month.

[47] This is an accurate transcription but did John Buxton intend Carver? See note no. 325, p. 147, below.

[48] Rhubarb (*Rheum*) was used as a purgative and basic treatment for many ailments. Sloan, p. 62.

[49] Aslacton, a parish and village, two miles from Channonz, in which John Buxton owned property bought from the Le Neve family. Laurence Le Neve died on 29 June 1724 leaving no children. Blomefield, V, p. 179.

[50] Loddon, a small market town ten miles south-east of Norwich on the Beccles road.

26 John Buxton to Robert Buxton [35/13]

Addressed: To Mr Robert Buxton at Mr D'Oyly's house in Playford near Ipswich, Suffolk
To be left at the Cross Keys, Ipswich
Channonz, July 23 1724

Dear Robert,

I have lately received two letters from you & am extreem glad to hear you are well. Those from hence with the parcel I hope are come safe to you. Your grandmother & aunt Buxton are with us, your mother has almost lost her cough but your grandmother Gooch continues ill, though a little better than when you left us. The weather I believe has been too cold for you to bath, you will do it I suppose when it grows warmer, but remember to be very cautious that you are perfectly cool when you go into the water. I mentioned in my last all that was necessary about your taking physick, the rhubarb may be had at Ipswich. You may get Tully's *Offices* there if you want one, I have a translation of S[*i*]r Roger Le Strange [51] which you may have if your master approves of it.

This cool season makes the country pleasant but the fruits will want a warmer to ripen them, you must therefore be cautious how you eat of them. Whiles I enjoy a perfect health my self & hear that you continue to do so, I assure you I do not envy the happy temperature of the climate at Lima, nor the beautifull ancient & modern scenes of the buildings & gardens &c of Italy, nor the politenes of France nor the riches of Holland, nor any thing els in England but what my own good fortune has already given me.

I am with my best wishes for your health, your most affectionate father,
Signed: John Buxton

Your mother sends her blessing, your grandmother does the same. Service at Whitnesham when you see any of [the] family.[52]

27 John Buxton to Robert Buxton [35/14]

Addressed: To Mr Buxton at Mr D'Oyly's house in Playford, Suff[*olk*]
To be left at the Cross Keys in Ipswich post p[*ai*]d: 3d.
Channonz, 5 August 1724

Dear Robert,

My being last week at the assizes prevented me receiving your letter & of

[51] See item 48 in Appendix A. [52] The Meadowe family.

answering it so soon as I would have done. I went to Norwich on the Monday & stayed till Thursday when your mother & aunt Hannah with Betty [*Elizabeth*] came for me in the coach & returned the same day leaving the beau monde at the assembly for a quiet night's rest at home without envying or even thinking of the people or the divertions we left behind. I hope the bathing has agreed with you & that you find no inconvenience from the rhubarb. The weather begins now to be somthing cooler so you must be cautious in the use of both, but your own experience will direct you & if any time you find any alteration in your health be sure to let your master know it at the first, whatsoever accident may have occationed it, & though it may seem but little, for a remedy applyed in time prevents a disease from doing much hurt.

My work here [53] goes forward leisurely, the staircase at present employs the joiners. Upon much consideration I have left the door there where it was & the steps are to begin at the great parlour door as first designed. The blue room is finished & the alteration to every ones liking as well as my own, which is somewhat unusual. The windows are all finished in the front of the house & the capitals or tops of the pillars at the corners all repaired & now stand in the same form they were first built in, the fanes only left out. The out side of the house is now entirely finished & seems so sound & firm to bid fair to remain two centurys more <if some> if no extraordinary accident happens to it.[54] Your grandmother Buxton is perfectly well again but your grandmother Gooch much as she was if not declining; your mother & the rest of the family in health, all joyning in wishes for yours.

I am your most affectionate father,

Signed: John Buxton

Service to Mr D'Oyly. I have sent the translation of Tully's *Offices.* Your mother sends her blessing. Betty desires to be perticular in her love to you & is very good natured. Sarah upon putting on Mrs Meadowes present & her new cloaths became very circumspect & carefull of her motions. The gardner much the same has abundance of cowcumbers but no melons; your mare very well. There is just 21 deer in the park, 7 young ones besides that from Whitnesham. Cozen Meadowes picture is ready to be sent.

[53] Remodelling Channonz

[54] John Buxton's view of the durability of Channonz was optimistic. The house survived for a little over 60 years. Two of its three wings were pulled down when the family completed its removal to Shadwell Lodge in 1786. A. Paget Baggs, 'Channons Hall', *Norfolk Archaeology*, 34 (1966–9), pp. 9–13.

28 John Buxton to Robert Buxton [35/15]

Addressed: To Mr Rob[*er*]t Buxton at Playford
5 August 1724

Dear Robert,

I sent a letter this day by the Harlston carrier before I knew of cozen Meadows servants coming hither. He brought one this night from you that gave us a great deal of pleasure. I wish you the continuance of your health & am your most affectionate father,
Signed: John Buxton

The book comes by this bearer.

29 John Buxton to Robert Buxton [35/16]

No address
26 August 1724

Dear Robert,

Your letter of the 9th inst. which gave me so good an account of your health gave me also the greater pleasure I can return you the same good account of all your freinds here except your grandmother Gooch who continues as she was.

Your desire to know how the work goes forward is too oblidging to me not to be gratified, I sent you a full account of it in the letter by the carrier directed to be left at the X Keys, which I suppose is lost, & least it should be so I will repeat what I said in that about the building, which in spight of my utmost dilligence goes on but slowly. All the pillars at the corners of the front of the house are repaired & all the windows there finished so it now appears as when first built. The brick peers at the bridge & end of the court wall are coped, & the drawing room chimney, a most tedious peice of work, just done & in the way of being made a good one. The great parlour ceiled & strings of the staircase just up, but upon much consideration the door left where it was & the steps begin at the great parlour door. The blew room has been a long time done & every way improved, I hope all will be finished some time before Xmas.

Your mother's pictures are not yet come but the box of glass & china is & very safe; your grandmother Buxton is now at Lady Ward's at Norwich, I expect her here again on Saturday. Your uncle Jacob [55] & all his family are now

[55] The Jacob family of Laxfield (Suffolk), related through the marriage of John Buxton's sister Elizabeth (1688–1756) to Nicholas Jacob.

here, I am just going with him to Winfarthing [56] to fish there. I have done nothing about the stables, it was well I took no more of the great barn for that use, for it will now scarce hold the corn of this year which my lands have yeild in very great plenty. The deer are all safe in the park to the number of twenty one, & your mare there in very good plight. I made your compliments to Mis[*s*] Meadowe & by letter to your aunt Han. They both give me the pleasure of speaking often of you, & send their service.

I must before I end this tell you how much Betty [*Elizabeth*] oblidged me. The contest about the wish[*bone*] in the lot of the merry thought fell between Betty & Sarah. Betty pulled the longest bone & when I asked her what she wished for she said it was that you might have your health. I kissed her for her kindness to you & shall always love her the better.

I am your most affect[*ionate*] father,

Signed: J[*ohn*] Buxton

30 John Buxton to Robert Buxton [35/17]

Addressed: To Mr Robert Buxton at Mr D'Oyly's house in Playford near Ipswich, Suffolk

To be left at the Cross Keys in Ipswich

Channonz, 2 September 1724: in the year [*16*]*66* on this day London was burnt <by>.[57]

Dear Robert,

I have received yours with the enclosed for Betty [*Elizabeth*] with which she is more pleased than with any other present you could have given her, & wishes she could write to thank you for your kindness. I have promised to assist her, at present she is a good deal taken up with your cozens from Laxfeild who have been here for some time. I told you in my last how much she oblidged me, I believe she will continue to do it by observing how much it pleases me when you all love & oblidge each other. Your grandmother Buxton is come from Stratton & is perfectly well again, but your grandmother Gooch continues much as she was. Mis[*s*] Meadows & your aunt Han are with me & at your service.

The drawing room chimney with that of the chamber over are quite finished & I hope by the care I've taken will not smoke, for the whole stack as

[56] Winfarthing, a parish and village in south Norfolk, three miles south-west of Channonz.

[57] The great fire of London began in Pudding Lane in the early hours of Sunday 2 September 1666. By the time the fire was checked on 5 September some four-fifths of the medieval city had been destroyed. R. Porter, *London: A Social History* (1996), pp. 84–7.

far as the roof was taken down & rebuilt, the diameter of the tunnels one third less than the old. The largeness of them has certainly been the occation of their smoaking. The stairs are up to the first landing & will now go on very fast.[58] I forgot to tell you I had hired another gardner to come to me at Michaelmas; the rest of my manservants stay. You've heard I imagine Mr Hare of Hargham[59] is near marrying a great fortune, a grocer's daughter of Thetford, & report says S[*i*]r Will[*ia*]m Holland[60] is marryed to a lady with a very small one; he has been so little at Quiddenham[61] & at such uncertain times that I have not found any to wait on him there. No more but my best wishes for your health from your most affectionate father,

Signed: John Buxton

Service to your master.

31 John Buxton to Robert Buxton [35/19]

Addressed: To Mr Robert Buxton at Mr D'Oyly's house in Playford near Ipswich, Suffolk
To be left at the Cross Keys in Ipswich
Channonz, 30 September 1724

Dear Robert,

I received your last letter a week after it came to Harlston by neglect of those that should have called for it, the pleasure was not less though a little deferred. You have anticipated my desires, I intended in this to have made some enquiry how you proceeded in your studies which you have very agreeably prevented. I am very sorry to hear of your master's illness, it is in general called a sickly time though thank God my family continue well, all but your grandmother who is much at the old rate. Your grandmother Buxton is gon to Laxfeild & is very well as a letter just now received informs me.

The trees planted this last year on Aslacton Common do not prosper so well as my gardiner assured me they would, about half will live. The staircase

[58] Remodelling Channonz.

[59] Thomas Hare of Hargham (1692–1736) married Mary, daughter of Joseph Sharpe of Thetford. Blomefield, I, pp. 412–9.

[60] Sir William Holland Bt, of Quidenham, married the daughter of Mr Upton, a Spanish merchant. Blomefield, I, p. 344.

[61] Quidenham, a parish and village eight miles west of Channonz. Quidenham Hall, built by the Holland family in 1606, was sold to John Bristow *c.* 1740 and he sold it to the third earl of Albemarle in 1762. Pevsner, *Norfolk 2*, pp. 596–7.

is not to be wainscotted higher than the rails, but only plaistered from the first going of the steps, the rest below to be wainscotted up to ceiling. Your letter to Betty [*Elizabeth*] gave her much pleasure & som pride, it will be no less to me to see you love each other & so to behave your selves as to deserve it. I am my dear Robert your most affectionate father,

Signed: John Buxton

Service to your master. I am glad Mr Cresham[62] is come again, he is by much the best master, the difficulty of the Greek which you are now to begin will soon be over, you must not therefore be discouraged at it at first.

32 John Buxton to Robert Buxton [35/20]

Addressed: To Mr Robert Buxton at Mr D'Oyly's house in Playford
Channonz, 15 October 1724

Dear Robert,

I have deferred to thank you for your letter of the 4th inst. till this oppertunity of sending by cozen Meadowe who came last Tuesday for Miss. I hope your cold is quite gon of & that you'l have no more returns of it, if you have let me hear <if you devel.>. If your astma should come in any great degree you must be content to lose a little blood, & a day or two after take about 12 grains of ippacacuenna[63] to vomit, but this only in case of necessity. I have sent your cloath cloaths by cozen Meadowes chariot, if you find the stuff too thin you may wear these, your fustian[64] had better be laid by till till [*sic*] the summer & your stuff[65] worn for every day instead of that. We all continue well here except your grandmother Gooch whose illnes seems tries old age & decay. The season has been exceedingly pleasant & the drynes so sutible to us as to make me wish its continuance.

I was yesterday at Thelveton, Mr Havers'[66], an old brick house somthing in

[62] A master at Mr D'Oyly's school.

[63] Ipecacuanha, the root of a South American shrub (*cephaëlis ipecacuanha*) possessing emetic and purgative properties.

[64] Fustian, a coarse cloth made of cotton and flax. By the date of the letter the term could refer to a thick twilled cotton cloth with a short pile or nap.

[65] Stuff, an unfulled fabric made from long-staple wool. By the end of the seventeenth century descriptive of a range of fashionable textiles manufactured in Norwich from worsted and mixtures with silk and linen. U. Priestley, *The Fabric of Stuffs. The Norwich Textile Industry from 1565* (Norwich, 1990).

[66] A Thomas Havers was lord of the manor of Thelveton in 1737, being the son of William Havers. It is not clear which man John Buxton met.

the manner of this but a very humble imitation of it. I had letter from Mr Branthwayt [67] since he got to Bristol where he intends to be some time for the benefit of the waters: he is much better than when he left Norfolk. I hope your master is so after his journy into this country. I had not the pleasure to see him then but I believe I shall in a little time do it at Playford. Mr Randal [68] & I have talked of coming together. There is no harm in your being a critick so long as you take care who you make your remarks to. The young man who was the subject of them will I hope mend his behaviour [*?word*] your school. He was sent from Bury[69] for some great misdemeanours which the master there was not able to check. If Mr D'Oyly is not acquainted with this you may show him what I have writ & with my service to him I shall conclude this from your most affectionate father,

Signed: John Buxton

Your mother sends her blessing, Betty [*Elizabeth*] & Sarah & Len their love.

33 John Buxton to Robert Buxton [35/21]

Addressed: To Mr Robert Buxton at Mr D'Oyly's house in Playford near Ipswich, Suffolk
6d. To be left at the Cross Keyes, Ipswich
Channonz, 27 October 1724

Dear Robert,

I have received yours of the 18th inst. with a small bit of intelligence enclosed from cosen Meadowe in which she says a great deal in a little, when she tells me her family is well. I have sent a Greek testament such as I learned by at Bury[70], with a lexicon, as also Ovid *Metamorphosis.* If your master approves of it I will send you the translation of Ovid by Dryden, Garth & others.[71] You will every day find less difficulty in the Greek, the rules in the grammer are absolutely necessary to be remembered & though you don't at present see the reason of them, you will in a very little time when you come to apply them. The sentence you quote from Terence is worthy of that Roman. Governed by such maxims what difficultys did not that people overcome by

[67] Arthur Branthwayt of Hethel. See note 72, p. 58, below.
[68] Not identified.
[69] An unnamed pupil at Bury School who transferred to Mr D'Oyly's establishment at Playford.
[70] John Buxton attended the Free Grammar School in Bury St Edmunds.
[71] See Appendix A, item 67.

degrees arriving to the highest pitch of glory, as high as human nature coud carry them.

I forgot whether I told you Mr Branthwayt went some time ago to Bristol to drink those waters, this day sennight I was surprised with an account of his death. His brother Miles is gone in order to have him brought to Hethel where he is to be buried privately.[72] I have lost a freind & the country a patriot. It is said S[*i*]r Will[*ia*]m Holland is married to a lady of no fortune.[73] He is very much censured by most people because there are a great number of women that have fortunes out of which he might have chose at will, indeed this is a point a man ought to be well advised in since the happiness of his whole life is concerned in it.

This year having afforded plenty of acorns I have taken the oppertunity of planting some, the plowed feild of 5 acres on the west side the home close is designed for a grove. You may thank me for the pleasure it may yeild you & I know not who for the profit but I flatter my self it may be some of your descendants. George & Jack came home this evening to morrow being holyday to assist in this agreeable work & I intend your sisters shall have a hand in it & even Nanny[74] is strong enough to carry an acorn. I will reserve some for you to set at Xmas well knowing what pleasure you take in planting. Your mother is well & sends her blessing, all your brothers and sisters their love. You have both from me who am your most affectionate father,

Signed: John Buxton

Your grandmother Buxton is well & all that family, your grandmother Gooch much as she was. Service to your master, I hope he is perfectly recovered. The flesh broth will be of much service, Dr Cheyny[75] advised me to it when last at Bath.

34 John Buxton to Robert Buxton [35/22]

Addressed: To Mr Robert Buxton at Mr D'Oyly's house in Playford Suff.
To be left at the Cross Keys in Ipswich
Channonz, 9 November 1724

Dear Robert,

Your letter to condole with me for the loss of my freind was very oblidging &

[72] Arthur Branthwayt died in Bristol on 17 October 1724 in his 38th year. He was buried in Hethel church. Blomefield, V, p. 104.

[73] See note 60, p. 55, above.

[74] A pet name for Anne, born 1721.

[75] See note 64, p. 18, above.

though I am deprived of one of my most agreeable ones it gave me some consolation as coming from one who gives me hopes of supplying all losses of this kind & who will be worthy of my freindship as well as paternal affection.

The books you desired were sent. If you want a lexicon I will send you one called Passers [76] peculiarly adapted to the Greek testament. S[*i*]r Edw[*ar*]d Ward [77] is in some danger of being made sheriff this year, an office not very agreeable to him. The heires[?s] at St Margretts[78] was lately in great danger also, if not dead. Thank God your mother & brothers & sisters continue well though all complain of the very sharp east winds. I hope you find no inconvenience from them. I have no more at present but service to your master from your most affectionate father,

Signed: John Buxton

Your mother sends her blessing, your sisters their service & best wishes.

35 John Buxton to Robert Buxton [35/23]

Addressed: To Mr Robert Buxton at Mr D'Oyly's house in Playford, Suffolk 3[*d*]. To be left at the X Keys in Ipswich
Channonz, 24 November 1724

Dear Robert,

Your letter of the 7th inst. laid above a week at Harlston, the market people are not so constant in their motions this winter time & trusting to them I omit sending a servant. The lexicon was not put up with the other books by mistake, you may take it with [*you*] at your return. I'm much pleased you begin to be reconciled to the Greek. That maxim you mentioned out of Terence will carry you through all difficulty, there are abundance more to be met with in that author not inferior to this. When you are more acquainted with the sages of antiquity you will meet with so much good sense, that your surprise will turn to esteem & veneration.

I have not yet finished planting but am daily engaged about it, till very lately we have not had rain enough to take up trees. I shall not now be able to see you before Xmas except I should come for you about which I am not resolved. I thank you for your care for the ennigo[?][79] root but shall not want

[76] George Pasor (1570–1637), *Lexicon Græco-Latinum* (London, editions from 1621 to 1650). See Appendix A, item 54.

[77] Sir Edward Ward, fifth baronet, of Bixley (d. 1737).

[78] Refers probably to a Buxton relative at South Elmham, Saint Margaret (Suffolk).

[79] Ennigo is possibly the root of Wild Indigo (*BaptisiaTinctoria)*, a plant native to North America, used medicinally.

any. Your grandmother has been ill again but is a little better, your mother & all ells well. This is all at present from your most affectionate father,

Signed: John Buxton

36 John Buxton to Robert Buxton [35/25]

Addressed: To Mr Robert Buxton at Mr D'Oyly's in Playford
11 December 1724

Dear Robert,

The badnes of roads & uncertainty of weather make me choose to send the chariot for you to secure you from the inconveniencys of both, & your mother's company will make it more agreeable than coming on horsback. I had thoughts my self of taking this oppertunity of waiting on cozen Meadowe but a multitude of workmen still oblidge me to keep near them. Before you leave Playford give my service to your master & let him know if he makes a tour into Norfolk that I shall hope for the pleasure of seeing him this Xmas. I wish you a good journy & am yours most affectionately,

Signed: J[*oh*]n Buxton

37 John Buxton to Robert Buxton [35/26]

Addressed: To Mr Robert Buxton at Playford
Wednesday, 21 April 1725

Dear Robert,

The lamenes of my horse kept me a day longer at Witnesham than I designed. I returned on the road as I came home and made me have a most tiresom journy. I was glad to hear so good an account of you by my servant. I hope you have entirely lost your cold. We have had abundance of rain here, the young oaks rejoyce at it. All here are well except your grandmother.

With love & blessing to George is all from your most affectionate father,

Signed: John Buxton

Your mother will send sheets &c for George very soon. Betty [*Elizabeth*] sends her love. She is got into her closet & much pleased with having the prospect of a room to her self. I hope yours is to your liking.

38 John Buxton to Robert Buxton [35/27]

Addressed: To Mr Robert Buxton at Mr D'Oyly's house in Playford, Suffolk
To be left at the Cross Keys in Ipswich
Channonz, 4 May 1725

Dear Robert,

I did not expect a letter from you sooner than that I received last Wednesday. I need not tell you what pleasure it gave to hear so good an account of your self & your brother. I hope George will take care to preserve the good character he has gained, & follow your example to observe & oblidge your master.

We have had frequent showers but not that plenty of rain you mention to have fallen about Playford, though enough to save the trees but the hedge is somwt doubtfull. I shall not be at the horsrace, I told you the reason in my last which came with some books & a letter for my cozen Meadowe: in Whitsun holy days I am to be at Laxfeild with your mother. We take Betty [*Elizabeth*], Sarah, Jack & Leny with us, our stay will be about 5 or 6 days. Let my cozen Meadowe know the pidgeons arrived safe at Stratton & were a novelty to my uncle who never had any of the kind before.[80]

Next week you may expect some shoes & the house lining on George's account which he should have brought with him at first. The weather has been too cold for you to think of bathing yet so your physick has not been sent. Convey the enclosed to my cozen Meadowes, the first convenience.

I am dear son, your most affectionate father,
Signed: John Buxton

Your mother joyns with me in blessing to you both. Your sisters & Leny in abundance of love. Your grandmother at Laxfeild is well & all freinds there.

[80] John Buxton refers here to the Marshams of Stratton Strawless. Buxton's uncle was Thomas Marsham (d. 1751) who married Dorothy Gooch, daughter of Leonard Gooch of Earsham and sister of Buxton's mother Elizabeth.

39 John Buxton to Robert Buxton [35/28]

Addressed: To Mr Robert Buxton at Mr D'Oyly's house in Playford near Ipswich
Channonz, 10 May 1725, the day I came to reside here

Dear Robert,

If Mr Mallom[81] continues his resolution of going this day to the horsrace you will receive this letter by his servant, which is to thank you for yours received last Friday when you were perticularly remembered. The little Virgil [82] had been sent with the other books but it was not come from the binders, you shall have it with the next parcel.

Since you love to hear of the planting I will often mention it & now I may with perticular satisfaction for it rains very plentifully just as the oaks begun to want it. The hedge looks seer [83] but I do not entirely give it for lost. The painter has this morning begun the rooms. Rob[*er*]t Phillips's[84] house [*is*] up to the chamber floor but I have yet began nothing of my stables or other works abroad. Only the terras is removed into the park. My horse has been lame ever since I came home & if I had designed coming to Ipswich horse race[85] that would have prevented.

Betty [*Elizabeth*] thanks you for the property you allow her in the closet. I believe she will not leave it without myne or your approbation. Both she & Sarah are learning to write & come on very fast in it but I believe Sarah will send the first letter to George having a perticular genious that way. I hear four of the new Knights of the Bath will be of Norfolk – L[*or*]d Lynn, Mr R[*obert*] Walpole & his brother Horace, with S[*i*]r J[*ohn*] Hobart.[86] The news you

[81] John Mallom (or Mallam) (*c.* 1670–1728) of Wacton, three miles north-east of Channonz Hall. He was educated at Wymondham (Norfolk) and Caius College, Cambridge, and married Elizabeth, daughter of Robert Suckling. Venn, part I, vol. III, p. 130.

[82] Appendix A, item 135.

[83] Seer: dry or withered. Now used only in a poetical or rhetorical sense but the word was current in East Anglia as 'Sare' or 'Sear', E. Moor, *Suffolk Words and Phrases* (1823), pp. 329 and 324.

[84] Robert Phillips was a Buxton tenant at The Grange. He was also John Buxton's bailiff. Appendix C.

[85] Ipswich race week took place every summer on a heathland course between the Felixstowe and Nacton roads. After a boom during the French wars, attributable to the presence of the military in the town, interest declined. The last flat meeting was held in 1883 and from 1902 the site was built over. Bishop, *Ipswich*, pp. 101–3. Bishop gives the earliest recorded date as 1727 but Buxton's letter precedes this. See also L. Redstone, *Ipswich through the Ages* (Ipswich, 1948), pp. 106–7.

[86] Two of these men were created Knights of the Bath: on 17 June 1725, Sir John Hobart Bt

send me of your self & brother is the best you can write, and if you can keep the *mens sana in corpore sano*[87] you will be happier than any knights in the world.

I am your most affectionate father,
Signed: John Buxton

Your mother joyns with me blessing to you both, service [to] your master. I am glad that [*?word*] is so much to your liking.

40 John Buxton to Robert Buxton [105/55]

Addressed: To Mr Robert Buxton at Mr D'Oyly's in Playford
Channonz, 17 May 1725 [*?*]

Dear Robert,

We have received two letters from you since I writ. I also heard of you by Mr Mallom and Mr Layman[88]. I hope the pain you complained of has left you. The box I mentioned will be sent to you next Wednesday with lining [*linen*] in it and two books. I could not get the Medulla[89] at Norwich. If it is to be had at Ipswich buy it there for your brother. If Mr D'Oyly thinks it proper, George may read in Fuller's *Lives*[90] sometimes. I knew no other book more suitable to him.

Tomorrow we set out for Laxfield. Your grandmother there has been very ill with an impostume[91] in her head attended with a feaver. Last Friday I sent and she was growing better. I hope to find her almost well.

We have had plenty of rain and the young oaks seem very prosperous. Yesterday in walking round to observe all in the home close I could not perceive

(1694?-1756) of Blickling (created Baron Hobart of Blickling in 1728 and first Earl of Buckinghamshire in 1746), and on 25 June 1725, Robert Walpole (1676–1745) of Houghton, first baron Walpole of Walpole (1723), prime minister, who became the first earl of Orford in 1742. Lord Lynn – Charles Townshend (1674–1738), second Viscount of Raynham and Baron Townshend of Lynn Regis – had been a Knight of the Garter, a more elevated rank, since 1724. Robert Walpole's brother Horace (Horatio) (1678–1757) was not honoured. He was created first baron Walpole of Wolterton in 1756.

87 A healthy mind in a healthy body.

88 Habakkuk Layman, a surgeon of Diss (*c.* 1678–1744), married Amy Barry in 1702 and their son, also Habakkuk, was baptised in 1708. Venn, part I, vol. III, p. 58.

89 Medulla = marrow, a term commonly used in the Latin title of books to indicate that the essential substance of a subject has been covered. The reference is not specific enough for the work to be identified.

90 Thomas Fuller (1608–61), *The Lives and Deaths of Moderne Divines* (1651).

91 Impostume: a swelling, cyst or abscess.

more than one but what seemed to grow. The acorns in the wheat close begin to come up but the hedge shews few signs of living. I will compound for that if the rest do well, though the oaks in that give me hopes of life.

I am very glad your room is to your liking. Did the other young gentleman quit it without offence? I saw Mr Nuttle[92] since he was at Playford. He spake much in praise of that place and of the order and economy of your master. Monsieur Christen says George is very good. It is a great pleasure to hear it. Your mother joyns me in blessing to you both, and our wishes for your health.

I am your most affectionate father,

Signed: John Buxton

Two pair of shoes for yourself and one for George come with the box. Service to your master.

Betty [*Elizabeth*] stands by me and desires her love. Jack, Sarah and An[*ne*] are at play but I will put in theirs which is always intended. The key of George's box enclosed.

41 John Buxton to Robert Buxton [35/30]

Addressed: To Mr Robert Buxton at Mr D'Oyly's in Playford near Ipswich, Suffolk
To be left at the X Keys in Ipswich
Channonz, 16 June 1725

Dear Robert,

I did not receive your letter with the perticular account of your illnes till last Wednesday. It should have come to me at Laxfeild where I had orderd all letters to be sent that week from Harlston, but the man who brought them from thence never delivered them. I hope you've had no returns. It was the effect of taking some cold at the horsrace. Last Saturday I shew S[*i*]r Benj[*ami*]n [*Wrench*] your letter: he says if a like disorder should return you should first be bled a little[93] about 4 or 5 ounces & then apply a blister[94] to your neck, keep warm within for a few days & forbear flesh meat.

The weather has been extreem wet here & unseasonable for every thing I think but the oaks. The roads as bad as in winter but we hope every day for God's blessing & the sunshine. Your mother is perfectly recovered of her illnes & by this time I believe your grandmother Buxton is so too, for the last

92 Not identified.

93 See note 66, p. 18, above.

94 Blister: a dressing applied to raise a blister.

account of her from Laxfeild was very favourable. You oblidge me in your good wishes for her, may they be successfull as I dare say they are sincere.

Mr England[95] dyed last Thursday after a weeks illnes but it was of the sort that made the doctor from the beginning of it despair of his recovery. He was gentile well bred man of sense & will be regretted by all that knew him. I hear that the chancellor refuses a licence to Mr Brooks that teaches Mr Preston's[96] sons so they will be to seek for another master. I have not yet got the workmen out of the parlour but the door next the stairs is now hanging & this day will conclude there. The stairs not yet plaistered. Let me know somtimes in general what books & exercises you are upon, & always the state of your health, is the humour out? The season has been as yet too cold for bathing. I am with love & blessing to Georgy & your self, your most affectionate father,

Signed: John Buxton

Your mother sends you both her blessing, your sisters their love. They with your brothers are well. Only Betty [*Elizabeth*] complains somtimes of the pain in her arm.

42 John Buxton to Robert Buxton [35/31]

Addressed: To Mr Robert Buxton at Mr D'Oyly's house in Playford near Ipswich, Suffolk
To be left at the Cross Keys in Ipswich
23 June 1725

Dear Robert,

I received yours of the 11th, it does in some measure answer what I desired in my last to you, haveing an account of the progress you & your brother make in your learning. You will find the Greek much easier than it at first seems to be. Pray let your master have my thanks for his invitation, I shall certainly wait on him as soon as the weather makes it tolerable travelling. At present we have scarce hopes of its being better, but we must not complain of any of the

95 Not identified.

96 The Act of Uniformity (1662) required clergymen and schoolmasters to swear the illegality of taking arms against the king, declare their conformity to the Church of England as by law established, and deny the binding force of the oath commonly called the Solemn League and Covenant. Catholic recusants and protestant nonconformists were particular targets. The act covered masters working in public and private schools, and those employed as tutors in houses or with families. Licensing was in the power of the bishop of Norwich, hence the involvement of the chancellor of the dioscese. The details of the objection to Mr Brooks are not known. H.M. Jewell, *Education in early modern England* (1998), pp. 4 and 37.

ways of Providence, & those that are planters have least of all reason. The weather has not been at all proper for bathing, & till it shews some good signs of change I would also have you forbear purging,[97] take care how you allow your self fruit, that which in other seasons were most wholesom is now pernicious, you can't be too cautious. You say nothing of your health in your last letter, I shall always take it that you are perfectly well when silent on that head, nor would I have you count a small indisposition enough for you to regard or me to know.

Your sisters & brothers were yesterday at Norwich guild[98] with great expectation & almost as much disappointment, for the weather that interrupts almost almanner of business does also spoil people's pleasure. I heard yesterday from Laxfeild that your grandmother is every day getting better, a letter from you will both please & oblidge her, as it has already done me by your intention. Your mother is perfectly recovered of her late illnes but not quite hardy against the effects of this weather. We both joyn in love & blessing to your self & George & from your most affectionate father,

Signed: John Buxton

I fancy the Pie road [99] is so bad that my cozen Meadowe can't come at us. These here are as bad as in the worst winters. Your thoughts about Shadwell[100] were never more seasonable [*sic*]. I will take care of Mr Clark's bill[101]. I don't reckon the last illnes you gave me an account of a small indisposition, however since it is of, you may make your advantage to guard against future inconveniencys.

[97] Purging: the taking of a substance, usually of plant origin, to promote the evacuation of the bowels. Sloan, pp. 61–5.

[98] Guild Day in Norwich, the Tuesday before the eve of the feast of the Nativity of St John the Baptist (24 June), was a day of civic ceremony on the mayor taking office.

[99] Pie or Pye Road: the main highway running south-west from Venta Icenorum, a few miles south of Norwich, across the county boundary towards Ipswich, a route now largely followed by the modern A140. T. Williamson, *The Origins of Norfolk* (Manchester, 1993), p. 38.

[100] For the development of John Buxton's thoughts about the building of Shadwell Lodge see above pp. 25–28.

[101] Mr Clark: possibly an Ipswich surgeon.

43 John Buxton to Robert Buxton [35/33]

Addressed: To Mr Robert Buxton at Mr D'Oyly's house in Playford
Channonz, 11 July 1725

Dear Robert,

I have received two letters from you, or three since I writ last, for which I thank you, being all extreemly agreeable to me. That you sent to your grandmother was received by her with a great deal of pleasure. Thank God she is finely well but the Suffolk roads are not good enough for her to travel in yet, & I fear the return of this bad weather will not mend them. I do not forget my promise of seeing you at Playford though I have not been able yet to perform it. Next week the sessions come on & the assizes so soon after that. Till they are over I shall scarce be at liberty.

I must not forget to commend your resolution of thinking at all times that all things are ordered for the best, but at some times you will have occation for all the force of reason & your best facultys to keep it, but endeavour if it be possible to keep it, it will make your life happy. The lightning was here as you described it to be at Playford, unusually firce & continued but not attended with any ill effects, unles it were a forerunner of this foul & stormy season. Georgy is much oblidged to you as well as my self for your care of him, & what ever the laughers say I believe you'l not easily depart from the rules of temperance. Unless they can support their jests with some reason is it not surprising that the little witlings[102] of this age should attempt to ridicule what the great sages of antiquity ever held a principal virtue, & accounted their wise men deficient though endued with justice, fortitude & providence if temperance also was not in conjunction with them, & they who now despise the latter are generally wanting in all the rest, so their opinion the less to be regarded. I woud say a great deal more on this subject but the author you mention has done it already, besides, your own reflections carry you so much into my way of thinking on this occation that it is entirely needless.

Your mother was at Bungay horsrace[103] with all your sisters. If anything

102 Whittlings; drunkards, contrasted here with temperate people.

103 Bungay: a market town in north Suffolk on the river Waveney, 14 miles south-east from Norwich. The races, for which the earliest extant advertisement dates from 1718, were held on Outney Common, north-west of the town. In the early nineteenth century as many as 10,000 people were reported to have attended. In 1725 there were not only races to divert the visiting Buxtons. In June an advertisement in the *Norwich Gazette* announced:

> This is to give notice that the late Mr Tollet's Company of Comedians is designed to be at Bungay Horse Race and Act that week and the following and no longer. N.B. They have provided a new handsome Building, and extraordinary Company and a good sett of Musick.

from that divertion is worth your knowing you will have it from her. Your grandmother Gooch is come from Denton[104] not much mended in her health, your aunt Herne something worse in hers. You have applyed your verse in Ovid with much propriety to the late season. The *madidis alis* [105]might be applyed to all the winds blowing continuall rain, but since the great disposes of the seasons is endued with infinite wisdom we must believe it is usefull perhaps necessary in the economy of the world, though through the narrowness of our understandings or partiality to our selves we do not perceive it.

I am dear son, your most affectionate father,
Signed: John Buxton

My service to your master. Your mother sends her blessing to your self & Georgy. You have both mine & your sisters love. Lenny gives me much pleasure. I hear little of your brother Jack but that he is well & got almost to the end of As *in presenti.*

I don't know whether I ever shew you the enclosed verses made for Col[*one*]l Fane's house in Kent[106], built after a model from Palladio. The house is supposed to speak them. *Dum Dominus Dominam Cupidis miratur ocellis sit*[?] *precor exclamat tam mihi pulchra domus. Votum erat immodicum, sed si sim proxima voto non foret in terris pulchrior ulla domus.*[107]

Your mother has sent two doses of rhubarb. If you are well I really think there is not much occation to take any, & if the weather be warm enough you may venture to bath in the sea water without the previous physick.

E.A. Goodwyn, *Elegance and Poverty. Bungay in the Eighteenth Century* (Bungay, 1989), pp. 81 and 86–8; E. Mann, *Old Bungay* (1934), pp. 245–6.

[104] Denton: a parish and village in south Norfolk, eight miles east of Channonz.

[105] Literally 'moist wings' from Ovid, *Metamorphoses*, i, 264.

[106] Mereworth Castle (Kent) was built for Colonel John Fane who succeeded as seventh earl of Westmorland in 1736. The architect was Colen Campbell and the house, completed in 1723, one of the first complete realizations in England of the Palladian style. C. Hussey, *English Country Houses: Early Georgian 1715–1760* (Woodbridge, 1988), pp. 58–65.

[107] The source of this verse, an epigram consisting of two elegiac couplets, has not been identified but it is an original composition and not a quotation from a classical author. The house is the speaker. It says that the master of the house was so taken by the charms of the mistress of the house that he said 'I wish I had a house as beautiful as she'. If (says the house) I could come anywhere near to being as beautiful as she is, I should be the most beautiful house on earth.

44 John Buxton to Robert Buxton [35/35]

Addressed: To Mr Robert Buxton at Mr D'Oyly's house in Playford
To be left at the Cross Keys in Ipswich
Channonz, 1 August 1725

Dear Robert,

Mr Gibbs's[108] son coming to Ipswich gives me an oppertunity of sending this with my thanks for your last of the 19 July, where I have the pleasure to see your judgement lead you into the best opinions, & which as you grow older you will still more approve your observation from Tully is very proper. Temperance is not confined to eating & drinking only, it should govern us in all our actions as well as passions, & when applyed to the mind procures the *mens sana*[109] as well as healthfull bodies.

Your grandmother is not yet come, the bad roads have prevented her. You will I hope have the pleasure of finding her here in September. Twenty little affairs keep me in some uncertainty about my visit to Playford though I think of it every day. Perhaps it may be defered till the time of your coming home. I have just begun a part of the stable which engages my present care, all last week I was at the assizes, where there was a most numerous appearance of gentry, among the principal S[*i*]r Tho[*mas*] Coke,[110] one of the Knights of the Bath.

Your writing without rule was as well as I could expect for the first time nor did I perceive it wors than your former with it. If you are much grown it will be difficult for the taylor to fit without a new measure. The next spring I have thoughts of your seeing London again, <and then> till then we may get a drugget[111] suit made up with your brothers when you come home at Norwich, which may serve for the winter. Your mother went last Thursday to Rolesby[112] & is to return to morrow; Betty [*Elizabeth*], Sarah & Len with her. I expect on Wednesday to hear the time is fixed for your grandmother coming hither. No more but service to your master from your most affectionate father,

Signed: John Buxton

Love & blessing to yourself & dear George. I hope the difficulty of the French is over with him. I've writ in much hast as you may see.

108 Mr Gibbs: see note 26 above. p. 43.

109 Healthy or sound mind.

110 Sir Thomas Coke of Holkham (1697–1759) was created a Knight of the Bath in 1725 and first earl of Leicester on 9 May 1744.

111 Drugget: a kind of stuff used for wearing apparel, woven from wool, or wool mixtures with silk or linen.

112 Rollesby: a parish and village 17 miles north-east of Norwich.

45 John Buxton to Robert Buxton [105/57]

Addressed: To Mr Robert Buxton at Mr D'Oyly's house in Playford, Suffolk. To be left at the Cross Keys in Ipswich
Channonz, 11 August [*No year. Catalogued as c. 1725*]

Dear Robert,

My being at sessions one whole week and at the assises another and your mother writing in the week between has been the occation of my silence. You may be well assured my affection is not lessened when you every day give fresh reasons for its encrease.

The horses shall be sent for you as you desire if the weather or very bad roads do not forbid and I have still thoughts of coming for you myself. This day I am to meet your grandmother Buxton at Mendham[113] in order to bring her hither tonight. I shall at the same time pay a visit to Mr Preston on the death of his mother[114] which happened about a fortnight since and has given him a fine enlargement.

I writ to you last week and hope you have received the letter. Betty [*Elizabeth*] has been very ambitious of making you her complements by way of epistle: you have it here enclosed. The news of your good health gives me perfect plesure. Pray God it may continue. You may now with tolerable care have as good a share as others.

The staircase was finished last night but the stables not so forward. Such a building season has not been known but as it favours planting we must not complain. More of the trees are dead than I expected in the spinney but as I have wherewith to supply them it gives me little pain and they are cheifly of the small sort that fail. The hedge is revived to a miracle for I thought it quite dead. Some of the oaks that appeared so are also come again.

I am, dear Robert, your most affectionate father,
Signed: John Buxton

Blesssing to dear George from me and your mother.

[113] Mendham: a parish and village in north Suffolk, near Harleston and nine miles south-east of Channonz.

[114] Possibly of the Preston family of Beeston St Laurence (Norfolk).

46 John Buxton to Robert Buxton [35/37]

Channonz, 23 August, 1725

Dear Robert,

I received two letters from you last Wednesday, & one by Ben last night. I have only time to thank you for them in general, & to say you give me as much pleasure as my affection makes me hope. I think to be with you on Thursday, I mean at Witnesham, & on Friday at Playford, to return on Monday. If the weather allows the horses shall come & George's white shall be remembred. Your mother & grandmother Buxton & all your freinds here are well wishing for fair weather & the pleasure of seeing you in it.

I am, dear Robert, your most affectionate father,
Signed: John Buxton

I'm glad the venison was good: it was the first killed in this old park revived, & being but four years old I was affraid it woud not have proved so well.

47 John Buxton to Robert Buxton [35/38]

Addressed: To Mr Robert Buxton at Mr D'Oyly's house in Playford
To be left at the Cross Keys in Ipswich
Channonz, 1 November 1725

Dear Robert,

I received your letter & with all the satisfaction you designed to give me by it, since it brought me so good an account of your health. This fine weather has been favourable toward your perfect recovery of your cold as well as to our country affairs here, though our roads are as bad as I ever knew them. I found the Pie roads as I returned the best part of my journey, those nere Whitnesham & my own home were exceeding bad. However, I came through without stopping any where, & very little tired.

Your grandmother Buxton & aunt Han went last Saturday to your aunt Ward's[115] to stay there till the next, Betty [*Elizabeth*] at the same time to Mrs Nuttle[116] for a longer time, & this morning I am going my self to Rushford, to stay till Friday. I saw Lady Selina Shirly[117] at Norwich. She is to leave this

[115] Lady Barbara Ward.

[116] Not identified.

[117] Lady Selena Shirley (1707–91) was the second daughter of Washington Shirley (1677–1729), second Earl Ferrers. She married Theophilus Hastings, ninth Earl of Huntingdon,

country next Wednesday & says she is to go very soon into France where her mother now is, I think at Paris. This young lady talks of crossing the sea & of all the fatigues & hazards of travell with great ease & indifference & makes as little of it as some people do of a Norwich journey. She has a fine temper of mind and body; what a fine thing would a right education have made her. I'm to write this post to cozen Meadowe which makes me end this the sooner.

I am, dear Robert, your most affectionate father,

Signed: John Buxton

Your mother sends her love & blessing to you & Georgy. Let mine be given to him with it, I hope he applies to his book. Sarah does very much to hers & is very good. I have heard nothing yet of the pictures.

A little book I've lately met with pleases me very much: conjectures concerning the planetary worlds.[118] If you have it not at Playford I'll send it. My aunt Marsham[119] is recovered as well as ever.

48 John Buxton to Robert Buxton [35/40]

Addressed: To Mr Robert Buxton at Mr D'Oyly's house in Playford
To be left at the Cross Keys in Ipswich
Channonz, 24 November 1725

Dear Robert,

The letter to your mother came last week to Channonz & gave us all the greatest satisfaction to find so good an account of your health I have received. None from you since I last writ where I mentioned a book I intended sending if you had it not with you at Playford. The people where your letters are left I believe are but careless, we must think of some other place for this trust.

We have had prodigious quantity of rain & this is but an uncomfortable addition to this worst season of the year. However, my cozen Meadowes's enlivening conversation within doors has made us take the less notice of what passes without, where I can neither walk nor ride to make a divertion of either, but so long as I have the choice of a removal to Rushford, upon these occations I bear the present inconvenience upon the hopes I may in due time get it

in 1728. Her father and mother (Mary Levinge) separated, which accounts for the presence of the latter in France. An evangelical Christian, she developed an independent church, her 'Connexion'. B.S. Schlenther, 'Hastings (née Shirley) Selina, Countess of Huntingdon (1707–1791)', *ODNB*.

118 Not identified in the list of books, Appendix A.

119 Aunt Marsham is Dorothy Marsham, née Gooch, at Stratton Strawless.

removed. I cannot yet come to a determination whether Shadwell or Birch Close[120] is to be preferred; if <these> water could be had at the latter there would be no room for dispute for the air & soil & prospect seem to give it an advantage over the other. It is difficult in all things to choose the best but yet we must not always be fluctuating for then there could be no action at all. However as much deliberation as the thing will permit of ought allways to be had before we enterprise, & if afterwards in the course of our lives we discover errors, we must not be surprised at it but make allowance for the weakness & incapacity of our judgements, & consider how much the accidents of life are out of our power & how far short our understandings come of that perfection required to enable us to <act &> judge & act in all things so as to have no cause for repentance.

Your mother & brothers & sisters are all well but your grandmother Buxton has had some return of an illness she is subject to, a sort of cholick[121], the effect of taking cold this wet season. Your grandmother Gooch holds as usual. They all desire their proper compliments. I am, my dear Robert, your most affectionate father,

Signed: John Buxton

My love & blessing to dear Georgy. I'm pleased to hear he minds his book. I've heard nothing yet of the pictures though every day expect them.

49 John Buxton to Robert Buxton [105/65]

No address

Stratton [*Strawless*], Friday. *No date. Catalogued 'about 1725'.*

Dear Robert,

The weather has not been favourable for our expedition to the sea since I came hither and my uncle having engaged me to try how it will prove for a day or two longer, you must not take it ill if I do not call you to go home so soon as I intended, and I am not certain whether it will be before the sessions. I am to be there on Wednesday and hope to be finished with busines I have that day and so take you with me home in the evening, if you don't contrive to travel some other way before. I am pleased to hear you behave yourself so well. I have so good an opinion of you to belive you will always do it that I may have always the greatest reason to be your affectionate father,

Signed: John Buxton

120 Birch Close: an alternative site for John Buxton's new house. The location has not been identified.

121 Colic: bowel pains.

50 John Buxton to Robert Buxton [105/60]

Addressed: To Mr Robert Buxton at Mr D'Oyly's in Playford. To be left at the Cross Keys in Ipswich.
No date. Catalogued 'about 1725'

Dear Robert,

I have received yours of the 6th inst. and do most heartily rejoyce with you upon your enjoying so good health. The continuance is one of the greatest blessings I can wish to myself or you.

I deferred sending the books till this oppertunity by Mr Bolton[122] who you know is a carefull person and I hope you will have them safe. The new coach horse proves a very good one and so does the pad but his uneasiness with the flyes makes me not like him so well.

I make your complements to your freinds here who are all well except your grandmother Gooch. She continues much as she was. Betty [*Elizabeth*] desires me to send her love. You will allways be sure of mine while you so well continue to deserve it.

From your most affectionate father,
Signed: John Buxton

Service to your master.

51 John Buxton to Robert Buxton [105/61]

Addressed: To Mr Robert Buxton at Mr D'Oyly's
No date. Catalogued 'about 1725'.

Dear Robert,

Mr Comarque's[123] visit was very oblidging and I wish he could have made it longer. I send you enclosed a guinea which you may present him with or not, as you shall think proper, but I think you mentioned something of that kind when you were here, and it would not be amiss to oblidge a very deserving man.

I am heartily glad to hear you continue so well. I received no letter from Mr D'Oyly and am at a loss to understand what you say in yours.

In hast from, my dear Robert, your most affectionate father,
Signed: John Buxton

[122] Not identified.

[123] A David Comarque (d. 1748) was admitted at Corpus Christi College, Cambridge, in 1717. He was headmaster of Colchester School (Essex) 1726–7. Venn, part I, vol. II, p. 376.

52 John Buxton to Robert Buxton [105/62]

Addressed: To Mr Robert Buxton
Friday morn. *No date. Catalogued 'about 1725'.*

Dear Robert,

I expect this will find you in Harling feild [124] where I intended meeting you but I am oblidged to be at Larlingford [125] upon the publick busines there. With my service to Captain Wright [126] you must make my excuses. I will be with you in Rushford in the evening. Let Richard return with you thither. It will be best for you to lye in the warmest part of the room where your sister lodged and Richard [127] in the other bed there. I will lye in the hall chamber. Let things be disposed accordingly. Take care not to ride too much to tire.

I hope to find you well as might from your most affectionate father,
Signed: J[*ohn*] Buxton

Love and blessing to your mother and sister and Georgy.

53 John Buxton to Robert Buxton [35/41]

Addressed: To Mr Robert Buxton at Playford
Saturday, 4 December 1725

Dear Robert,

I received your last letter which was perfectly agreeable to me without any other news than that of your being both perfectly well. My cozen Meadowes when you see her will let you all this part of the world affords. She has desired that you & your brother may be with her a fue days in Xmas. I leave it to your self to oblidge her. Betty [*Elizabeth*] is still at Norwich with Mrs Nutthall & meets with great civilitys from her. Be you as oblidging to master Nuthall as the ways of the place will allow. Your grandmother is almost quite well again. I'm in hast though always your most affectionate father,
Signed: John Buxton

Your mothers blessing with mine is with you both.

124 East and West Harling: parishes and villages in south-west Norfolk, five miles from Rushford.

125 Larlingford or Larling is a parish and village, eight miles north-east of Thetford and two miles north of Harling, at a crossing of the river Thet.

126 Captain Wright was a landowning neighbour of the Buxtons in Rushford.

127 Richard: a Buxton servant.

54 John Buxton to Robert Buxton [105/63][128]

No address
No date. Catalogued 'about 1725'.

Dear Robert,

I have sent you ten shillings which you may dispose of to Mr D'Oyly's servants as an Xmas gift. If there is but three servants you will have half a crown left. I wish you a good journy to Channonz when I shall be glad to see you and expect to do it before dinner.

I am your affectionate father,
Signed: John Buxton

55 John Buxton to Robert Buxton [105/58]

No address
Channonz, 21 December 1725

Dear Robert,

I have received yours by Mr Christian; that to your sister was sent to her at Norwich and has since been received at Channonz with great approbation and I do assure you whatever your progress may be in Greek, your English is perfectly good and your handwriting in it so much improved that I make no doubt your care and dilligence in the other matters you are now to follow will make you perfect in them also. Let not the difficulty of the Greek discourage you, your pains will be well recompensed by the pleasure that charming language will give you when you have got a tast of it. If Virgil is all over admirable, Homer is wonderfull. I speak this from the report and general consent of mankind. I mean that part of it that have qualified themselves to talk of these matters. Tully's *Offices* is as instructing as the others diverting. You will do well in all parts of life to mix the *utile* and the *dulce*[129] as often as you can and if it be possible to let business and pleasure by turns engage you, but let both be manly.

The season continues very unpleasant which with a little cold I have lately taken keeps me within doors. The return of the sun will bring us health and fair weather: two blessings that makes a heaven on earth. However, I have not been idle. Really, I have never studied so hard in my life as I have lately done

[128] Two letters are catalogued with this reference number.
[129] Useful and sweet or pleasurable.

in scheming about Shadwell. I have built forty houses there which were no sooner finished and thoroughly examined than immediately pulled down and soon after a new one erected.[130] I built one this morning out of the materials of the old ones which at present I think without a fault. It cost me four hours contrivance as I lay in bed from four to eight a clock. An expense I should very much grudge upon any other occation and I pray heartily it may stand since I have bought it at so dear at rate, and trust it will meet with your approbation. I have not forget you in the design where you have allotted you a very handsom bedchamber and study.

Captain Draper[131] has met with an adventure in town and is come lamely. Of what inconveniencys does folly draw upon us. How safe, how glorious to be conducted by wisdom.

I writ you word in my last that you were at liberty to dispose of your time there always as you should choose. You will be very agreeably entertained at Witnessham and I shall sometimes wish myself a party. I was extreem glad to hear my cosen Meadows arrived so safly to her home. My fears were much worse than the roads, though they are bad enough everywhere, but, as you observe about Thetford, and who would not when it is their power have have [*sic*] a place to escape to upon these emergent occations.

I send you beside these enclosed all blessing, love and good wishes from all your freinds here in which Georgy has his part, and I am my dear your most affectionate father,

Signed: John Buxton

I correct an error in your letter: you write version for verification.
Betty [*Elizabeth*] thanks you much for her letter. She will answer it when her closet is warm enough to write in. Sarah plays at shuttlecock as well as any one. I look upon this to be no mean accomplishment and is rather before playing on the spinet.[132]

[130] John Buxton's high rate of generation of designs for Shadwell is confirmed by the number of sketches surviving in the Buxton Papers for which he used any available scrap of paper including old letters.

[131] Not identified.

[132] Sarah Buxton was then ten years old. The comparison between prowess at a game and a keyboard instrument is a rare example of ironic humour in John Buxton's letters.

56 John Buxton to Robert Buxton [105/63]

Addressed: To Mr Robert Buxton at Playford
Monday. *No date. Catalogued 'about 1725'.*

Dear Robert,

I will write a line or two by Monsieur [*Christian*] to let you know we received your last letter and that we are all pretty well. Your grandmother Buxton is much better. Betty [*Elizabeth*] is still at Norwich which agrees with her extreem well. She is improved in her writing as much as I could expect.

The wet season continues to make our country unpleasant. I shall know this winter the worst of Channonz. No more now but the blessing of your most affectionate father,

Signed: John Buxton

Love to George.

57 John Buxton to Robert Buxton [105/59]

No address
31 December [*no year. 1725?*]

Dear Robert,

Ben[133] is [*in*] so much hast I've only time to tell you I received your letter of the 24th inst. with my usual pleasure when I hear you are well. We continue so here, notwithstanding the badness of the season. Least your fortune should not have been good this Xmas I send you the enclosed and am, dear Robert, your most affectionate father,

Signed: John Buxton

The gold is for yourself, the silver for Georgy with my blessing.

58 John Buxton to Robert Buxton [105/54]

Addressed: To Mr Robert Buxton at Playford
Channonz, 24 January 1726

Dear Robert,

I have received yours of the 15th inst. and am glad to find you have been proof against the cold of the late very severe season. I did not think you could get

133 Ben, a Buxton servant.

from Witnessham after I saw so much snow fallen. Thank God we are here all pretty well after it, though it is as yet unpleasant riding or walking.

I had a thought of going for a week with your mother and sisters to Rushford, but the late great floods that must now surround the house there have discouraged me and must render that place not so wholsom till the winds have a little dryed the morrasses. And I heard yesterday Charles Slappe's [?][134] family have not escaped the effects of these unusual floods, two or three of his servants being dead and others ill of a feavor that carrys them of[*f*] very quickly. This was not Mr Braksly's[135] case though, too much liquer was his overthrow. Will this be a warning or an example for his son.

Your aunt Han is still at Norwich. The next morn I am to bring her home, for our roads are passable if not as good as any of our neibours. Last Thursday I went to Banham[136] in the morning and returned by the Longton[137] before dinner and I did it with ease. Saturday Mr Brown of Moulton[138] dyed. He also might have lived longer if he had been temperate. I have heard Mr Needham[139] will succeed him.

Mr Harry Branthwayt[140] from whom I lately had a letter sends particular service to you and is well. I dare say you take such pleasure in oblidging your freinds and making yourself acceptable that you will always meet with love and esteem from them as well as the greatest affection from me, who am dear Robert, your most affectionate father,

Signed: John Buxton

Your mother and grandmother and sisters all send you proper complements. I must find no fault with your writing, my own being but a scrawl, besides, when I can read an account of your health I shall never blame the hand. Give Georgy my love and blessing. My present will be bestowed if it makes him industrious.

[134] Charles Slapp rented Buxton land in Rushford and Harling. See Appendix C.

[135] Not identified.

[136] Banham, a parish and village five miles west of Channonz.

[137] The Longton. This route has not been identified.

[138] Thomas Brown of Moulton. Moulton St Mary and Moulton St Michael (or Great Moulton) are parishes two miles north-east of Channonz. He was buried at Great Moulton, 23 January 1726.

[139] Not identified.

[140] Henry Branthwayt was a younger brother of Miles who had succeeded their elder brother Arthur on his death in 1724.

59 John Buxton to Robert Buxton [35/43]

Addresed: To Mr Robert Buxton at Playford
Thursday, 17 February 1726

Dear Robert,

I received your letter yesterday at Harlston by which I perceive the bad weather has its effect on you as well as others for I think few escape it. The uncertainty of hearing by the carrier makes me send to enquire how it is with you. I make no doubt of your being carefull of your self but that will not always do as I find by my self having now a cold though not very bad that came I know not how. I believe you have not forgot S[*i*]r Benjamin's directions in the managing of these colds. If your lungs should continue much oppressed by all means bleed 4 or 5 ounces, if it is come to a cough & you raise with it, it will go of[*f*] that way without bleeding. When your cold is gone & the weather favourable, I believe it would do you good to take a dose of rhubarb.

Your last letter by C[*h*]ristian was very agreeable. Surely I've taken notice to you of the receipt of your play you sent your aunt: the posts & carriers are very careless. Your mother or my self have not missed writing once a fortnight at least & sometimes oftener. Your grandmother Buxton has been something indisposed with her old illness, but is now better. She with your mother joyns with me in sending you our blessing & best wishes from your most affectionate father,

Signed: John Buxton

Love & blessing to George. I've sent you some potatoes for your master which are to be given him with my humble service.

60 John Buxton to Robert Buxton [35/44]

Addressed: To Mr Robert Buxton at Mr D'Oyly's house in Playford
Channonz, 21 February 1726

Dear Robert,

I hope this letter will find you perfectly recovered of your cold though the weather will put you in mind of being carefull. Mine was but a little one has almost left me. Your grandmother Buxton is also much better but not yet hardy enough to venture to Laxfeild. I shall be glad to hear from you by every oppertunity but the ways of sending are so uncertain that I know not which is best. We have not yet received those letters you say were left at the popinjay. Your letter to your aunt Marsham was very kindly taken, she has mentioned it in one to my mother & will soon send you her thanks. I think she is better in her health & more composed in her temper than I've known her for some years. Your sisters are now dancing & do both give me great pleasure in their endeavours to make the best improvements. Jack[141] is come home for the time of Shrovetide & as he growes more like you, has you may believe not less of my good opinion. You will meet him at Easter & when that's over he is to be placed at Bury school. Not that I prefer that to the place you are in, only the views I have in life for him being different I have judged it more proper for him to be brought up at a publick school & in the more common method. Besides, another reason which weighed very much with me, that if George & he were at the same place one of them might have been discouraged as I found by the little time they were together.

This dismal season has made me come to a resolution of doing something at Shadwell. I have bought materials for this design & hope to put it into excecution the spring after this. Capt[*ain*] Draper's projects seem at a full stop: they were but ill begun & so not likely to succeed. Your mare is well & has been in the stable all this winter [*and*] will be fit for service.

After all the tryalls of the several ways of sending [*letters*] we must come to the old one of the Harlston carrier which I believe most safe & certain, if trusty Ben does his part in delivery & calling for letters. In due season liquorice[142] is so good for colds I can't help putting it in your mind though it comes in here very abruptly & it is best left in the roots if you can reconcile your self to use it so.

My love & blessing joyned with your mother's to you both shall end this from your most affectionate father. Betty [*Elizabeth*] is at my elbow & sends her love,

Signed: John Buxton

Jack sends his love to you & Georgy. His cozen[143] your namesake is come home with him & is a good promising boy.

141 Jack (John) Buxton, then in his ninth year, is at an unidentified school before attending the Free Grammar School in Bury St Edmunds.

142 Liquorice: a medicine or sweetmeat made from the evaporated juice of the root of the leguminous plant *glycyrrhiza glabra.*

143 Robert Marsham (1708–1797) of Stratton Strawless, the eldest son and heir of Thomas Marsham and Dorothy Gooch. In his twentieth year he joined his cousin Robert Buxton at Clare Hall, Cambridge, as a fellow-commoner. At an early age Marsham developed a passion for natural history and especially the planting of trees, interests that remained with him throughout his life. He married Mary Browne of Yaxham and a son and heir Robert was born in

61 John Buxton to Robert Buxton [35/45]

Addressed: To Mr Robert Buxton at Mr D'Oyly's house in Playford, Suffolk
To be left at the Cross Keys in Ipswich with a parcel
Channonz, 1 March 1726

Dear Robert,

Your letter by Mr Hare's[144] servant has given us some pain: I hope for one to morrow that will by a good account of you take it all away, & this very fine weather is as favourable as I could wish. I make no doubt of your case till you are perfectly recovered, nor of your knowledge how upon these occations to order your self. If the cough continue as it has sometimes done you are to be let blood about four or five 5 ounces. I will very willingly send Mr Layman[145] if you are desirous of his seeing you, though I think the Ipswich surgeon Mr White has as great a reputation as the other.

Two letters that have layn so long at Hall's[146] were received last Saturday with that from Georgy inclosed. He has oblidged his mother as you have me by yours, & we think he has writ a very good hand much better than was expected. I'm sorry yours did not come sooner that the book you desired might have come to you in season. It comes now though perhaps too late for your occation. Your kind taking my advice will be an encouragement to me to offer it whenever it is wanted but I foresee your own good sense will make it but seldom wanted. The pains you take to master the Greek tongue will be overpaid by the pleasure those authors will yeild you when you are arrived at a tolerable degree of knowledge in them. Geography is play to you now, & so usefull that few books as you observe can be well understood without it.

Your judgement of Bransly[147] is I fear too just. He discovers a very strong inclination to drinking & he will find as well as in Harlston people to favour him in his debauches. I will refer our discours of Shadwell till I see you, we must upon the spot determine whether that is not the most proper place to build on, for as we cannot have every thing in a scituation we ought to take that with most advantages. Channonz now begings to be pleasant. It would

1749. His first wife died in the 1750s and he then married Elizabeth Newby of Stratton Strawless. In 1755 the elder Robert began the rebuilding of the family seat, Stratton Strawless Hall, but it was incomplete on his death and was finished by his son. R.W. Ketton-Cremer, *A Norfolk Gallery* (1948), pp. 149–161

144 Possibly of the Hare family of Hargham.

145 See note 88, p. 63, above.

146 Halls, a collection point for post, in New Buckenham perhaps.

147 Not identified.

have been more so if your good grandmother Buxton had continued here still. She left us this morning in pretty good health & she has my sincerest wishes for its continuance. She would be pleased to hear from you that you are well again having joyned with us in our concern for your illness. If you have time write also to your aunt Ward, she may expect this perhaps if she hears that you writ to your aunt Marsham & she has a right to it as your godmother.

I have writ this in some hast & am a good deal tired having been out all day at Banyds Hall[148] & other farms setting out wood. I am my dear Robert, your most affectionate father,

Signed: John Buxton

Your mother joyns with me in love & blessing to Georgy & your self. Your mother wants to know in what perticulars the shirts you sent do not fit. You intended some account of this but she has not yet received any.

62 John Buxton to Robert Buxton [35/46]

Addressed: To Mr Robert Buxton at Mr D'Oyly's house in Playford, Suffolk
To be left at the Cross Keys in Ipswich
Channonz, 15 March 1726

Dear Robert,

I received last Wednesday the letter that ought to have come the week before, with another at the same time confirming the good account of your health which I met with in the <other> former & they have given me the greatest satisfaction, & though your humour is a little out still, I would have you think it one of the least concern so long as you find your self otherwise in perfect health. Your letter to Lady Ward is taken very kindly. You have an acknowledgement for it enclosed in this in which I must also bear a part for your so readily doing what I only hinted to you.

Nothing ever more surprised me than the unfortunate account of poor Harry Branthwayt[149] & it is thought he met with unfair usage & his freinds will carry on the prosecution with the utmost vigour. If the weather is but tolerable fair your horses shall be sent that you may come at the time you desire & I will if nothing prevents come with them my self, & this will be a much pleasanter journey to us both than the last I made with you, though in spite of all I am to suffer on such occations such things must be for your advantage.

[148] Banyards Hall in Bunwell.

[149] See note 34, page 46, above. The nature of the misfortune is not known.

Your grandmother bore her journy much better than could be expected & had the finest weather for it we have had this 9 months. She will be oblidged by your letter & much pleased to find you are well again. I've now no more to add but blessing to both my dear sons from their most affectionate father,
Signed: John Buxton

If your account of the Bury usher proves right I would by no means put Jacky there.[150] Your mothers blessing is always joyned with mine. Service to your master. I hope he has lost his pain as well as a tooth, & even so I think it is buying it of at a dear price.

63 John Buxton to Robert Buxton [35/50]

Addressed: To Mr Robert Buxton at Mr D'Oyly's house in Playford in Suffolk
To be left at the Cross Keys in Ipswich
By Ipswich carrier
Wednesday, 18 May 1726

Dear Robert,

My Lady Ward's man took your letter from the Beccles[151] post & gave it me as I was on Trowse[152] bridge, so I met it part of the way, & I'm oblidged to you for contriving so soon to let me hear of you. I did expect the ruffle of a journey would a little disorder you; I hope by this time it is over & that you'l quickly find the benefit of change of air as I perceive by your mother's master Nuthall has already done, & by your own there is a beginning of some amendment in your self. Thank God my cold is just gone though I don't believe the weather at all favourable towards a cure, the excessive heat in some p[*ar*]t of the day with a constant n. east wind that S[*i*]r Benj[*ami*]n [*Wrench*] says makes against us. I saw him yesterday & shew him your letter which he interpreted as a good account, leading to a better & I hope your mother will bring it at her return.

I came last night to Channonz about a quarter after 10 aclock having dispatched our affair at Norwich sooner than I expected. Next Tuesday I have appointed to go with Mr Bardwell[153] to Rushford there to settle the important point with Charles Slapp.[154]

150 Bury Grammar School.

151 Beccles: a north Suffolk market town on the river Waveney, 18 miles south-east of Norwich.

152 Trowse Newton: a parish and village on the river Yare, two miles south-east of Norwich.

153 Mr Bardwell (or Bardswell?) was John Buxton's steward.

154 Charles Slapp was a tenant of John Buxton in Rushford.

Your freinds here continue *in stata quo.* Betty [*Elizabeth*] is oblidged for your perticular concern for her: the tooth ach will not yet leave her, she had a return yesterday but not any last night, so I hope the humour has spent its self. Sarah is heart of oak, & now <her> disengaged from company minds her work very diligently. No rain yet nor the appearance of any here; so dusty about Norwich that I almost think it more troublesome than the dirt with us in winter. Your sisters joyn in love & duty to your mother & their two brothers to which I will add the blessing of your most affectionate father,

Signed: John Buxton

I saw Mrs Osborn of Seething[155] at Norwich who enquired particularly of you. Service to Mr D'Oyly.

64 John Buxton to Robert Buxton [35/29]

Addressed: To Mr Robert Buxton at Mr 'Oyly's house in Playford in Suffolk
To be left at the Cross Keys in Ipswich
Channonz, 24 May 1726

Dear Robert,

I received with the greatest pleasure the good account your mother brought me of your great amendment. Both your letters also came to me in due time & I hope you have received mine. The enclosed I send your master <for> as a specimen of the performance of the young man Mr Kidman[156] mentioned to him, which I think very extraordinary for his years. The occation of this speech was his being chose president of a club of young men at Ipswich which he there set on foot for your mutual improvement &c. He would be now glad to be with Mr D'Oyly & Mr Kidman with his service to him. Desired me to let him know if the unhappy news of my cozen Buxton's[157] catastrophe having I suggested by this time reached you at Playford. I have learned very fue perticulars of it only that about three aclock in the morning on Saturday he rose from his lady, went to a pond in the yard, strip himself & layed his clothes near it, & then took the fatal leap. There is great riding & sending

[155] Not identified.

[156] Charles Kidman of Norfolk was a celebrated tutor of Corpus Christi College, Cambridge. Admitted sizar in 1679, he graduated in 1682–3 and was fellow from 1685–1710. He became president of the college. Rector of Banham (Norfolk) until 1735, he died in 1740 and was buried at Diss. Venn, part I, vol. II, p. 15. See also letters nos 70 and 117, pp. 90 and 136, below.

[157] Robert Buxton of South Elmham, St Margaret. His burial was recorded in the parish register (SRO) 22 May 1726.

expresses for his courts. Mr Branthwayt[158] is to succeed him in mine. I'm just going to Rushford with Mr Bardwell & in much hast but always your most affectionate father,

Signed: John Buxton

May the 25. I returned last night from Rushford by eight, not at all tired though I rid a good deal when there about the grounds. The tenant is not yet come to my terms. I believe in time he'l think them reasonable. That country is not less pleasant now than in the winter. I find by Mr Christian you have not received the letters I sent; yours by him gave great satisfaction. My cold is quite gone & your sister Betty [*Elizabeth*] much better. Your mother has also lost her cold: the air here may have the credit of that.

65 John Buxton to Robert Buxton [35/51]

Addressed: To Mr Rob[*er*]t Buxton at Playford
1 June 1726

Dear Robert,

I have received yours of the 23rd May & do heartily congratulate you upon the great alteration you have found in your health. Whether it is Playford air or any other accident that has made this is very hard to guess, people are apt to judge by success. For my own part so long as you can obtain that greatest blessing, I do not much care how you come by it, but I hope time will make you strong enough to bear this air or a worse upon occation.

This dry season has given us the advantage of the dry soyls that are now so scorched as to envy the verdure of our feilds though we have had very little rain to refresh them. The trees in the avenue hold out beyond my expectation; though the weather has been very hot, yet the wind has been constantly east. This when you come on the sea shore you'd be so sensible of as I believe you'd hardly thing it proper to bath. I think your cold too should be entirely gon first. Thank God mine has left me some time, I believe told you of it in one of my letters. You ought to have had three since you went from me, besides one that came to your mother. This need not be returned, cheifly concerning your self & is therfore at your disposal.

The sudden death of my cozen Buxton has given us all much concern. I mentioned it in my last & who was to succeed him in my courts. Last night & the night before I observed the appearance of a great tempest to the south. We

158 Miles Branthwayt of Hethel.

had a little of the thunder, a prodigious deal of the lightning, but scarce a drop of rain. I judged it reached Playford but I hope with none of its bad effects.

All your freinds here are well. Jacky is come home & very well pleased with his new school. He is 2[*n*]d boy on the form but expects very soon to go on to the third. Your mother joyns with me in blessing to you & Georgy with hearty progress for both your healths from your most affectionate father,

Signed: John Buxton

66 John Buxton to Robert Buxton [35/52]

Addressed: To Mr Robert Buxton at Mr D'Oyly's house in Playford
Channonz, 5 June, 1726, Sunday afternoon

Dear Robert,

Mr Mallom gives himself the trouble of this letter & has promised to send it in due time. The enclosed is from Mr Jermy.[159] I was with him when he wrot it & we both agreed in our opinion that it woud not be proper for our children to go to Ipswich horsrace.[160] I think when you were at home you had the same thoughts. Tell Georgy it is my love & care of him occations this. The day may nevertheless be made holyday & pray my dear give him a shilling out right to dispose of as he pleases.

I had designed answering yours by giving you a perticular account as you'd asked of our domestik affairs, & I thought to have done it while my neibour had been at church: he chose to stay with me & I must not leave him too long. I hear by him my cozen Buxton has made a will & given all to his wife & child & if the latter dyes the estate to go to his wife to dispose of. From his brothers & their children this is worse than the other action if true.

We have had plenty of rain but no ill effects of the thunder though it was violent. I make no apology to you for preventing you of this divertion of the horsrace because you already believe whatever I do is designed for your intrest, & that I am your most affectionate father,

Signed: John Buxton

Mr Comargt[?][161] complained of the length of the road from Norwich & well he might for he came three miles out of his way as I heard by those that saw him come through our street. Service to your master: I've not received his letter you mentioned.

159 Mr Jermy of Stansfield near Wymondham.

160 See note 85, p. 62, above.

161 See note 123, p. 74, above.

67 John Buxton to Robert Buxton [35/53]

Addressed: To Mr Robert Buxton at Mr D'Oyly's house in Playford
To be left at the Cross Keys in Ipswich
14 June 1726

Dear Robert,

This day was fixed for my coming to Whitnesham, an accident prevents me, which I shall not take up this paper to tell you, designing the next week to do what I intended in this. Your letter by Mr Mallom to your mother gave us great satisfaction. I saw him yesterday & never with so much pleasure heard him talk while he gave me so good an account of your health, how well you looked, how cherfull, &c., till he was interrupted by some new incident, & you know how very apt he is to digress.

I'm glad to see that good tast will not let you mistake an horsrace for a divertion when it is atten with those inconveniencys you take notice of. It is a sort of good genius that will keep you company all your life, by which you will distinguish, *quid sit pulchrum quid turpe, quid utile, quid non,*[162] & learning will every day improve it.

The late rains came very seasonably for every thing. The young trees wer not the least sensible of the benefit, it came time enough to save abundance that were very sick but not to produce much more grass in the meadows when it is very short. The clover was pretty good & well ended, & the wheat would claim a large offring to Ceres was her divinity in any repute. Let the great Father of all things receive the sacrifice of an humble & a thankfull mind, for this & every other blessing of life.

One of the [*brickmaking*] clamps[163] at Rushford is by this time on fire. The season has been such as brickmen pray for. I hope they have not so good an intrest in heaven as those who made Pharoah's bricks: they are an vile generation of people & one would be apt to suspect *quod ab illis orientur.*[164] The new stables & coachhouse are floored, the gardners house being 3 rooms with a large colebin adjoyning are built up to the roof & this morning I am to mark out the foundation of a slaughter house, & house for swine & poultry in the new wood y[*ar*]d. I have a little altered the plan for Rushford in the principal floor without changing any thing at all in the other. I shall have time enough when wee meet to tell you this scheme, & till then I must refer wtever I have els to say I am with love to dear Georgy your most affectionate,

Signed: J[*ohn*] B[*uxton*]

162 What may be beautiful and what foul, what may be useful and what not.

163 John Buxton's accounts for building at Shadwell include the making of 270,000 bricks at 7s. per 1000, not including the cost of fuel and carriage. CUL Buxton Papers, 124/3.

164 What arises (comes forth) from them.

68 John Buxton to Robert Buxton [35/54]

Addressed: To Mr Robert Buxton at Mr D'Oyly's house in Playford near Ipswich
To be left at the Cross Keys in [*Ipswich*]
22 June 1726

Dear Robert,

I received yours by Mr Christian. You will always have a good subject when you can tell me you are perfectly well. I must not talk of seeing you since I am so often disappointed & though I every day design it you must not expect me till I come. I'm going this day to Harlston upon a meeting for the land tax: some appeals about that make it necessary for me to be there. My Lady Ward talks of coming hither very soon: this will again prevent my journey. Jacky is gon to school & the first that returned. I'm in hopes he will also be every way the first among his school-fellows.

I am, my dear Robert, your most affectionate father,
Signed: John Buxton

Love & blessing to Georgy. I fear you'l want the books before I come.

69 John Buxton to Robert Buxton [35/55]

Addressed: To Mr Robert Buxton at Mr D'Oyly's house in Playford, Suff[*olk*]
To be left at the Cross Keys in Ipswich. Car. paid
29 June 1726

Dear Robert,

I will venture to fix another time for my journy to Witnessham though I've so often been prevented coming when I designed. I hope nothing will do it next Monday. Your mother goes that day to Laxfeild, with your Aunt Ward, who is expected here to morrow to make some stay with us. I will refer all I have to say till wee meet only that I am always your most affectionate father,
Signed: John Buxton

70 John Buxton to Robert Buxton [35/56]

Addressed: To Mr Robert Buxton at Playford
26 July 1726

Dear Robert,

Your mother having told you the ill news of your cozen Tommy,[165] I will say no more of that only that I could wish a more temperate regimen had been observed in the course of that poor child's diet, which possibly might have prevented his untimely fate.

Don't you think I was much surprized when I last returned from you to find the addition to the family here.[166] Their foolish management is no less to be blamed than their vice. I have determined for example sake that Richard shall leave my service, my Lady Ward's man comes in his room.

I shewed your freind Mr Darb[*?*][167] the Quaker your exercise, with which he was much pleased & since writ me the enclosed letter. I took it in good part as it is meant it had the approbation also of a better judgment; Mr Kidman was pleased when I shewed it him. I have read the poem of Cadenus & Vanessa[168] with great delight after the assizes. I hope to make good my promise of seeing you at Playford.

I am, dear Robert, your most affectionate father,
Signed: John Buxton

Love & blessing to Georgy.

71 John Buxton to Robert Buxton [35/57]

Addressed: To Mr Robert Buxton at Mr D'Oyly's house in Playford, Suff[*olk*]
To be left at the Cross Keys in Ipswich
4 August 1726

Dear Robert,

I was much pleased with your letter by Mr Cretien [*Christian*], both from the good account you give me of your health & of the method you take to preserve it, & though it may seem troublesom at the first a little time will give

[165] Not identified.

[166] Seemingly a reference to an illegitimate birth resulting from a liaison between Buxton servants.

[167] Not identified.

[168] A poem written by Jonathan Swift (1667–1745) in 1713 for Esther Vanhomrigh and published in 1726, three years after her death. Drabble, p. 156.

you such a habit in it, that it would be as much trouble to leave it of. Such influence has custom on our minds & bodys; how much then does it concern us to establish good ones early?

We did not see any thing of Mis Meadowe or her company; I heard only of their lodging at the popinjay.[169] I suppose they are returned. I've little news to send, only that I'm not so great a sufferer by this bad weather as some of my neibours, having ended a great deal of wheat in very good condition, though the crop not so large as I hoped for, but the wet season was the hindrance. I hope to find liberty after the assizes to see you; shall take Laxfeild in my way if the roads are not made very bad.

The oldest buck is kild. He became for the last month a continual out lyer; proved very good but not so fat as if he had kept quiet at home. The mayor of Norwich[170] had a haunch & Lady Ward the plate, the rest was eat at home. I believe I shall kil no more this year. I hear my Lord Townshend has sent one of his sons to Clare Hall under Mr Wilcox.[171] The influence of your new master has done this. Dicky Fuller[172] keeps the character he brought with him of a very bright youth; if his discretion keeps pace with his fine genius he may become very considerable.

I am, my dear Robert, your most affectionate father,
Signed: John Buxton

Your mother joyns with me in love & blessing to your self & Georgy. He can't please me more than by improving himself & using his best endeavours.

72 John Buxton to Robert Buxton [35/58]

Addressed: To Mr Rob[*er*]t Buxton at Mr D'Oyly's house in Playford
To be left at the Cross Keys in Ipswich post paid
Laxfeild, 19 August 1726

Dear Robert,

The time of your coming home is now so near at hand that I shall not see you

169 Popinjay was an early name for parrot. An inn sign.

170 The mayor of Norwich was John Custance. Cozens-Hardy, p. 116.

171 No record of a Townshend entering Clare Hall at this date has been found in the college archives. If John Buxton's information was correct it is possible that the son attended the college but did not matriculate. John Wilcox (d. 1762), born at Grantham (Lincs), was admitted to Clare Hall as a sizar in 1708. He graduated in 1712 and was fellow 1714, taxor 1720, and master 1736–62. He left his fortune for the building of the college chapel. Venn, part I, vol. II, p. 405.

172 Dicky Fuller: the servant recruited from Lady Ward to replace the disgraced Richard. See note 166, p. 90, above.

till then, & I design three or four days before to be with you at Playford if nothing falls out to prevent me. Your freinds at this place are all well, though the loss of their son lyes yet heavy. Time will wear it away. I'm going with your aunt to a small assembly at Yoxford.[173] Your sister Betty [*Elizabeth*] is come to make some stay with Mrs Kemp at Ubbeston;[174] I hope she will make advantage of seeing good company. To morrow I return to Channonz, where I left your mother & all last Wednesday very well.

This is all I've to tell you at present; more than that I am, my dear son, your most affectionate father,

Signed: J[*ohn*] Buxton

Service to your master. Tell him I've pd his bill to Mr Chase.[175] Your grandmother sends you her blessing. You have also the compliments of the rest of this family. Love to your brother.

73 John Buxton to Robert Buxton [35/59]

Addressed: To Mr Rob[*er*]t Buxton at Playford, Suff[*olk*]
Sunday 29 August 1726

Dear Robert,

An unaccountable mistake was made about the time of sending for you but it is rectified very critically this morning. Though I loose the pleasure of my journy I shall hope for that seeing you both perfectly well to morrow. With service to Mr D'Oyly, I am your most affectionate father,

Signed: John Buxton

/Turne over/[176]

[173] Yoxford: a north-east Suffolk parish and village, nine miles south-east from Laxfield where John Buxton was staying with his cousins.

[174] Ubbeston: a Suffolk parish and village, two miles from Laxfield.

[175] William Chase was the proprietor and printer of the *Norwich Mercury*, and as book and music seller and stationer could have supplied goods for Mr D'Oyly's school.

[176] A letter to Robert Buxton from his mother was written on the reverse of the sheet.

74 John Buxton to Robert Buxton [35/60]

Addressed: To Mr Robert Buxton at the Lady Ward's house in Norwich
Channonz, 3 September 1726

I hope this letter will find my dear Robert in perfect health again since I left you in so good a way towards it. My Lady Ward's kindness & agreeable air of Norwich will I dare say engage you to think well of that place, & make you pass your time there with a great deal of pleasure. We got home about a quarter after twelve, our guests had been come an hour before; they came in Mr Barry's[177] coach which also brought his eldest daughter with them. But the greatest stranger was your mother's picture which you know has been expected this two years. It is so like her & in so good a manner that I am fully recompensed for the long delay. These pictures of your parents will one day be yours & when we are no more will serve to keep in your mind an idea of the persons you have given so much reason to love you.[178]

The books you receive with this letter may be an amusement when you have no better & returned to Mrs Oliver[179] befor you leave Norwich, which I will not fix to any day though I think of the latter end of the week. Among the visits you have on your hands I belive you'l not foget somtimes an enquiry after your little pad[?],[180] and though she is in carfull hands it will not be a miss to see her now & then as you pass that way. Your brother is quite well again; a voluntary abstinence yesterday from flesh meat together with meeting some of his schoolfellows have been his cure, & as in this so I hope in all things he is capable of he will make your actions the rule for his own. I shoud be glad to know how long the master of Clare Hall stays in Norfolk. Perhaps you may learn it from Dr Herring.[181] Pray put Kerridge[182] in mind of bringing your news papers. I shall end this with your mother's & my own best wishes for you which include all manner of blessings & am my dear Robert

[177] Not identified.

[178] Portraits of John Buxton and his wife Anne, attributed to Michael Dahl (1656–1743), are in the Castle Museum, Norwich (catalogued as of *c.* 1710). They are reproduced here as the Frontispiece and Plate 1. Portraits of later generations of the Buxton family are discussed in Moore, *Family and Friends*, pp. 19, 115 and 122–3.

[179] Not identified.

[180] A pad-nag, a road horse or an easy paced horse.

[181] Dr William Herring (d. 1762) of Norwich, the cousin of Thomas Herring (1693–1757), who was appointed chaplain to King George II in 1728, and became archbishop of York in 1743 and Canterbury in 1747. R.T. Holtby, 'Herring, Thomas (1693–1757)', *ODNB*, describes William and Thomas as probably brothers but this is not the case. See notes 262, 289 and 355, pp. 129, 135 and 159, below.

[182] A John Kerridge was a Buxton tenant and his clerk. Appendix C.

your most affectionate father,
Signed: John Buxton

All our service waits on Lady Ward with abundance of thanks for late favours. Let me hear of S[*i*]r Edw[*ar*]d for I have great pleasure in knowing he is like to regain a good state of health.

One quarter of oats a day will be sufficient I believe for your mare.

75 John Buxton to Robert Buxton [35/61]

Addressed: To Mr Rob[*er*]t Buxton at Playford near Ipswich, Suffolk
To be left at the X Keys in Ipswich
25 October 1726

Dear Robert,

I have received two letters from you with great satisfaction, with the present of apples from your master for which I return him my thanks. I was last week at Rushford when I should have writ to you, & though the weather was but rough it did not hinder me from being abroad. I have fixed the scituation for Shadwell Lodge though the plan of the house not yet resolved on. Capt[*ain*] Draper's steeple[183] comes to view in the the [*sic*] right point, the line that goes from that takes the lower part of the close in a very proper part, & may have a handsom peice of water in the view, when opportunity serves. You may think I was much pleased with this good fortune, & shall proceed with the greater alacrity when a scituation is so much to my liking.

Your cozen Marsham[184] told me he had a letter from you; your correspon-ding sometimes with him will be very proper. I think it would not be amiss if you were to wrte once to your Aunt Ward to thank her for favours to you & to give an account of your health. You may do it by Christian.

Yesterday we all dined with S[*i*]r Rob[*er*]t Kemp,[185] both young & old of my family. I am going this day to Bunwell Courts[186] to meet our new steward. Dr Herring has had no answer yet about your chambers. I am very glad to hear of Georgy's improvement; he will now begin to think he is born for some employment, & that he must by industry & study endeavour to qualifie himself. Your Brother Jack is very well again. Pray God continue you all in

[183] Steeple = tower.
[184] See note 143, p. 81, above.
[185] Sir Robert Kemp of Gissing Hall, two miles south of Channonz.
[186] Bunwell manorial courts. A parish and village four miles north-west of Channonz.

health, & that you may one day obtain what my hopes now flatter me.

With the agreeable hopes of your most affectionate father,

Signed: John Buxton

Mrs Mallom has borrowed the poem[?]. I will send it next week.

76 John Buxton to Robert Buxton [35/62]

Addressed: To Mr Rob[*er*]t Buxton at Mr D'Oyly's house in Playford
To be left at the X keys in Ipswich
Channonz, 9 November 1726

Dear Robert,

I received your letter by Mr Chretien [*Christian*] with perfect pleasure; your good account of your health & of the use you make of it will allways give such. I know not what makes my letters fail of coming to you in due time, but you ought to have had one every week either from your mother or my self. The last week she writ & I did the same the week before. This will tell you we are all pretty well, as is your grandmother at Laxfeild & your aunt at Norwich.

Our affairs at Shadwell go on as well as the rainy season will permit; I think it favours schemes within doors. I am come to an absolute resolution in them & since I can't make one without some objection I must take what I think there can be fewest made against. I've sent you small sketch enclosed, & pray be so free to make yours against it. Coming through the hall to the eating room is the only on[*e*] I can find, but there so many good things both in the offices & above stairs to ballance this that I shall pass it over. Besides, the eating parlour is to the south, which I could not have without the other objection of coming through the hall. Capt[*ain*] Draper is come again & pretty full of projects. His scheme is now to pull all down & build a quite new thing 100 foot in front upon the same spot, but I've no more time than to tell you, I am, dear Robert, your most affectionate father,

Signed: J[*ohn*] Buxton

77 John Buxton to Robert Buxton [35/63]

Addressed: To Mr Rob[*er*]t Buxton at Playford near Ipswich in Suffolk
To be left at the Cross Keys in Ipswich
22 November 1726

Dear Robert,

I have your letter by Mr Chresten [*Christian*] and have sent those enclosed as directed. I dare say your cozen Marsham is pleased with your correspondence, & it will be of use to you both to exercise your talents that way & bring you by practice to an exactnes in writing upon any occation, an accomplishment to be aimed at as much as any other belonging to a gentleman. Your master Horace[187] who you seem so much delighted with is both an excellent rule & example for you, & leads one into a very just way of thinking in almost every thing relating to the affairs of life, & it is happy for you that you have so early a tast of him.

Your objections to the plan [*for Shadwell*] I foresaw you woud make, but I think it is almost impossible to produce one so perfect as I woud wish. The closet window will command the backyard, which I like better than that the eating parlour shoud do it, where though I shall keep for the most part my self, yet sometimes company will be there for whom the prospect of a back yard woud not be so agreeable. As to the other objection of the distance of servants, I think in a very small house the difficulty is generally to prevent them being too much heard in the rooms we keep in, & this inconvenience we shall not find in our plan where the back stair case is extremely well placed both for privacy & for communication. The offices under & the chambers above are without objection & the whole, though a pretty large plan, well enlightened with only three windows in each front. The closet to the study makes the latter of double use. I am now supplying the defects in the walks of oaks in the home close & hope they will succeed.

Last Thursday your sister Sarah had some symptoms of a feaver; she has been bled since & with two or three things besides by S[*i*]r Benj[*ami*]n's [*Wrench*] order done for her. I hope she will escape this that is now so epidemical. Yesterday S[*i*]r Rob[*er*]t Kemp's family dined here. I entertained them with some beef of my own grazing, & the first that bled in the new slaughter house. My lady complimented it with the name of venison, & I this day with dining entirely on the sir loyn the best I ever eat. This advantage at least our dirty country gives us.

[187] Quintus Horatius Flaccus (65–8BC). See Appendix A, items 80, 81 and 133.

Your grandmother with the rest of your friends at Laxfeild is perfectly well as she writ me word last Wednesday & gives me hopes of seeing her at Xmas. If the weather is very fine perhaps you'l venture there the pye road to see her for a fue days: I leave it to your choice. Your mother's cold hangs still upon her; the rest are well. Love to Georgy is all from your most affectionate father,

Signed: J[*ohn*] B[*uxton*]

78 John Buxton to Robert Buxton [35/64]

Addressed: To Mr Robert Buxton at Mr D'Oyly's house in Playford, Suff[*olk*]
To be left at the Cross Keys at Ipswich
30 November 1726

Dear Robert,

The letter I writ last week gave you an account of your sister Sarah's illness; this will tell you she is very well again. Betty [*Elizabeth*] had a little of the same disorder & hers also is going of. I am very glad to find by yours you escape this common sicknes & that you are also free from the others you have been troubled with. I did not see your master though I was at Norwich when he was there, nor hear of him till I was just coming away. You mentioned somthing of George's performance to be enclosed in your letter. What came of it for none appeard upon opening it.

Your mother went with me yesterday to Hethell.[188] Our neibours there will live in a very elegant manner, great alterations in the house & avenue, though the first can never be made what one would call a good one. Shadwell is no less changed since I last writ, & front again turned south which in some sort brings us back to the old plan. Your objection to the nearnes of 3 doors in hall was what I did not think of but very just, for the rest it is good, but will you not come into my opinion when you observe there is but two windows to the south in this plan. The south! so comfortable in the gloomy season in which this place is to be inhabited. I have taken notice that during November, December & January the sun comes very little upon the east or west side & then so faint at rising or setting that scarce yeilds any warmth or spirit. The south then must be courted in our scheme, nor shall we loose any other advantage by this alteration, for I keep the same point of situation, for house & garden, & the views of Harling &c as well commanded from the study & common parlour.

[188] Hethel, the Branthwayt's seat.

I mentioned in my last that your mother would be glad to see you at Xmas if the weather & roads can encourage your journey, which I should leave entirely to your discretion. I expect your grandmother & relations from Laxfeild; you will certainly be a welcom guest to all of them though to none more than your most affectionate father,
Signed: J[*ohn*] Buxton

Love & bless of your mothers joynd with mine to you both. If you come Georgy will bear you company, but there is very few hares for coursing. His freind Jo the coachman has left me.

79 John Buxton to Robert Buxton [35/65]

Addressed: To Mr Robert Buxton at Mr D'Oyly's house in Playford, Suffolk
To be left at the Cross Keys in Ipswich
13 December 1726

Dear Robert,

You had a letter from your mother the last week if the post was not unjust. I have the pleasure in this to let you know your sister Sarah is pretty well again & that the illnes has gon no further in the family; only your grandmother Gooch has been confined to her chamber a fue days with an aguish illness, the effect I believe of this very cold <season> weather.

We were very much pleased with Georgy's performance. I make no doubt he will proceed in learning such things as distinguish gentlemen from the common herd. I am glad you are proof against the night air. I hope you will every year find an encrease of health & I dare say you will know the value of it. I'm affraid this severe season will discourage our freinds at Laxfeild from making us the visit they intended this Xmas, as it has already done your aunt Han who will keep where she is till the sessions are over. If you continue your resolution of coming I shall hope for more favourable weather.

It is determined that the front at Shadwell be south though I can't for that aspect contrive a plan altogether so agreeable to my mind, the advantages as to scituation & prospect are the same, & the offices will be better disposed than the other way. Nothing I believe is to be made perfect by any one but the deity. I have endeavoured to bring this little plan as near to that point as I could & will content my self if I can see no more faults than are usually to be met with in other buildings, & if it serves the uses it is intended for. I have just before the frost began made an end of planting where the former trees failed;

no busines of that sort can now go forward, & I fear I shall be prevented doing what I design'd this year, which was a walk to the common.

I don't certainly know who was the author of the play you mention: I have a notion it was Mr Farquar, no first rate poet.[189] I've lately been reading one that is so among men, Milton,[190] & see a thousand beautys I had overlook in former readings. Most other poems are really but ballads compared with his.

With mine & your mother's blessing to you both is all at presen from your most affectionate father,

Signed: J[*ohn*] B[*uxton*]

80 John Buxton to Robert Buxton [35/70]

Addressed: To Mr Robert Buxton at Mr D'Oyly's house in Playford, Suffolk
To be left at the Cross Keys in Ipswich
Tuesday, 28 February 1727

Dear Robert,

Last night to our great joy your mother was safely brought to bed of a daughter & both are like to do well.[191] Thank God I am in the same way my self though the progress I make is but slow, I mean as to strength, for the sore is within a very fue days of being perfectly healed. I hope when warm weather gives me leave to use exercise in the open air I shall also recover my former strength both of mind & body. It is with great pleasure I hear of your continuing so well. I leave room for your aunt to write on the other side & will add no more but my blessing to you both from your most affect[*ionate*] father,

Signed: John Buxton

[189] George Farquhar (1678–1707), born in Londonderry, wrote a number of successful comedies, including *The Recruiting Officer* (1706) and *The Beaux Stratagem* (1707), still regularly performed. Drabble, pp. 339–40.

[190] John Milton (1608–74). See notes 250 and 295, pp. 126 and 137, below.

[191] Isabella Buxton (1727–52). In 1750 Isabella became engaged to Richard Gardiner (1723–81), described by Ketton-Cremer as 'a busybody, a sponger and a cad'. After her death Gardiner harboured grievances against the Buxton family and their Sotherton and Branthwayt friends and in 1754 published a malicious novel *Pudica* in which the characters are thinly disguised versions of those persons he believed had wronged him. R.W. Ketton-Cremer, *Norfolk Portraits* (1944), pp. 110–39.

81 John Buxton to Robert Buxton [105/64]

Addressed: To Mr Robert Buxton at Mr D'Oyly's house in Playford, Suffolk. To be left at the Cross Keys in Ipswich.
Tuesday 4 o'clock. *No date. Catalogued 'about 1725' but probably March 1727.*

Dear Robert,

You will think me grown strong when I tell I'm this moment come in from taking the excersise of my coach, for indeed the air was mostly excluded and so long as the east wind prevails I will not fail to be very cautious. Thank you for your letter and the care you express for me in it. This is the first time I have ventured out since the cold winds.

Your mother and her little one are in a very fair way of doing well. Next Monday is designed for the christening. Lady Ward, your grandmother Buxton, and Mr Branthwayt the gossips.[192] Thank God your grandmother is recovered from her illnes.

I should be glad to see the papers you spake of. This day the old house at Banham went to Shadwell.[193] I must not venture thither myself till the weather change. The sore place is not yet quite healed. I believe this cold season retards a little but it every day grows towards it. Having no news I'll not trouble you or myself with a longer letter from your most affectionate father,

Signed: John Buxton

Our blessing to yourself and Georgy. Have you a plan of Gibraltar?[194] I'm in some doubt about the plan for Shadwell, whether the sketch under is not to be prefered.

Sketch of the ground floor plan of a house 52 feet by 46 feet. Reproduced as Plate 6.

[192] Gossips: godparents or sponsors.

[193] An old Buxton house at Banham was pulled down and salvaged building materials sent for reuse at Shadwell. This action is confirmed by a letter dated 28 Feb. 1727 to Robert Buxton from his aunt Hannah. CUL Buxton Papers, 35/70.

[194] Gibraltar was captured from Spain in 1704 and British possession confirmed by the treaty of Utrecht (1713). There seems to be no special significance in the Buxton interest other than in relation to Robert's education.

82 John Buxton to Robert Buxton [35/72]

Addressed: To Mr Robert Buxton at Mr D'Oyly's house in Playford
Channonz, 6 March 1727

Dear Robert,

We were all very glad to hcar by Mr D'Oyly of your being well though he stayed not long enough for any one to tell you so for your Aunt Han had writ a letter which through his hast was left behind. I hope his troubles are over ere this time & your house in peace. Your mother is like to have a fine getting up & will be well before me, though I'm also in a very good way, & have been twice abrod without taking any cold. The sore place is not yet healed but neare the matter.

I said nothing in my last of your French letter which I'le now thank you for. I could easily make out the greater part of it. Your plan was also very well contrived, & as you think would answer all that a moderate person could wish, when this is exceeded our schemes will have no bounds.

Your grandmother Buxton is recovered of her little indisposition or what she makes little of being the least complainer of illness. Since your mother's being in bed your little sister Sarah has been both nurse & surgeon & is very expert. Lenny continues his part & is very dextrous at the candle. Betty's [*Elizabeth*] part is now with your mother & performs it with great assiduity & care. It is pleasant to see them give me such hopes of their being of some use in the world, a thing the ladies of this age do little think of.

Mr D'Oyly speaks so well of George that I must let him know how much it pleases me to hear of it. My blessing is with you both from your most affectionate father,

Signed: John Buxton

83 John Buxton to Robert Buxton [35/73]

Addressed: To Mr Robert Buxton at Playford
Thursday 8 a clock morn[*ing*] 16 March 1727

Dear Robert,

Last your agreeable packet came to the great satisfaction of all your freinds here. I am glad this weather has no ill effects on you; I find none from it myself only that it prevents my going out, though I've ventured once without any hurt. Thank God I grow better every day though the sore is not quite dryed but very near. Your mother is also finely & the rest of your friends.

The foundations of Shadwell were not begun to be layed as Mr D'Oyly told you but only to be digged. The soyl not loam but a firm chalk which is far better. By the end of next week the digging will be ended so the week following perhaps we may begin. Have you thought of somthing to be inscribed on the stone to be put somwhere in an obscure part of the wall.

The key of the bureau is not yet found: you are desired to look in the linings of your breeches & coat where possibly it may be lodged. Mr Cooper[195] wrot to Mr Wilcox about his son, & has engaged him not to oppose his being your sizer,[196] so I hope it will be to both your satisfaction. I send you another play that I have not read nor yet the poem of summer, only dipt into it, but so far I'm much pleased.

I'm oblidged to you for the tender & affectionate things you say in your letter but forbear to say what my heart would dictate to you again because at present it makes too great an impression on my spirits, but without this you are assured of being your most affectionate father,

Signed: John Buxton

Your mother joyns with me in love and blessing to your self & Georgy. It is a great pleasure to find his genius turns to figures. Two draughts for fronts have been made for Shadwell, one with three windows [*bays*] the other with five. The latter is rejected and the last plan you saw here again approved.

I writ yesterday by the post.

84 John Buxton to Robert Buxton [35/74]

Addressed: To Mr Robert Buxton at Mr D'Oyly's house in Playford, Suffolk
To be left at the Cross Keys in Ipswich
Channonz, 21 March 1727, Wednesday morn[*ing*]

Dear Robert,

Mr Christian makes him self very acceptable by the intelligence he brings with him; may we never want these good accounts of each others health to make us happy. Yesterday the christining was performed in form & the weather being cold we had it in the hall. Mr Branthwayt & family were here. Your mother is finely well & the little one as thriving as possible. I am not quite well my self,

[195] Not identified.

[196] Sizer or sizar: a poor student admitted to a Cambridge college who, in return for the payment of his expenses, performed certain duties as the servant of another, more affluent, undergraduate. This practice provided a way round the regulation that banned the keeping of personal servants in colleges. V. Morgan, *A History of the University of Cambridge*, II, 1546–1750 (Cambridge, 2004), p. 330.

some fungus or other accident in the sore retards the cure: the warm weather will I hope finish it, for it is healed quite out of sight. I am otherwise much recovered & have great addition of strength every day, & recruit of the flesh my illnes had pulled from me.

[I] don't know whether Mr Layman's coope [*Cooper*] is at all related to the young man that is to be your siser. Have you any perticular character of him more than what you had from us?

Your judgement of plays is not ill grounded & you are much in the right to be very cautious of shewing it, for experience will certainly make you alter in many things what you may now think of them. When your own opinion agrees with that of the established judges you may boldly proname it & when you have good reasons to support it.

No bricks are yet laid at Shadwell; the earth not yet removed, & indeed as the weather has been, had they began they could not have gon forward. Georgy's hand is much improved, I will take care to send the letter to his brother. Your mother will expect to hear from you next post being now so well, & I suppose you will let us know the time of your vacation.

I am returned to the old plan again which all together is the best I can think of. I would send you that of Gibraltar but your leaving Playford is so near that it is not worth while. Thank God the N. E. wind is gon, so I will end this with S[*i*]r Will[*ia*]m Temple's[197] three wishes that we may have health, peace & fair weather.

I am, dear Robert, your most affectionate father,
Signed: John Buxton

85 John Buxton to Robert Buxton [35/75]

Addressed: To Mr Robert Buxton at Mr D'Oyly's house in Playford, Suffolk
To be left at the Cross Keys in Ipswich
28 March 1727

Dear Robert,

I opened the enclosed supposing it to my self by mistake & beg yours & your correspondent's pardon. I have little of news since my last only that your mother & all freinds here are well. I get around every day though some but little, the sore not healed, but have hopes of no further since this rainy weather, though warm, does not agree with me. I'm out every afternoon in the coach though the country about us is as wet as in the depth of winter. This

[197] Sir William Temple (1628–99), diplomat and essayist. See Appendix A, items 72–4.

may perhaps discourage your seeing us here, but you may be at Rushford or dispose of yourself as you like best. I hope to be able to meet you there when you are come or a fue days [*after*]. I expect to know by your next when we are to send for you. The roads to Rushford will be better than the Pye road, & your directions at Shadwell very usefull now I can't be there so soon my self. The foundations if not yet dug nor will be ready for the masons this ten days or a fortnight, so you may be at the laying the first stone. The inscription I found but must leave out a good deal of it least we be accused of vanity; we will contrive some other when we meet. I hope it will be in health.

I am dear Robert, your most affectionate father,
Signed: John Buxton

86 John Buxton to Robert Buxton [35/76]

Addressed: To Mr Robert Buxton at Rushford
10 April 1727, Monday morn.

Dear Robert,

I hope this will find you freed of the little indisposition you lately complained of. The weather forbidding me to come I have sent to enquire of your health. My cold is not quite gone but much better. In two or three days I think of being with you, if no accidents happen. I have not yet seen Mr Bucknam[198] since the people want him, are they not fit to begin to lay bricks. With my love & blessing to you both is all affections.

From your most affectionate father,
Signed: John Buxton

87 John Buxton to Robert Buxton [35/77]

Addressed: To Mr Robert Buxton at Mr D'Oyly's house in Playford, Suffolk
To be left at the Cross Keys in Ipswich
Rushford, 1 May 1727

Dear Robert,

I received your letter by Abraham[199] the same day he came from Playford & am glad you had so good a journy after your fears about the weather, in which

[198] John Buckenham, Buxton's surveyor. He carried out an estate survey in 1719 (CUL Buxton Papers, 96/49) and measured building work at Shadwell Lodge (CUL Buxton Papers, 96/50, undated).

[199] Abraham, a servant.

I had some part for you, but it soon cle[*a*]r[*e*]d up & has since been so fine that I believe you have been almost tempted to bath in the sea. If it continues thus & you have no cold or indisposition that forbid I think you should not loose the oppertunity but do it with discretion, staying but little time in the water, going in not too warm, dressing and rubbing your self imediately upon coming out &c.

I have [*been*] out on horsback every day since you left me, both forenoon & after & have great in that most agreeable exercise, but I do not indulge myself in that freedom I have formerly taken but I hope in time I may. I don't find much abatement of the discharge from the sore but sometimes more sometimes less, though riding I think does rather encrease it.

The building goes forward very well, & thank God I've yet strength enough to be with the workmen six or seaven hours in the day & find much occation to be there, not knowing how to depend upon the surveyor, who is often absent & as often when there liable to blunder. The pump man, after sinking about 18 foot through an entire rock of chalk, is come at water & as free a spring as he says & he ever met with. Three of the elements have conspired to make Shadwell lodge a most agreable place & I am every day more charmed with the situation, & see every day where new schemes may be put in excecution in their order, and time & opportunity will give us leave.

I have fixed Whitson week for your Cambridge journy if nothing falls out between to prevent us. Sarah is with me still and wants your company as well as my self but I shall always content my self to be without it when it is either for your health, your improvement or your pleasure, to be absent in all which I have great satisfaction.

I will say nothing from Channonz supposing you will hear from thence by your mother, for whom I'm much concerned on account the fright she met with in the chariot. I've some hopes of seeing her here to day. I hear your grandmother Buxton & aunt are well at Norwich & your grandfather Gooch at Quidenham. If I write more I shall want room to tell you I am your most affectionate father,

Signed: J[*ohn*] Buxton

88 John Buxton to Robert Buxton [105/27]

Addressed: To Mr Robert Buxton at Mr D'Oyly's house in Playford, Suffolk. To be left at the Cross Keys in Ipswich
Monday, 8 May 1727

My dear Robert,

I am drove in by the rain from my usual exercise and amusement which I have been constant to both forenoon and after ever since you left me. I have now nothing to do but write so begin my letter three days before it will be sent. Riding is become very easy to me and I can be on horseback six or seaven hours, moving from one workman to another, and I find myself very necessary among them all. I imagined when the foundations were layed the chief case of putting matters right had been over but I find a busier scene every day as the walls advance. It is more in the offices where I would take advantage of every inch for some account or other, than it will be in the upper rooms. They have not yet layed the first floor. The vault took up the time and it will be two or three days before they will be fit.

The subject I began with has led me too far before. I rejoyce with you on the good account you send me of your health, pray God continue it to give you. In all places the weather is now so much altered you'd hardly venture to bath [?]. The season has been exceeding fine for our purpose here and this change serves also for the clover.

I am every day more pleased with my schemes at Shadwell. The taking the air and amusement of building has greatly contributed to making me well. I hope it will hereafter when the building is done with continue to agree with us that we may think our trouble well bestowed. As to myself, I am grown much stronger and I may say almost the same as usual, but the discharge continues though not so much. I hope by degrees it will quite close. In the mean time I believe my constitution receives much benefit from it. Yesterday Mr Slater[200] dined with me here and I like the man very well though he is not yet quite so courtly as we might expect from a quality chaplain.

Wednesday morning from Channonz, 10 May 1727.

I came last night hither when I found your aunt Jacob with her family and all my own well, only your mother has got a cold. I had the pleasure also of hearing you were so, which will always be the greatest addition to all I meet with in life. I have left the workmen for a day or two and I must not be longer

[200] Not identified.

absent because they are very apt to deviate. A months absence has made this place new to me and its being of so different a kind makes the change vastly agreeable, though I think the other more to my taste: the extensive openes of the country fills my mind with the idea of greatness. Here the views are sweet and charming but all confined and the park that used to seem a large wide place is contracted to a small field of an acre or two. I shall expect you at Rushford the latter end of the week before Whitson day, for in the beginning of Whitson week I think to go with you to Cambridge. I would not have you bleed without a necessity, the warm weather will carry off your pains I hope, and the exertion [?] of your journys. I have no more room than to say I am your most affectionate etc.

Not signed

Service to cozen Meadow and thanks for her information about the ordering of the pheasants.

89 John Buxton to Robert Buxton [35/78]

No address
Channonz, 15 May 1727

Dear Robert,

I hope this will find you so well as to think of your Cambridge journy in Whitson week. I shall expect tomorrow to hear from you & according to the account you give shall send the horses that you may come to me at Rushford by Saturday or Sunday night. Dr Herring will be there to go with us & your cozen Marsham has allso got leave of his father to see Cambridge though not to stay there.

No more till I see you but that I am your most affectionate father,
Signed: John Buxton

Your aunt Jacob is just now going home but desires her service to you.

90 John Buxton to Robert Buxton [35/79]

Addressed: To Mr Buxton at Clare Hall in Cambridge[201]
Rushford, 1 June 1727

Dear Robert,

I found my self & horses so little fatigued with coming to Rushford on Monday morning that I proceeded the same day to Channonz where all are well except your grandmother Gooch, & she is so ill every letter I write you may expect to hear of her departure. By the next return of the Cambridge carrier you will receive the parcel of books, & in Lock[*e*]'s *Essay*[202] before the blanke leafe is sent the catalogue, but I came in such hast this morning that I do not know whether the purs is put up.

I hope your cold is quite gon; mine will not quite leave me till the fine weather returns, but it is so much abated as to be no manner of trouble. I come hither to meet a person about hiring the farm here & to take a little view of Shadwell if the weather gives leave. I've no more at present but that I am always your most affectionate father,

Signed: John Buxton

My service to Mr Wilcox. You must get a Boyers dictionary[203] & what other books you want. I could not find a Greek grammer nor Grotius:[204] I have the latter only in English. Direct your letters to Channonz. There are six parcels of books. As you are like to be a custimer to this carrier I hope he'l not impose on you for carriage, of which you had best inform your self the rates &c. Jacky is with me & sends you his love & service. We had yesterday a letter from Georgy. He is well & so is Len[205] though he said much concerned for losing you at Playford.

[201] The first letter addressed to Clare Hall. Robert Buxton was admitted to the college on 25 May 1727 and matriculated in 1728. Clare Hall, founded in 1326, became Clare College during the mastership of Edward Atkinson (1856–1915).

[202] Appendix A, item 120.

[203] Appendix A, item 5.

[204] Appendix A, items 94, 156 and 172.

[205] Leonard Buxton (1719–88), the third of John Buxton's sons to be educated at Playford.

91 John Buxton to Robert Buxton [35/80]

Addressed: To Mr Buxton at Clare Hall in Cambridge
Channonz, 12 June 1727

Dear Robert,

I have read both your letters with the wig from Cambridge, & have returned the latter being too little for me in the caul,[206] nor do I at all like the fashion, so if the barber expects any thing for the return, though I think nothing due, you may give him half a crowne. I shall furnish my self with a wig from Norwich more to my liking.

If your cold was not extreem bad I shall hope this find you quite freed of it. If it continues very troublesom your remedie is to bleed a little & if upon that it should not cease you must for a while change air & come to me at Rushford or to Mr D'Oyly's at Playford. Thank God I continue pretty well as does your mother also & the rest of our family except your grandmother Gooch who every day declines though she holds beyond expectation.

I have let Rushford to one Mr Gent,[207] a substantial tenant, the whole farm except that part designed to go with the lodge farm, & have not abated the old rent making only allowance for what I take for my own use. This has eased me of some cares and if I hear you are well I shall have very fue to disturb me. Till you are perfectly well don't omit to let us hear every post <when>. The carrier will bring the Greek common prayer book;[208] let me know if you shall want any others.

The weather has been much against you & others that are subject to colds; I've yet scarce got rid of mine. I belive Rushford air will quite cure it. I'm going thither this morning, shall call at Bucknam[209] in expectation to have a letter from you till when I will defer ending this.

Rushford, 2 a'clock.

I met your letter at Buckenham & wish the contents had been more agreeable. You must not defer bleeding since your cold gives you so much uneasines, nor to change air for some time, & you shall have either the chariot or a horse which you like best to come to me here. If your cold abates you shall defer the bleeding till you come hither; the usual quantity you know I suppose, about 4

206 Caul: the netted substructure of a wig.

207 Richard Gent was the most important of John Buxton's tenants, paying £350 per annum rent in 1729, representing thirty per cent of Buxton's rental income. Appendix D.

208 Appendix A, item 145.

209 New Buckenham.

or 5 ounces, if now necessary. I send Abraham, that if you are well enough you may take his horse, he hiring another to come to me at Newmarket[210] on Thursday afternoon in order to come thither. I will be there, or send the chariot, if a letter by the post that day does not tell me you are like to get [rid] of your cold.

I've no more but my best wishes from your most affect[*ionate*] father,
Signed: J[*ohn*] Buxton

92 John Buxton to Robert Buxton [35/81]

Addressed: To Mr Buxton at Clare Hall in Cambridge
Channonz, 19 June 1727

Dear Robert,

You will be glad to hear your mother with her little one came safe home on Saturday. As I was then at the good account she gave of your being in the way of health again, I hope this will find you in possession of that great blessing. I believe it was an accidental cold & not any thing from the disagreeableness of air.

We were as every body els much surprised with your news of our king's sudden death.[211] As to mourning, I would have you do as other gentlemen where you are, & suppose almost every one puts on black cloath & made up as strict mourning as for a parent. I believe you had best line the <body of your> westcoat with chagrik[212] silk cloath els would be too hot this summer.

Your grandmother Gooch continues yet though not all mended, nor does she give any hopes of a recovery though she may possibly hold a little longer. I've not heard from Laxfeild since your grandmother left us. Dr Herring told me he had received a letter from you last Monday & designed answering it on this; you have a very good correspondent of him, as well as a very good friend.

I am your most affectionate father,
Signed: John Buxton

It was extreemly well judged of you not to remove from Cambridge without necessity for upon your return again you might have been liable to some inconvenience upon the change of air which does generally at first affect most people.

[210] Newmarket (then part in Cambridgeshire, all now in Suffolk), a market town thirteen miles from Cambridge on the road to Norwich, a further 55 miles distant.

[211] King George I (1660–1727, reigned from 1714) died on 11 June.

[212] Possibly related to chagrin, now commonly spelled shagreeen, in this case an imitation of an untanned skin or leather with a rough surface.

93 John Buxton to Robert Buxton [35/84]

Addressed: To Mr Buxton at Clare Hall in Cambridge
Rushford, 1 July 1727

Dear Robert,

The weather has been so exceeding bad that I do not wonder your cold still continues upon you, & I was apprehensive it would have encreased. If from change of weather you do not find your self better you must try the change of air, but we have had so much rain in Norfolk that we can scarce tell where to set our feet dry. Though Shadwell feels little of the effects being all over the close where the building is perfectly dry, while here at Rushford we are surrounded with water.

This week we proclaimed the king at Harlston & Diss[213] with such numbers of people & such demonstrations of joy as I did not expect in those places. I met S[*i*]r Edm[*und*]d Bacon[214] at Diss & Mr Sayer[215] who both enquired much after you, but they know they could not make me a better complement. I shall stay at this place till Wednesday but you must direct still to Channonz being the surest way of hearing of you & I will hope for good accounts.

I am, my dear Robert, your most affectionate father,
Signed: John Buxton

My humble service to your master & Mr Wilcox. I do not forget what I said I would send when I kill a deer.

Let me know when you would have your quarter's allowance & I will send it. The chamber floor is to be raised on Monday or Tuesday. I like every thing perfectly well; no water has ever stood after the most violent rains in the foundations. Mr Fuller's[216] affair cast some reflections though unjustly on your master. He is an indiscreet young man; it is of infinite disadvantage at setting out in the world to make such fals steps, the most regular conduct hereafter

213 Diss: a south Norfolk market town on the Suffolk border, 19 miles south-west of Norwich and six miles from Channonz.

214 At this date there were two Sir Edmund Bacon baronets active in Norfolk. One (1693–1738), commonly known as the 'Gillingham Sir Edmund', was the fifth baronet of the Gillingham (Norfolk) line. He was Whig member for Thetford 1722–38. The other Sir Edmund (*c.* 1680–1755) was the sixth baronet of the Garboldisham (Norfolk) line. He was a Tory, the member for Thetford 1710–13 and Norfolk 1713–15. He was elected unopposed for Suffolk in 1728. John Buxton met the former of these gentlemen. Sedgwick, I, p. 426.

215 Not identified.

216 The details of Mr Fuller's indiscretions are not known.

will scarce set him right in the good opinion of people of such force is early prejudice.

Your grandmother Gooch is as she was.

94 John Buxton to Robert Buxton [35/86]

Addressed: To Mr Buxton at Clare Hall in Cambridge
Rushford, 4 July 1727

Dear Robert,

I am glad to find by your last which I did not receive here till Monday that you cold is not worse. You shall whenever you'l appoint the time have your horse sent that you may come either to me at Rushford or to Playford. I hope the waters here will be fallen in a weeks time; they have been very high ever since I came last, & make me wish I could have lodged at Shadwell. I am there every day now but go on but slowly through several little impediments. The chamber floor will be raised this week & then I hope we shall proceed with more dispatch.

I think you will want a sort of riding coat to wear with your black westcoat. If you come into the country it should be of dark grey cloath lined with black. The late rainy season disagreed much with me but I think I gain ground & hope the old complaint will in time go of & that yours may do so too is my hearty wish, from your most affectionate father,

Signed: John Buxton

You take no notice of a parcel lately sent you by the carrier of tea &c. from your mother. Your grandmother Gooch continues yet but without any hopes of her overgrowing this illness.

95 John Buxton to Robert Buxton [35/85]

Addressed: To Mr Buxton at Clare Hall Cambridge
9 July 1727

Dear Robert,

I give you joy of the return of your health & the prospect you have of the continuance of it in the place you find every way so agreeable. I have not yet received your letter sent last to Shadwell but shall do it tomorrow. The floods at Rushford had no ill effecs on me only the gnats intollerably troublesome from the plenty of water. Having taken a little phisick to day makes me end this the sooner. from your most affectionate'

Signed: J[*ohn*] Buxton

I would have you get the bible new bound. /turn over/ Bind only the bible & singing psalms, leaving out the littergy that is part torn.

96 John Buxton to Robert Buxton [35/87]

Addressed: To Mr Buxton at Clare Hall in Cambridge
Rushford, 17 July 1727

Dear Robert,

I came this morning from Channonz where I left your mother & the family well & your grandmother not worse, and all very glad to hear such good accounts of your continuing so well, as we perceive by your letter of the 14 inst. As also that you approve of the rules of your colledge & the acquaintance it affords, which I believe are both the best in the university, & are much mended since I was there. But you will hereafter as your observation shall direct you, sometimes converse out of your own society & always let the worth & good charactre of the person justifie you.

I am heartily sorry for Mr Fuller's indiscretion. You observed very right in the letter you writ Dr Herring this is a blot will scarce ever be wiped out. The imputation of atheism or prophaness is absolutely to be avoided. If your master at Playford is like to suffer for this folly of Fuller, <and> for it is said he was trained up in such principles at school, though this I know is fals, yet calumny though never so much so will stick, & therefore you that have been under the same master must be more particularly on your guard & if any thing in talk should happen among young people about religion, as it often does, I would advise you to take the orthodox side of the question, but always without affectation for that will be as much suspected. The next time you write to Dr Herring you may say something in defence of Mr D'Oyly about Fuller; it will be to both your advantage & his.

You must buy those books you mentioned for I have none of them, & St Everment's works [217] in French which you'l be much pleased with. I hear there is a new edition of Mr Bayes dictionary[218] coming out in French &

217 Appendix A, item 185.
218 Pierre Bayle (1647–1706), *Historical and Critical Dictionary.*

English: enquire about the price &c. I have not read Ker of Kersland's memoirs[219] but have often heard of them.

I don't hear who stands for Suff[*olk*] beside S[*i*]r Will[*ia*]m Barker; I believe S[i]r Rob[*er*]t Kemp has an inclination. S[*i*]r J[*ohn*] Hobart & S[*i*]r Tho[*mas*] Coke I believe will be for Norfolk, Mr De Grey having declined in favour of the former.[220]

I shall remain here till Saturday so you may direct accordingly. The work rises slowly without I'm here often; I will attend now till the assizes. Your freinds at Laxfeild are well as I heard last Wednesday. I've nothing more to add but my best wishes for you at all times being your most affectionate father,

Signed: John Buxton

I left your sisters last Thursday at Mr Chretien's [*Christian*].

97 John Buxton to Robert Buxton [35/88]

Addressed: To Mr Buxton at Clare Hall in Cambridge
Rushford, 22 July 1727

Dear Robert,

I just now received yours & will take care very speedily to return you some mony. It will be very proper to get a duroy[221] frock; as you mention in these matters you are a fit judge for your self & must do as you find occation. I will send you Clarendon[222] as soon as I get to Channonz which I expect to do on Monday, with a late authour that has criticized upon him.

You are oblidged to Dr Herring for his correspon: the freindship of an honest man is no small happiness. S[*i*]r J[*ohn*] Hobart joyns with S[*i*]r

219 John Ker of Kersland (1673–1726), *Memoirs* (1726). Ker, born in Ayrshire, was a government spy who died in a London debtor's prison. His memoirs were published in three parts, the third posthumously.

220 At the election of 1727, Sir William Barker (?1685–1731) fifth baronet of Grimston Hall (Suffolk), a Tory, was re-elected for the county. Sir Robert Kemp (1667–1734) third baronet of Ubbeston (Suffolk), a Tory, represented Dunwich at various times in the period 1701–15, but did not sit for the county until 1732. Thomas Coke (1697–1759), of Holkham (Norfolk), sat unopposed as a Whig for Norfolk 1722–28, when he was raised to the peerage at the coronation of George II. Sir John Hobart (1693–1756), fifth baronet of Blickling (Norfolk), a Whig, was the member for St Ives (Cornwall) 1715–27 and was returned for Norfolk in 1727. Thomas de Grey (1680–1765) of Merton (Norfolk), a Whig, sat for Norfolk 1715–27 but did not stand for re-election. Sedgwick, I, pp. 434, 564 and 608; II, p. 142.

221 Duroy: a coarse woollen fabric, typically of west country manufacture.

222 Appendix A, item 151.

Tho[*mas*] Coke for our county; Mr Holt opposes S[*i*]r Will[*ia*]m Barker & S[*i*]r Jer[*e*]m[*i*]ah Davers in Suffolk. The two latter joyn but it is thought Mr Holt will be one.[223]

The 1st chamber floor at Shadwell commands Thetford hil and part of the town; I was upon it this morning & laid out the several partitions. The appartments will be very commodious.

I am in hast, your most affectionate &c.,

Signed: J[*ohn*] B[*uxton*]

98 John Buxton to Robert Buxton [35/89]

Addressed: To Mr Buxton at Clare Hall in Cambridge
The Green Man near Shadwell Lodge, 31 July 1727

Dear Robert,

The above written bill you are to endorse & either your tutor or alderman foul[?][224] will take it; if you want any more let me know it. As I came through Buckenham I received yours of the 24[*th*] as I did the packet before & have sent the enclosed to your grandmother who is as well as the rest of your friends at Laxfeild, are those at Channonz except your grandmother Gooch are so too. She is now so bad as I have not yet seen her; I left the doctor there this morning. I think she can't continue many days.

You will receive with this Clarendon's *History.* I will send the other book I mentioned whe I go to Rushford which will not be now till after the assizes. Ther'se no opposition in Norf[*olk*] but it is said there will certainly be one at Norwich as well as in Suffolk. I wish good success to Mr Holt [225] who meets with great encouragement.

I will enquire for the book you desire at Norwich but fear if neither London nor Cambridge afford it, it will scarce be found in Norwich. Dr Herring is with me & sends you his service so I will take my self no longer from his company than to assure you I am your most affectionate father,

Signed: John Buxton

It is a great pleasure to hear Cambridge agrees with you so well; you need not

[223] See note 220 above, p. 114. Sir Jermyn Davers (*c.* 1686–1743), fourth baronet of Rougham and Rushbrooke (Suffolk), a Tory, was the member for Bury St Edmunds 1722–27 and sat for the county 1727–43. Sedgwick, I, p. 606. The unsuccessful candidate in 1727 was Mr Holt of Redgrave.

[224] Alderman Foul[?] has not been identified.

[225] See note 254, p. 127, below.

be perticular in the accounts now of your being so, I shall always suppose it when I see nothing from you to the contrary. I am also much pleased with your design of continuing there without coming into the country.

99 John Buxton to Robert Buxton [35/92]

Addressed: To Mr Buxton at Clare Hall in Cambridge
Norwich, 16 August 1727

Dear Robert,

The little disorder since it is so well of will I hope prevent a greater & may perhaps be a means to secure you from the illnes of the season. Mr Cooper brought your letter on Monday to Channonz. I am glad to hear you are every way so well for I was perticular in my enquiry, & had great satisfaction to find the humour had also left you.

I am very willing you should have the books you mention, Rapin's *Hist*[*ory*][226] &c. If you can have them on better terms at the auction you may get them there, but take care they are perfect for at auctions they often bring imperfect books as I have found more than once.

I am come hither with design to go tomorrow to Blickling[227] and shall take Dr Herring and Mr Barnard[228] with me. Your mother continues well & your brothers & sisters, your granmother as she was. At Laxfeild they are all well but Mis Betty Jacob who has that feaver that is now very much among the country people.

I am, dear Robert, your most affectionate,
Signed: J[*ohn*] Buxton

100 John Buxton to Robert Buxton [35/93]

Addressed: To Mr Buxton at Mr D'Oyly's house in Playford Suff[*olk*]
To be left at the Cross Keys in Ipswich
4 October 1727

Dear Robert,

I hope this will find you as it leaves us in the mending way; your brother George was so ill the day you left us that we feared he would have the common illnes but it is gone quite of & he is brisk again.

226 Appendix A, item 196.
227 Blickling Hall, 16 miles north of Norwich, the seat of Sir John Hobart.
228 Not identified.

Mr Ralph Hare[229] dined with me the day after you left us & Mr D'Oyly came the same night; [*he*] went away yesterday morning to Mr Partridge's.[230] The weather has [*been*] very favourable for your hardening; I make no doubt you have made use of it. Sarah has been a little out of order at Norwich but is well again; they are all so at Laxfeild as I hear to day by a letter from your grandmother.

I have not been at Shadwell since you went from us, the alteration among my servants keeps me at home to see them setled in their posts. I do not like a change if it could be avoided. If you find your self hardy enough to endure the ceremony of a visit I think you should see Major Churchill [231] befor you leave Playford & when you do, give him my humble service. Perhaps my cozen Meadowe would meet you there. It may be expected you should do the same to our relations of the Acton[232] family but I think it is not due, but if by any accident you meet with any encouragement you may make them a short visit. I leave it to your own choice, for there's nothing in it either advantageous or agreeable.

With your mother's & my love & blessing is all from your most affect[*ionate*] father,

Signed: J[*ohn*] Buxton

Georgy gives you his love & often mentions you as if it was sincere.

[*Ann Buxton to Robert Buxton*][233]

Your father leaveing this little room, must tell my dear Rob[*er*]t how much my low spirits are raised by hearing you bore your journey so well; may we have the same good account to night. My dear Fib I think was merrier that day you left us then ever I see her, that she would not let any one wish her be mallen-

229 The forename Ralph occurs in the Hare families of both Stow Bardolph and Hargham. The latter connection, near neighbours of John Buxton, is more likely. Hargham Hall was built by Hugh Hare in 1689 (Pevsner, *Norfolk 2*, p. 382). The house is also attributed to Ralph Hare (d. 1709) whose eldest son, of twelve children, was Thomas Hare. The Ralph who dined at Channonz may have been a younger brother. Anne Carter, *The Beevor Story* (Norwich, 1993), p. 2.

230 Of the Partridge family of Buckenham Tofts Hall (Norfolk).

231 Not identified.

232 The Actons of Bramfield (Suffolk) were distant cousins as a result of the marriage of John Buxton's grandfather's sister Isabella Buxton (1628–64) to John Acton.

233 Robert Buxton's mother Anne wrote to him regularly. This short letter on the same sheet as John Buxton's letter is included here as an example of the style and content of her correspondence.

coly. Oh how happy is she is in this troublesome time where so fue enjoy any thing.

My family still continue in great disorder; & one of my new cookes came a Sunday so ill that I was forced to send her home againe; & now my maid Bab have heared of a place & is a going. But with all these small disapointments I hope in time to go throu with every thing, & will send your brothers to Playford some time next week but not afore Thursday though your marster would have had them sooner. I can't git well my self but hope to hold up; your grandm[*other*] better, your aunt Herne not well but may be about a gaine tomorrow. I'm in some concern for your sister Sarah; I hope to be able to see her soon though she was finly well yesterday.

Wishing you health & pleasure, am your ever affect[*ionate*] mother,

Signed: Ann Buxton

101 John Buxton to Robert Buxton [35/94]

Addressed: To Mr Buxton at Playford
Saturday, 16 October 1727

Dear Robert,

Your brothers, notwithstanding the season continues sickly here, return in health to Playford. I shall be glad this finds you so & that the air of Playford has had its usual effect. Your mother has a return of her illnes but I hope it will be but little. The sicknes continues yet in the country about us; God knows when it will cease & we must with patience wait his time. My uncle Marsham is ill, & your cozen Robert carried the ague with him to the coronation, & some bark[234] also in his pocket, but I think he puts too much upon a good constitution. Your aunt Han is come to Norwich; I saw her there last Thursday well. She left your grandmother & aunt so at Laxfeild. This you'l be pleased to hear as I was.

If it was not for the unhealthynes I should think the season extreem fine but the lodge is yet uncovered, but next week I expect to put on the roof; the walls are finished & dry as fast almost as in the summer. A good account of your health will give us great satisfaction & I hope you'l be able to send it to your most affectionate father,

Signed: J[*ohn*] B[*uxton*]

Your grandmother Gooch is something better & your aunt Herne very well.

[234] See note 65, p. 18, above

102 John Buxton to Robert Buxton [35/95]

Addressed: To Mr Buxton at Mr D'Oyly's house in Playford in Suffolk
To be left at the Cross Keys in Ipswich
1 November 1727

Dear Robert,

Though we had no letter from you the last week, I heard at Norwich on Saturday of your continuing well. You will be pleased to hear we grow better here; your mother has not had any more returns, & your little sister is finerly recovered again, though not quite free of the illness. The servants too who have been very bad with this feaver are also like to do well, & even your grandmother Gooch has been for some days below stairs every day, but is now confined again having I believe got some cold.

This is the state of my own family & I have the satisfaction to hope in a little time we shall all be perfectly well but it is not thus with our neibours. The sicknes rather encreases as well as the mortality occationed by it, & we have dayly sad accounts from all parts. Poor Bardswell,[235] the ingenious country-man whose assistance I have often taken in country affairs is dead, & my new tenant at Rushford[236] has buried both father & mother of his wife since Michaelmas, & his own is so ill that they have but little hopes of his recovery. Last Saturday I heard of the death of the bishop of Norwich, S[*i*]r Lambert Blackwell of Sprowston, & Sukey Cooper, a favourite of Mrs Harbord's. On Sunday morning Lady <Bacon> Kemp died not of the feaver but the stone with which she hath been long afflicted. S[*i*]r Edm[*un*]d Bacon of Garboldsham has this feaver and is very bad with it. Several of the doctrs are dead, as Dr Aldis near Walsham & Dr Hepburn at Lynn. Layman is very ill, but S[*i*]r Benjamin [*Wrench*], with more fatigue I believe than he ever went through with, holds perfectly well.[237] Col[*one*]l

235 John Buxton's steward.

236 Richard Gent, see note 207, p. 109, above.

237 This melancholy account of sickness and death refers to (1 Nov 1727) John Leng (1665–1727), Bishop of Norwich 1723–27. Sir Lambeth Blackwell baronet of Sprowston was one of the younger of the seventeen children of Captain John Blackwell of Mortlake (Surrey). He was knighted in 1697 and from 1698 to 1705 was envoy to Tuscany and Genoa. He was M.P. for Wilton 1708–10 and a governor of the South Sea Company. He was created a baronet in 1718 and died on 27 October 1727. Lady Kemp may have been Martha, daughter of William Blackwell of Mortlake (Surrey) the third wife of Sir Robert Kemp (1667–1734). He married four times. See note 185, p. 94, above. For Sir Edmund Bacon of Garboldisham see note 214, p. 111 above. The chapel of St Nicholas, King's Lynn has memorial inscriptions for members of the Hepburn family including medical practitioners but none can be related to the death reported by John Buxton. E.M.W. Hovell, *A complete list of the inscriptions on the slabs tablets and monuments in the*

Windham[238] is also extreem ill, but amidst this sickly account of our neibours & acquaintance I have the pleasure to tell you your grandmother & freinds at Laxfeild, except Mis Betty, continue well & Lady Ward & your aunt Han at Norwich are so to.

I suppose you begin to think of Cambridge if you are perfectly well, for I would have you be so before you remove from the place you are in, & I leave it to your own choice & discretion to stay or remove as you like best, as also the way of travelling to Cambridge. If you come by way of Rushford your mother will one day see you there. As to the affair of your board &c. at Playford, I will take care of that, only do you give half a crown a piece to the servants at your departure, or if more than three servts use your discretion.

I have no more to add but my best wishes for you & my blessing in which your brothers must have their share & am your most affectionate father,

Signed: John Buxton

103 John Buxton to Robert Buxton [35/96]

Addressed: To Mr Buxton at Mr D'Oyly's house in Playford, Suffolk
11 November 1727

Dear Robert,

I did not receive your letter till yesterday but had it come sooner you could not have had an answer before this. I am sorry to hear the disorder you complain of is not gon of; your mother has acquainted Sir Benj[*amin Wrench*] with it & has sent you what he ordered with proper directions. If you find your self strong enough for the journey it would be most proper to go to Cambridge before you begin taking the phisick but you must be carefull of being overtired, otherwise riding, the doctor says, is not at all hurtfull. If you think the journey will be too much & you like it, you may continue where you are for I know no place agrees with so well & perhaps you will not be so easily accommodated in Norwich. You will take care to write time enough to Mr Cooper[239] to have your bed & lodgings well aired, if you go to Cambridge, & I must still leave it for you to choose which way you move. I say nothing to encourage your going sooner than you find it convenient, & that you are sure you can do it without prejudice, & you will find by the

chapel of St Nicholas, King's Lynn, existing in the year 1937 (King's Lynn, 1937), p. 37. For Mr Layman see note 88, p. 63, above and for Sir Benjamin Wrench see note 63, p. 71, above.

238 See note 30, p. 9, above.

239 Mr Cooper, Robert Buxton's sizar.

returns of illnes whether you are in condition or not to travel. If you begin the medicine first you must stay to see what effects it has & send us word that, if there be occation, any alteration may be made in the method.

I've just new company come in that prevents my say more than that I am your most affect[*ionate*] father,

Signed: J[*ohn*] Buxton
11 November, 1727

Shadwell is not yet tiled. Blessing to Georgy & Len. We have considered that if you go to Cambridge it will be best for you to take the way of Bury or Rushford. Let us know your motion & care shall be taken of the beds &c. at Rushford where you may also rest a day or two if you find need.

104 John Buxton to Robert Buxton [35/97]

Addressed: To Mr Buxton at Clare Hall in Cambridge
Norwich, 10 December 1727

Dear Robert,

I was very glad to meet your letter here yesterday with so good an account of yourself after having had some fears for you for want of hearing. I have not received any letter from you since that by John Fuller[240] who found me on the top of the building at Shadwell, as he came home with your mare. She is well recovered of her cold as are the rest of my horses though all have had this distemper. My family is also recovered, & S[*i*]r Benj[*amin*] Wrench like to do well.

The things you sent your sister Sarah came safe & are forwarded as directed. I am now at Lady Ward's, shall be at Channonz to night. To prevent your letters going wrong you must direct to me hear [*here via*] New Buckenham & though I always hope the best when I do not hear of you I shall like it once a week till you are quite recovered.

I have sent a bill for twenty pounds & had got it yesterday before I received your letter; Mr Alderman foul[?] will exchange it. Dr Herring is well & sends you his service, so does your aunt Hannah who is here with Lady Ward & well though the latter has been much otherwise. I thank God I am am [*sic*] as well as I could expect to be in such weather when I am confined from the air & exercise abroad, nor could use my coach till yesterday, of three weeks.

You will hear very soon again from your most affect[*ionate*],

Signed: J[*ohn*] Buxton

240 John Fuller, a Buxton servant.

105 John Buxton to Robert Buxton [35/100]

Addressed: To Mr Buxton at Clare Hall in Cambridge
17 December 1727

Dear Robert,

Last night I received yours of the 15th inst. & the book also that should have come long before. This treatise of planting I had not among mine & I'm much pleased with it. Whenever you happen of any thing of the same kind & can get it reasonably as you did this, I should like to have it.

I hope this will find you better than when you writ. I'm concerned for the trouble this humour gives you, but I think it is better as it is safer for you that it takes its old course. I have great encouragement to try what the Bath will do, & hope in the spring to find oppertunity of going thither. You will receive with this a hare & a pheasant, a brace of partridges & some small foul, which you are obliged to Jack Mallom for, who brought them himself this morning. S[*i*]r Benj[*amin*] Wrench is recovered but not yet able to go out, but Mr Layman continues ill.

Your aunt I believe went last Monday to Laxfeild, though the season was not very tempting to leave the town for that country. If you like to have some game now & then I will if can get it send you some, & next week if I can find a fat doe among my little herd I will send you a part of one. The cold weather pinches me though I make a tolerable shift with & now the shortest days are over I shall a least fancy myself better & warmer. The family continues well which is all the news I can send you. If I can hear the same of you I shall not wish for better, being your most affectionate father,

Signed: John Buxton

106 John Buxton to Robert Buxton [35/101]

Addressed: To Mr Buxton at Clare Hall in Cambridge
Channonz, 31 December 1727

Dear Robert,

Yesterday we received two letters from you by way of Norwich, one to your mother & the other to your sister Betty [*Elizabeth*]. I need not tell you how much to our satisfaction when you let us know you are well. You will have the same good account of your freinds here, only Betty has had a very little of the common illnes that has not quite left the country though it is every where abated.

I am glad the eatibles we sent you were acceptable: you made the best use of them if you can oblidged your friends. Upon examining among my small herd of deer I could find none fit to kill: the does have all of them young ones & this hinders their being fat in their season. In the room of venison you will receive a hare by the next return of the Cambridge carrier.

You shall have the books by Mr Cooper, & Wingate's *Arithmetick*[241] if I have it. I suppose you are entring into a course of the mathematicks, a study I believe will be agreeable to you, & I'm sure of as much use in life as any other if not a great deal more. I thank you for the pamphlet you sent, but not having read Kers memoirs[242] I do not so well enter into the design of the former.

I have no manner of news & have scarce been out of doors for some time. Shadwell Lodge was covered the week before Xmas & has received no manner of injury from the weather; I have not been there since. Your friends at Laxfeild continue well. I am to expect your grandmother some time this spring but that will not hinder me from going with you to the Bath if it is thought proper for you, & I should with greater pleasure than ever take that journy with the hopes of its freeing you of the humour. Your brother Jack is much come on in his book, & begins to shew good tokens of doing well. I shall not fail to encourage this disposition in him & your good example is no small spur to them all. I make this reflection with abundance of pleasure being your most affectionate father,

Signed: John Buxton

Your mother sends her blessing, all your sisters & Jacky their best wishes for a happy new year.

107 John Buxton to Robert Buxton [35/102]

Addressed: To Mr Robert Buxton at Clare Hall in Cambridge
Channonz, 14 January 1728

Dear Robert,

I have deferred ansuring yours of the 5th inst. till I could do it by Mr Cooper who with this brings you the books you desired or as many of them as I could remember. I rejoyce with you upon the good hopes you have of being freed from your complaints & hope you will have no more returns. Betty [*Elizabeth*] has had one of hers, it comes now as an ague, she is in a course of

241 Edmund Wingate (1596–1656) published a number of books with arithmetic in the title, including *Arithmetique made easie* in 1650.

242 See note 219, p. 114, above.

the bark for it. The rest of my family are well as are also your freinds elsewhere in Suffolk & this county. Only Bob Marsham can't yet loose his ague which has made him extreem thin. The weather has been as bad as it could be yet thank God I escape the ill effects of it as well as most.

I am much pleased you find a disposition to the mathematicks; there is not any study more usefull in the practick part nor that affords more pleasure in the speculative. I have not seen Chamber's new book[243], only the specimen of it in the memoirs of literature, but I belive I shall be tempted to buy it. Langley's book of gardning[244] I have sent for, being willing to see everything on the subject; I have always delighted to read of though I have done nothing considerable in it myself. I have been taught by these books of gardning to see the extravagance of it & so have confined myself to a little of the usefull. Only the travells of Cyrus[245] I have just dipped into & returned them again, enough to know <they> it is a pretty book; will you not choose to have the French edition of it? Mr Gibbs's book of architecture[246] will tempt me I fear, though I've no great opinion of him <*word?*> There is something good in most, but in Jones's works[247] only nothing bad. The country affords as little news to send you as divertions to us in it. I live upon the hopes of what the spring & sunshine is to give us. Very little company at sessions, neither of the representatives being there. Mr Preston told me his son is with a private tutor in London, that he is master of the Greek, & also of classical learning & is now entring upon the mathematicks; the other son is prentice with a linen draper. I am glad the hare proved so acceptable but for the sawciges I know not from whence you had them nor can we guess except from Laxfeild.

I've now no more to add but my best wishes for you from your most affectionate father,

Signed: John Buxton

Wingate's *Arithmetick* is lent out. Pray what was the piece of red earth sent me by John Fuller? When he left you he said it came from Mrs Meadowe. Was not Wellwood's *Memoirs*[248] one of the books you desired? Proposals are

[243] This book cannot be identified from the unspecific reference.

[244] Batty Langley, *New principles of gardening or the laying out and planting parterres ... with ... directions for raising fruit trees etc* (1728).

[245] Appendix A, item 240.

[246] James Gibbs (1682–1754), *A book of architecture, containing designs of buildings and ornaments* (1728).

[247] Buxton is presumably referring to the work of the architect Inigo Jones (1573–1652), many of whose designs were published in two folios by William Kent (1684–1748) in 1727.

[248] Appendix A, item 161.

published here by one Corbridge [249] for an actual survey & map of this county on two sheets of atlas paper. I will send you these proposals as soon as they are printed. It meets with good encouragement; you may be sure I shall be a subscriber.

108 John Buxton to Robert Buxton [35/103]

Addressed: To Mr Buxton at Clare Hall in Cambridge
5 February 1728

Dear Robert,

I have received two letters from you since you had any from me for which I am to thank you. When you hear nothing from us you may think we are well & I allways hope the same of you, & that this fine season will ease your cold.

Last night your mother had your letter & I will next Saturday pay Dr Herring 25li [*£*] for you, by the next post you may expect a bill. That good man spent four or five days with me last week; two or three such neibours would make the country pleasant. We are now to expect that from the season, that society denys us. Mr Branthwayt is now at London: I had a letter from him yesterday that says he is but ill there. I saw your cozen Marsham at Norwich: he has lost his ague. It will be news to you to hear your aunt Jacob & family are coming to live at Norwich for the education of her children. I have sent you the prism & two or three little books. If you would have Wellwood's *Memoirs* let me know. If I can't find the craftsmen I think you mentioned them once.

If you have any perticular complaint or any remnant of your old one write to S[*i*]r B[*enjamin Wrench*]. I asked him yesterday if he had answered your letter, but as it came in the middle of his great illnes they did not give it him & have never since thought of it. He is perfectly recovered & looks I think better than I have seen him do a great while.

I am your most affectionate father,
Signed: John Buxton

249 The land surveyor James Corbridge published a prospect of Great Yarmouth in 1726 and a plan of Norwich in 1727. His county map, published in 1730, was based upon a new survey. It was successful in spite of the efforts of the Norwich booksellers William Chase and Thomas Goddard to obstruct Corbridge's sales while they prepared a pirated edition. D. Stoker, 'An eighteenth-century map piracy', *Norfolk Archaeology*, 37 (1978–80), pp. 123–6.

109 John Buxton to Robert Buxton [35/104]

Addressed: To Mr Buxton at Clare Hall in Cambridge
Norwich, 10 February 1727

Dear Robert,

I have only time now being at Norwich to let you know we continue well, only your mother had last week a little return of her ague but but [*sic*] hopes it will come no more. She is now with me & brought your youngest sister to have the doctor's opinion upon a weakenes she thinks she is fallien into. I hope this warm weather will make you perfectly well. All at present from your most affect[*ionate*] father,

Signed: John Buxton

Your grandmother Gooch begins to be ill again. All at Laxfeild are well.

110 John Buxton to Robert Buxton [35/106]

Addressed: To Mr Buxton at Clare Hall in Cambridge
Channonz, 15 February 1728

Dear Robert,

I had a great deal of reason to be pleased with your last letter, as I always am to hear you are well, & among the many delights fine weather affords us it is not the least to think it is also so favourable to you. I begin to be sensible of the approach of the sun towards us & as Milton says feel his soveraign vital lamp.[250] Channonz feilds are now dry enough for me to walk where I please in them, which thank God I am able to do long & frequent. The roads & even the long row as I found yesterday not unpleasant to ride in; this exercise I begin to use also with more freedom, & the season for setting out wood to my tenants calls me out, in which I take no less pleasure than my neibour does in hunting.

I am glad the books proved agreeable to you: I have a better edition of Bacon's *Essays* but I thought this might serve for your pocket. Would you have the large book of maps sent? Prideaux' *Connexion*, Caesar's *Commentarys* & Wellwood's *Memoirs* shall be sent: the other books you mention I have not as I think, though I'le make a second search. Thank you for the care you take to olidge me in getting books of agriculture &c., I have all but Ray's *Catalogue* &

[250] John Milton (1608–74), *Paradise Lost. A poem written in ten books* (1660) III: 'Hail Holy light and feel thy sovran vital lamp since God is light'.

you do not say whether it is a folio or not. What is the French book *L'antiquitie de temps* &c?[251] I never heard of it; you will be better able to judge of it than I.

I must unsay what I told you in my last of their schemes at Laxfeild. They have altered their thoughts & continue where they are. Your freinds there are all well as is your mother here & sisters. Little Tib[252] grows brisk again: it was feared she was falling as they call it into some weaknes but her disorder proves only a small hurt by a bent on the thigh bone which being timely looked to will do well. Dr Peck's[253] freinds rejoyced much that he was to succeed the late chanceller & thought it past doubt; he is a very worthy man & desirves much greater things.

I forgot to tell you some time since Dr Herring shew me a handsom letter of yours to him & is pleased with your correspondence. It will be proper on the notice, it is only my own observation. I heard your brothers are well at Playford & at Bury. I had lately a well writ letter from Georgy & at the same time an account from Mr D'Oyly that he is very itndustrious though slow, & that Lenny begins to mend his application, & is very quick. I please my self with hope all will do well in time, & that I may live to see you in your several ways serviceable to each other, the best and most certain band of friendship.

I am your most affectionate father,
Signed: John Buxton

Mr Holt[254] who has been extreem ill is well recovered. S[*i*]r Will[*ia*]m Holland has also been ill, as are very many again who lately had this feaver. I think you have Osborn's *Advice to his son*;[255] you'l find it well worth reading again & as in Bacon's *Essays*[256] many things that escaped your observation when you were too young to apply them.

[251] Appendix A, items 158, 160, 2 and 161 respectively. John Ray (1627–1705) published *Catalogus Plantarum Angliæ* in 1670. This was reissued in 1690 in a revised form as *Synopsis Methodica Stirpium Britannicum*, the first systematic British flora. *L'Antiquitie de temps* has not been identified.

[252] A pet name for Isabella, born 1727.

[253] Dr Wharton Peck (d. 1777), son of John Peck of Bracondale, Norwich. Admitted scholar at Trinity Hall, Cambridge in 1711, he graduated LLB in 1716, was admitted to the Middle Temple in 1712 and gained his LLD in 1722. He was a fellow 1718–31 and chancellor of Ely 1728–77. Venn, part I, vol. III, p. 334; R.W. Ketton-Cremer, *Country Neighbourhood* (1951), p. 64.

[254] Mr Rowland Holt of Redgrave (Suffolk).

[255] Appendix A, item 22.

[256] Appendix A, item 158.

111 John Buxton to Robert Buxton [35/107]

No address
Monday, 19 February 1728

Dear Rober[*t*],

We received your letter by last post & are all glad to heer you are so well & I hope proof against this chilly[*?*] of weather which seam are here. Your mother still complaining of something like an ague, I have also a little cold.

I have sent what books you desired that I have. I think I have not Puffendorf *Law of Nature &c*,[257] but it is at Rushford if I have it: I shall enquire the next time I go. I have not Phaedus[258] so you must get what you want & if your mony does not hold out let me know how much you'd have more.

The <post> carrier will stay so I conclude in haste your most affect[*ionate*],
Signed: J[*ohn*] Buxton

112 John Buxton to Robert Buxton [35/108]

Adressed: To Mr Buxton at Clare Hall in Cambridge
Ash Wednesday, 6 March 1728

Dear Robert,

I have now two letters to thank you for: you will never want an agreeable subject when you can tell me you can continue well as I find by your last. The first is at present mislayed or in your mothers pocket, so if there was any thing unanswered in this I must desire you to repeat it.

I will send Burnet's other parts & Osborn's *Advice* [259] by the first opportunity. Though the weather has been extreem fine yet in this season it is so uncertain that I think you did well to put of your journy till Easter when I shall be glad to meet you at Rushford. In the mean time since riding always agree so well with, I would have you take as many oppertunitys of using this exercise as you can.

I was much pleased that Mr Burrough's[260] approved of Shadwell; his oppinion will weigh down all the little criticks who are so free to dislike what

[257] Samuel Puffendorf, (1632–1694), born in Saxony, made natural and civil law academic studies for the first time and published, *inter alia, De jure naturæ et gentium* (1672).

[258] Plato, *Phædrus*, is a dialogue between Socrates and Phædrus, originally published in 360 B.C. Alternatively, John Buxton could be referring to *Phædri Augusti Cæsaris liberti fabularum Æsopiarum libri quinque*, published in London in various editions from 1668 to 1672.

[259] Appendix A, items 164, 166 and 22 respectively.

[260] See note 84, p. 23, above.

they don't understand. I cannot get it in that forwardness I would & fear it will scarce be habitable next Michaelmas. I have altered my scheme a little in the disposition of the offices which I shall shew you when wee meet.

It was a son of Mr Rudge you mention chosen for Ailsbury[261]; Dr Herring's brother is married.[262] I was afraid it had been the fine preacher till I heard yesterday from the Doctor; I shall remember your compliments to him. You never mentioned any thing of the book *Antiquitates* you saw in Magdalen library [263]. I have seen a new play lately, *The provok'd husband or journy to London*,[264] & like the humour extremely.

Your method of taking mony of your tutor as you want is certainly best. Mr Layman was here yesterday & says they begin to practice the London way of street robbery in Cambridge; the good hours of your colledge will be your security. Our country people have again relapsed of the feaver & ague; five or six of my se[*rva*]nts were bled a few days ago. Your sister Nanny who stood out so long has had this illnes at last but is got well again; I believe your aunt Herne has also somthing of it. The rest well & Tib in the way of being so & very brisk though her nurse maid is one of the sick. Sarah rid your mare yesterday: I think that creature is of an excellent temper that neither great rest makes skittish nor excercise dull. She will be ready to come for you at Easter. Your grandmother is well at Laxfeild though your uncle there & aunt Han have both been ill. He had the feaver I think, hers only a cold. Dr Whitfeild of Dickleburgh[265] is very ill; a diabetes is part of his illnes & is thought in danger. Mr Marcon[266] the brewer is in more having lately been tapped for a dropsy. Oh intemperance! What a plague art thow to mankind.

I am my dear your most affect[*ionate*] father,

Signed: J[*ohn*] Buxton

[261] Not identified.

[262] Dr William Herring's brother has not been identified. 'The fine preacher' is presumably Thomas Herring who never married. See note 181, p. 93, above.

[263] *Antiquitates*: not identified.

[264] *The Provok'd Husband or a Journey to London*, a comedy by Sir John Vanbrugh (1664–1726), completed by Colley Cibber (1671–1757), and first produced in 1728. Drabble, p. 794.

[265] Dr Whitfield, rector of Dickleburgh since 1724, survived this illness and died three years later on 16 October 1731. Venn, part I, vol. IV, p. 393.

[266] John Marcon, barrister-at- law was lord of the manor of Ellingham in Edgefield and of Holverstone. He died in 1723 aged 38 and on the death in 1727 of his wife Rebecca, daughter of Sir Benjamin Wrench M.D., his property passed to John Marcon of Swaffham, the grandson of Edmund Marcon (d. 1709) and son of Edmund Marcon of Forncett. Rye, p. 526. John Buxton could have been referring to the younger Edmund or his son John. No wills of Marcon identified as brewers were proved in the Norwich Consistory Court in the period 1687–1750.

You did not say Mr Thornhill[267] had been at your colledge. I remember him in town when I lived in Grey's Inn.

113 John Buxton to Robert Buxton [35/109]

Addressed: To Mr Buxton at Clare Hall Cambridge
18 March 1728

Dear Robert,

Your letter of the 14th found us well though the sicknes is pretty much in our neibourhood. Mr Mallim's family is at last fallen ill, the two youngest ladies are very much so, as your mothers says who saw them yesterday. You may compound for a little cold which I hope be all you will feel now, having already had your share of this general disorder. The winds are somtimes pretty sharp & though riding is what I would encourage you in, yet it will not be amis to be little cautious as there is such a disposition in the air to make us sick. I have often thought as you do now of your constitution that the tenderness of it under a discreet management may be no disadvantage. Perhaps you may loose your enjoyment of a fue riotous pleasures, but at the same time you have this satisfaction that while the robust who pursue those are spoiling a good health, you by your temperance are in a way of improving yours, & by that means laying a foundation for the most solid & lasting pleasures.

Thank you for the subscription paper, the subject tempts me to encourage it though I have some doubts of the author's abilitys for an undertaking of that sort unless he has good assistance. I know nothing of Dr Smith[268] nor of his proposals you mention so shall leave it to you to do as you like or have encouragement from the character of the gentleman. I have not Bently's *Horace* nor an Italian dictionary;[269] you must procure them where you are. I think there are two or three sorts of the latter, you'l be advised to the best but whether Torriano's[270] or the others have the preference I know not. I have sent you Burnet's abridgment & Osborn's works[271] in which his advice is included, & is so good that I can give you no better than to read it though great allowance must be made for the style, but the good sense can never be out of fashion. I have lately seen a piece that excells in both & that gave me very great

[267] Not identified.
[268] Not identified.
[269] Appendix A, items 201 and 208.
[270] Appendix A, item 107.
[271] Appendix A, items 164, 166 and 22 and 167 respectively.

pleasure. It was a letter of the late L[*or*]d Shafstbury to the L[*or*]d Somers about the art or science of design. You'l find it in the present state of the *Republick of Letters* for the month Feb[*ruary*].[272] You did not tell me whether you would have the large book of maps sent you, I mean that which wants to be new bound.

Have you made any acquaintance with Mr Burrows[273] or did you hear by a third person what he said of Shadwell? I should like to have a further account of the book you mention in Magdalen library: is it not a manuscript? I want to compleat my Monfaucon,[274] enquire of your bookseller about it for I have none in town I can depend on.

My Lady Ward enquired last time I was at Norwich very kindly for you, & invited you to be with her when you come into the country. If you can pick up any thing of news or tattle you think will divert or amuse her, you take an oppertunity to write to her but be sure not to forget your complements to Bixly.[275] S[*i*]r Edw[*ar*]d [*Ward*] has had a return of his illnes and has an ague every day, but no more now but my best wishes from your most affectionate,

Signed: John Buxton

Your aunt Herne is recovered again; your mother is pretty well but still takes the certen by way of prevention. Your grandmother at Laxfeild is well but your aunt Han has been ill; I think she is now grown better.

114 John Buxton to Robert Buxton [35/111]

Addressed: To Mr Buxton at Clare Hall in Cambridge
1 April 1728

Dear Robert,

I have yours of the 28th with one inclosd to your mother & the poem which is a pretty performance for a very young man, as I suppose the author, though I can't find a great deal of the sublime in it. I had the pleasure also to meet two of your letters last Saturday at Norwich, that to Lady Ward will not be lost,

272 Republic of Letters was an expression describing the collective body of those engaged in literary pursuits, first used by Joseph Addison (1672–1719) in his *Dialogues upon the Usefulness of Ancient Medals*, written about 1703 but published posthumously. Drabble, pp. 6 and 819. The expression was adopted as the title of a periodical addressed to that literary group.

273 James Burrough (1691–1764), architect. See note 84, p. 23, above.

274 Bernard de Montfaucon (1655–1741), *L'antiquité expliquée et représentée en figures* (Paris, 1719). A supplement was published in 1724.

275 The Ward family at Bixley Hall.

she means kindly towards us but is not always happy in a way of expresing it. We must take people as we find them & make the best use of all occations of keeping as many freinds as we can; some time or other they may be of service.

You could not have a better opinion than Dr Peck's about the books & I would by all means have you get the best, which you say is that of Alken.[276] I shall never think your mony ill layed out when it is done with any view towards your improvement, though at the same time I approve your caution.

I find you are all much taken up with the expectation of your royal gue[*st*].[277] Whatever you find necessary on this occation pray do not omit to furnish your self with, the moderate of your own order will be a rule. You will want somthing for riding when you come into the country, a good drap[278] colourd cloath made frock fashion, or as you find is worn will be as proper as any. This I only hint to you leaving things of this nature altogether to your own choice.

I have lately employed a bookbinder at Norwich who does things so well that I think to get the maps I mentioned to you bound by the same hand. Have you seen an Essay on Critisism by author of the Critical Hist[*ory*] of England? [279] If you meet with it you may bestow the reading <of> it. Boerhoave was a famous botanist but I incline to get a book of that kind that comes out monthly, if I can have a good character of it, that it is what it pretends to be a good & perfect collection from Tournfort, Ray & other celebrated botanists.[280] If you meet with any oppertunity of learning this, pray inform me.

I am glad to hear your cold gives you no more trouble. I make no doubt of your care to preserve your health, & sure more is at this time necessary than ever. We have had so much rain here that our fields are covered with water; I

[276] Seemingly an author or publisher but not identified.

[277] Concerning the visit of King George II to Cambridge.

[278] Drap = drab: a woollen cloth or a dull light-brown or yellow-brown colour.

[279] John Oldmixon (1673–1742), historian and pamphleteer, published *The Critical History of England* (1724) and *An Essay on Criticism* (1728). His writing reflected his belief that Clarendon's works (Appendix A, item 151) were biased towards the parliamentarian side.

[280] Herman Boerhaave (1668–1738), professor of medicine and botany at Leiden, published numerous works describing plant species. For John Ray see note 251, p. 127, above. Joseph Pitton de Tournefort (1656–1708) studied at the university of Montpellier. His *Institutiones rei herbariae* (1700) included his principles of classification and descriptions of some 7,000 species in over 700 genera. D.Isely, *One hundred and one Botanists*, (Iowa, 1994), p. 71. Cheap partbooks, or editions sold a few pages or a chapter at a time, and distributed every week or month, were common by the 1730s. London publishers used provincial agents to help disseminate their works. J. Brewer, *The Pleasures of the Imagination. English Culture in the Eighteenth Century* (1997), p. 133.

never saw these at Channonz so wet as now. Rushford, I mean about the old colledge,[281] is worse, but I hope the waters will be fallen before your time of coming thither, which I suppose will not be till the week after Easter. That is also sessions week & <will> I shall be obliged to be there so perhaps you'l put of your journy till the week following. The country will still be the pleasanter.

I am your most affectionate,

Signed: John Buxton

You are desired to send us the length of the bodys of your shirts & of the sleves, & whether you would have them made longer than those. You need not send the measure of the collars or waistbands because they will not be ready to work on before you come, & then a more exact measure may be taken.

It will not be amiss if you were to make a journal of the most minute particulars, while the king is at Cambridge, of the transactions of the day for your own satisfaction only.

Your mother & sisters are all well.

115 John Buxton to Robert Buxton [35/112]

Addressed: To Mr Buxton at Clare Hall Cambridge
Friday, 12 April 1728

Dear Robert,

Your letter of 5th was received but yesterday; it had made the tour of Norwich before it came hither. To prevent this you had best say on the superscription near New Buckenham by Attleburgh[282] bag. I hope this which comes by Mr Walpole[283] will find you perfectly well again as it leaves us here. The wet season has had no other ill effect than to spoil our roads that were beginning to be tolerable.

I am much pleased you have entered on the learning Italian: it will amply recompense your trouble. I have but very fue <Italian> books in that language:

[281] Rushford College was founded in 1342 by Sir Edmund Gonevile (or Gonvile) for a master and five chaplains. The institution was dissolved in the 1530s and the site bought in 1601 by Robert Buxton from Lord Howard of Walden. The collegiate church was largely demolished but the nave continued in use by the parish and contains memorials to Robert Buxton (d. 1691), Elizabeth Buxton (d. 1730) and John Buxton (d. 1731). Blomefield, I, pp. 287–93.

[282] Attleborough: a market town, 15 miles south-west of Norwich on the road to Thetford.

[283] A John Walpole was a Buxton tenant. Appendix D.

what there are shall be laid by for you. Serlio's *Architecture*[284] is one & I think I have also a bible. Vasari's *Lives of the Architects & Painters*,[285] if you could get it on any reasonable terms, would be a proper book.

I shall make so little a stay at Norwich in the sessions week that another time for your visit there will be as proper & your mother has then thoughts of seeing you at Rushford. However, I do not determine any thing about it: this may be done when we see you. I think you will want somthing handsomer & cleaner for riding (which is the way you will be seen in) than what your old riding coat will afford. Therefore it will be as well to let that be as it is at present, & make up a <coat> cloath coat such as I mentioned last of some light drap colour, but not drap. This may be worn with your black or drugget westcoat, & will be a long time serviceable, nor will it be yet too hot, more especially on the leaving of your gown at your first coming into the country. If you should be put upon getting your proper habits on the king's coming I shall think you make a very extraordinary complement, & will have more than your proportion of the expense of entertaining his majesty. However, you must by no means be singular: take your tutors & the masters advice in this affair. I shall be satisfied with their appointment. As to bands, there is a mystery in the making them beyond the capacity of our people in the country, you must provide them where you are, for a very small error in the fashion is very material in such a distinguishing part of dress.

I have thoughts if you like it to send a servant with your mare, on Easter Monday, that you may have the oppertunity of seeing the divertions at Newmarket with more satisfaction than on a hack, & may then take your own time of coming to Rushford. After the ceremony is over at Cambridge, let me know by Mr Walpole how you like this scheme, & what day you choose to have the servant come. The craftsmen you formerly mentioned are come to light & sent with this which I have nothing more to add to but my best wishes.

Your most affectionate,

Signed: John Buxton

[284] Sebastiano Serlio, sixteenth-century Italian architect and writer, published *Regole generali di architettura* in 1537, the first treatise to deal with the five classical orders in a systematic way. Serlio's books 1–5 of the 1551 Venice edition were translated into Dutch in 1606 and from this edition into English (*The Five Books of Architecture*, 1611). It was hugely influential, with no English architect writing or publishing a work between John Shute's *First and Chief Groundes of Architecture* (1553) and Colen Campbell's *Vitruvius Britannicus* (1715). R. Wittkower, *Palladio and English Palladianism* (1983), pp. 100 and 111. V. Hart and P. Hicks, eds, *Paper Palaces. The Rise of the Renaissance Architectural Treatise* (Nerw Haven and London, 1998), p. 170.

[285] Giorgio Vasari (1511–74), *Le Vite De Piu Eccellenti Pittori, Scultori Et Atchitetti* (1551).

[286] Desiderius Erasmus (1469–1536), Dutch humanist. His *Proverbs or Adagies* were published in 1539. See Appendix A, items 47, 95, 143 and 159 for other works.

Erasmus *Adagies*[286] are sent with the parcel. I just now met with a seasonable Italian proverb: *Aprilone. Aprilone tu non mi furai metter qui il pellicione Aquilone.*[287]

116 John Buxton to Robert Buxton [35/113]

Addressed: To Mr Buxton at Clare Hall in Cambridge
Monday, 15 April 1728

Dear Robert,

I did expect the bad weather would have some influence on you. It was very right that you were let blood, it might have been six or seven ounces as you are now grown stronger but I hope this will answer the end. This fine weather favouring, the horses shall be with you on Sunday. I had thought of this, as you perceive by the letter I sent by Mr Walpole, as safer & better for you than to trust to a Cam[*bridge*] hack.[288] I hope your mare will behave with temper in the crowd. I suppose you will [*be*] at Rushford the Monday or Tuesday after Easter week. Your mother will be there about that time, but you will let us know how you move.

I have lately read *The Beggars Opera*; the noise that has been made about it raised my curiosity.[289] I think it is a mean low performance. You will see by the publick prints Mr Herring has thought fit to take notice of it in one of his sermons, & I don't wonder he should meet with censure for it, considering how much the town run after the other performance. However, he is as much applauded by the wise & the good who have condemned this play as tending to make the world if possible worse than it is. Mr Herring took his text out of

287 This Italian peasant proverb refers to the uncertainty of the weather in April. Aprilone is a 'cosy' name for April and pelliccione an equivalent term for fur coat. Aquilone is the north wind. Essentially, the meaning of a modern Italian form of the proverb is: 'April. Keep on your jacket. If you take it off you will regret it'.

288 Hack = Hackney horse, a horse hired out for riding.

289 *The Beggar's Opera*, a ballad opera by John Gay (1685–1732), was produced by John Rich (?1692–1761) at the New Theatre in Lincon's Inn in 1728. The play combined burlesque of Italian opera and political satire, notably of Sir Robert Walpole. Thomas Herring (see note 181, p. 93, above) achieved notoriety for attacking the work as immoral, a stance with which John Buxton clearly agreed. Pearce argues that Herring's essential objection was political, describing him as a 'rabid Hanoverian' and asserts that his career benefited from his new prominence – he accompanied King George II to Cambridge later in the year (see letter no. 117, p. 136, below) and became archbishop of Canterbury in 1747. However, the debate provided publicity from which the production profited. C.E. Pearce, *Polly Peachum. The Story of Lavinia Fenton and the Beggar's Opera* (1913, reissued 1968), pp. 152–63 'Puritanism up in arms'.

the St Paul's Epist[*le*] to Romans Cap. 1st verse, the last which was very judiciously chosen.[290] I will refer what I have to say till I have the pleasure of seeing you, which will be very great if you are perfectly well.

Your most affectionate,
Signed: John Buxton

117 John Buxton to Robert Buxton [35/114]

Addressed: To Mr Buxton at Clare Hall Cambridge
Friday, 19 April 1728

Dear Robert,

Yesterday Mr Walpole brought me your letter with the epistolary poem to Mr Fowlks[291] & gave me much pleasure in telling us he saw you well. I write now being to go tomorrow to Norwich: if any thing falls out before sealing this I shall add it. I fancy it would oblidge your Aunt Ward to send her the remarkables of the day, the king passes at Cambridge: a short account of such things as you think women can understand or be pleased with.[292] I just now received a letter from Mr D'Oyly who says your brothers are both well, though some fue of his family have had this general ague. I sent to Laxfeild last Tuesday & heard they were also well there. This howdee was on your Aunt Jacob's account, who had lately miscarried.

You will see Mr D'Oyly at Cambridge he comes with a view of being dignified if it is permitted to more than the k[*ing's*] chaplains. I send you five guineas by Abram: your expenses must on this occation be encreased. As to his board wages I shall take care of that, only do you discharge the expense of horses. You may also allow him a little sizing on your head in the buttrys[293]: not exceeding 3d. a day I think will be sufficient. You must take care to be very oblidging to all strange[*r*]s: I mean those you know who come from town or country to see the solemnity, & let not the most inconsiderable escape your notice of some kind or other, & those you are more particularly accquainted with shew a perticular regard. It would be very proper if you could make a party of such as Mr Kidman, Mr D'Oyly, Mr Herring (who I hear is to be there) &c. to dine with you, at the same time inviting the master or your tutor

[290] Romans 1 v. 32: 'Who knowing the judgement of God that they which commit such things are worthy of death, not only do the same, but have pleasure in them that do them.'

[291] Not identified.

[292] See note 295, p. 137, below for John Buxton's views on the role of women.

[293] Payment for the servant Abraham's board.

if they happen to be unengaged. This will oblidge your freinds & get you credit in the coll[*ege*]. These are only hints for your discretion to make use of as occation serves. If the persons I have mentioned should be engaged, as it is likely they will among so numerous an acquaintance, your invitation will neverthe less be taken as a civility.

I am, dear Robert, your most affectionate,
Signed: John Buxton

Saturday, nine at night.
I am returned from Norwich where I saw your cozen Marsham, & he bid me tell you he intended being at Cambridge on Wednesday night & hopes the place in your bed is not engaged. He desires also you would bespeake a room for his two horses; I have told Abraham of it. I am glad to hear you have lost your cold & hope you'l be carefull of its return.

118 John Buxton to Robert Buxton [35/115]

Addressed: To Mr Buxton at Clare Hall Cambridge
Wednesday, 9 a clock, 8 May 1728

Dear Robert,

Least I should be misunderstood having writ in haste, what I said in your mother's letter I repeat it to you here: as well as my great satisfaction to hear your cold is better; if weather or indisposition does not prevent I would have you come to morrow to diner to meet Dr Herring here, & you may return again to Rushford the same night. On Friday we will dine with you there, & I will stay with you then, the Dr will either go to Norwich that night or come back to Channonz, at his choice. Come by Mr Blomfeild's grounds[294] which I think is now the best riding way, & keep either Tom or John Fuller with you.

Your sisters will stay at home to morrow to take care of household affairs: this is the province will fall to their lots. I hope they will one day well acquit themselves for this, as Milton says, is woman's first highest praise.[295]

Your most affectionate,
Signed. John Buxton

[294] An Edward Blomfield was a Buxton tenant. Appendix D.

[295] John Buxton clearly approves of Milton's expression of a woman's role in *Paradise Lost*, IV: (Eve to Adam) 'Gold is thy law, thou mine: to know no more is woman's happiest knowledge , and her praise.' And in *Paradise Lost*, IX, in a reference to Eve: 'For nothing lovelier can be found in woman than to study household good, and good works in her husband to promote'.

119 John Buxton to Robert Buxton [35/116]

Addressed: To Mr Buxton at Clare Hall in Cambridge
Channonz, 3 June 1728, Monday

Dear Robert,

I am very glad your journy had so good a conclusion. I hope this warm weather will prove so favourable that you'l soon be quite rid of your cold. Your mother did not go to Laxfeild till yesterday in the afternoon; I was oblidged to take <it> the chariot to Norwich on Saturday: it was expected then we should know who were to be our candidates for the ensuing election but they came to no determination. I believe there is a general approbation of S[*i*]r Ed[*mund*] Bacon,[296] but the difficulty is to find him a proper partner, & till such a one is found he does not care to declare himself. The scrutiny at Norwich is like to end in favour of Mr Harwood.[297] Abundance of people have been talked of for candidates for the county, among others Mr Woodhouse [298] if his father will not stand. I do not much trouble my self about it though should like to see our selves represented by gentlemen of worth.

I just now received a letter from cossen Meadow. She writes no news only that she intends to put in execution the journy to Shadwell & it is to be as she says incog[*nito*]. The country here is now exceeding pleasant & I find the air no less agreeable than that at Shadwell. Your mare I saw this day & she shews very little if any thing of her lameness. However, she shall rest till the cure is confirmed. Your grandmother Gooch is just as she was. I shall be glad to hear from you a little the oftener now on the account of late disorder. If you grow better write as you used to do, or as suits your inclination.

I am your most affectionate,
Signed: John Buxton

[296] See note 214, p. 111, above. Sir Edmund Bacon replaced Sir John Hobart who was called to the upper house, and Harbord Harbord (?1675–1742) replaced Sir Thomas Coke for the same reason. Sedgwick, I, p. 289.

[297] Thomas Harwood, a goldsmith, was mayor of Norwich in 1728. Cozens-Hardy, p. 116.

[298] The Tory William Wodehouse (?1706–37) of Kimberley Hall, son of Sir John Wodehouse, fourth baronet (1669–1754) was MP for Norfolk from 1734 until his death. He was succeeded by his younger brother Armine (*c.* 1714–77), later fifth baronet, who represented Norfolk from 1737 to 1768. Sedgwick, II, p. 553.

120 John Buxton to Robert Buxton [35/117]

Addressed: To Mr Buxton at Clare Hall in Cambridge
10 June 1728

Dear Robert,

I did but just now receive your letter by Mr Gibb's servant,[299] not sending for them so soon as we ought by some mistake. I am glad to hear your cold is on the mending; I have hopes the air at Cambridge will agree with you, but if upon a longer tryal you should find it other wise, you must change for some favourable. Your mother is come from Laxfeild & has brought her family home safe & well though they had an overturn near Pullham[300] by the axel tree of the coach breaking.

I have not been at Rushford this week being taken up by publick meetings &c; at Norwich there was one last Saturday of the principal gentlemen of the county & it was agreed there to set up S[*i*]r Edm[*un*]d Bacon & Col[*one*]l Harbord[301] & I believe there will be no opposition. The gent. you mention is disqualified by a very good place which I suppose he would not care to quit for the empty honour of being a representative of our county.

To morrow I am to expect your grandmother from Laxfeild with your aunt Hannah, & the week following your aunt Jacob with her family, & for their divertion they are to go with mine to the guild[302] at Norwich, which Mr Cosgrove[303] says will this year be kept with unusual splendour. Mr Harwood[304] is declared mayor & the tories are much exalted upon their victory.

I thank you for your wishes of health which I return you as the best I can make, though whenever I think of you I make abundance that you may in all things prosper. Your most affectionate,

Signed: John Buxton

Your mother sends her blessing. Jacky is come home, says he is on the usher's high form & had had the honour to be a monitor, & 2nd or 3rd on the form. I hope he keeps his post.

299 Buxton's neighbour. See note 26, p. 43, above.

300 Pulham St Mary Magdalen (commonly called Pulham Market) and Pulham St Mary the Virgin, parishes and villages, 15 miles south of Norwich, four miles from Channonz.

301 See note 43, p. 48, above.

302 See note 98, p. 66, above.

303 This may have been Henry Crossgrove, proprietor of the *Norwich Gazette*.

304 See note 297, p. 138, above.

121 John Buxton to Robert Buxton [35/118]

Addressed: To Mr Buxton att Clare Hall in Cambridge, with a plate of venison by the carrier
1 July 1728

Dear Robert,

This comes with a peice of venison killed this day, & I hope will arrive in due season. You will make my compliments to Dr Morgan[305] & I desire his acceptance of it; your mother puts you in mind to save the cloath it comes in.

I have a letter from you that shall be answered when I'm more at leisure. I had the pleasure to hear you were well last Saturday by your cozen Marsham. It is said the small pox is a little in Cambridge: if it increases much I think it will be proper for you to remove.

I can ad no more but my best wishes, it being late. Your most affect[*ionate*],
Signed: J[*ohn*] Buxton

122 John Buxton to Robert Buxton [35/119]

Addressed: To Mr Buxton at Clare Hall in Cambridge
Sunday, Rushford, 7 July 1728

Dear Robert,

Though I have not heard from you since I sent the last letter with the venison I will hope your cold is not worse & that morrow I shall have a good account. Last Friday I left Channonz as your mother did at the same time to set out for Witnesham. We had both a warm journy, it was the first time I attempted to come on hors back since my misfortune. I bore it pretty well though the weather was too hot to make it pleasant but the feilds about Shadwell were very much so covered with an exceeding fine crop of clover that is all now made into good hay.

I have just got the plaisterer to work, the joyner goes on with his, the back stairs are done with the floors of both the chambers on the first floor at the east end of the house, & they are now wainscotting, which I have at last prefered to plaistring. Considering the uses that are designed for, nothing is begun about the yards or outhouses. Our labourers are so taken up with the

305 Dr Charles Morgan (1678–1736). Born in London, he was admitted pensioner at Clare Hall in 1693. He graduated in 1697–8 and gained his D.D. in 1728. He was a fellow 1700–20 and master of Clare Hall 1726–36, being vice-chancellor 1732–3. Ordained in Lincoln in 1704, he held livings in Suffolk 1714–36. Venn, part I, vol. III, p. 211.

husbandry affairs that I can't yet spare them. Rushford is in *status quo* even to the branches of vines & other trees you remember laid slovenly in the bleech that were lopped last spring. They are in the same place.

Jacky returned yesterday to school & I think comes on very well & his master encourages me to think so. Your grandmother Buxton went with me in the coach on the election day to Norwich. I got out in Swardeston feild[306] to head my party, & to joyn S[*i*]r Edm[*un*]d Bacon at Harford Bridges,[307] where we were met by Mr Branthwayt, Mr Mallom, Mr Sayer & abundance of other gentlemen & freeholders who came in compliment to Sir Edm[*un*]d to wait on him into the town, & he entered with upwards of 1200 men. Colonel Harbord from the other side of the county came in like manner attended though not so numerously. I saw Mr Prideaux[308] on this occation who told me he saw you well. Len Mapes[309] confirmed this account as I heard by your cosen Marsham. I left your grandmother with Lady Ward & she is now with her at Stratton, & is the same good woman, & I think as healthy as I have known her.

You have a great deal of pleasure I make no doubt in reading Milton, & you will find no abatement upon doing it often, he is all over wonderful, the part you mention is truly sublime, makes the soul feel that holy rapture it ought ever to be filled with when we address the deity, almost to a degree if inspiration. I have read Ralph's poem on night,[310] which would be thought very well if we did not think of Milton. I have not yet seen Thomson's *Spring*[311] but by a small specimen in the *Memoirs of Literature*[312], which promises well.

Your mare is perfectly recovered & as fat as the buck you had part of; you will in the vacation bring it down a little. A Bath journy would effectually do it & perhaps do you both good. I have this in my thoughts but without any determination yet.

306 Swardeston: a village, four miles south-west of Norwich.

307 Harford Bridges: on the road into Norwich from the south where it crosses the river Yare, about two miles from the city centre. See note 296, p. 138, above.

308 Edmund Prideaux (bap. 1693–1745), son of Humphrey Prideaux D.D. (1648–1724), Dean of Norwich. He was admitted to Clare Hall in 1711. He married Hannah, daughter of Sir Benjamin Wrench M.D. Venn, part I, vol. III, p. 398.

309 Leonard Mapes of Rollesby was admitted to Caius College, Cambridge at the age of 18 in 1682. He died in 1733. He was the father of another Leonard Mapes (d. 1775), educated in Norwich and admitted to Trinity College, Cambridge, at the age of 18, in 1727, and therefore a contemporary of Robert Buxton's. Mapes entered the Middle Temple in 1733. Venn, part I, vol. III, p. 138.

310 James Ralph (d. 1762), *Night* (1728). A poem in four books.

311 James Thomson (1700–48), born and educated in Scotland, came to London in 1725 and published *The Seasons* from 1726–30. Drabble, p. 979.

312 Seemingly a periodical but not identified.

Monday
After this was writ I received your letter with your file for which I am to thank you. I hope you have by this time perceived the benefit of bleeding; if the cough continues you had best change air. I will procure lodgings for you at Thetford for I think this place will be too moist though you may try it first: it agrees perfectly well with me, & gives me what I scarce knew anywhere els, a stomach that makes me forget the ill cookery. I am glad the venison came in time; I'm sure it was good if your cook did it justice, but it could not be too good for the occation.

I am your most affectionate,
Signed: John Buxton

I have made an entire alteration in my scheme about the offices, though adapted to the last thought of the garden & court & of the lawn if you remember.

123 John Buxton to Robert Buxton [35/120]

Addressed: To Mr Buxton at Clare Hall in Cambridge
Channonz, 15 July 1728

Dear Robert,

Yours of the 12[*th*] found us all well here. Your mother & sisters returned from Whitnesham on Saturday after much divertion on their journy, but it would have been more pleasure to them to have had a better account of your cold. I hope you will find riding & change of air a cure for it. I will send your horses the beginning of next week. The rains have not been enough to affect Rushford at all, so you may come thither, & if you find the air agreeable we will content our selves with the rest, in the mean time I will make enquiry for lodgings at Thetford to be provided with if we should want them. This air was once of much service to the [*p*]resent Sir Andrew Fountain;[313] I shall be glad you find it as favourable.

Col[*one*]l Harbord is going to Scarburgh Spaw[314] for the benefit of those waters [*?word*] if he should not meet with that from them he talks [*?word*] going into France. Your grandmother Buxton comes to us on Saturday with

[313] Sir Andrew Fountaine (1676–1753) of Narford (Norfolk), a noted scholar, traveller and collector. Ingamells, pp. 376–7.

[314] Scarborough (Yorkshire, North Riding) was visited by Celia Fiennes in 1697. The first spa buildings were erected three years after her visit. C. Morris ed., *The Illustrated Journeys of Celia Fiennes, 1685–c. 1712* (Stroud, 1995), pp. 100–1.

your aunt Hannah. I shall bring them in my return from the sessions where I am to be tomorrow. On the other side I have writ a bill for £30.

With my service to the master & Dr Wilcox is all at present from your most affectionate,

Signed: John Buxton

124 John Buxton to Robert Buxton [35/121]

Addressed: To Mr Buxton at Clare Hall in Cambridge
Sunday, 21 July 1728

Dear Robert,

Though I have not heard from you this week or more I will hope this will find you well as it leaves us here, your grandmother Buxton & aunt making now a part of my family. If your cold is not quite gon it will be best for you to take up your quarters for the present at Rushford till you can be better accommodated elsewhere. Mrs Buxton has latly fitted up the old farm house at Snare Hill[315] for the tenant's use so there is now an appartment of two rooms on a floor empty. I have writ to her about hiring of it till Shadwell can be made fit to inhabit & expect to know her mind tomorrow. This place will be extreemly convenient for us, which I would not have her too sensible of because I've heard she is oft a temper to delight sometimes in people's disappointment.

Mr Pearce[316] who gave me the first design for the front of Shadwell was last week in the country. The milk & vegetable diet in which he still continues has made so great an alteration in him that of an very infirm he is become a very healthy person & has recovered both his plight & colour which were once entirely lost. He begins to be taken notice of as an architect & I believe will soon make a figure in that profession & he follows it *con studio con dilligenza & con amore.*[317] You see I venture at Italian, but I think it is a phrase that expresses more than an English one can on the subject, but I will refer what I have to say on this & others till I shall see you, only wishing this may find you in health and that you may have a good journey.

I am your most affectionate,

Signed: John Buxton

I desire you'l make my complements to the master & Mr Wilcox. I writ last week and sent you a bill for £30 – thirty pounds. Dr Herring's brother is now

[315] Snare Hill, an extra-parochial unit associated with Rushford parish.

[316] See note 83, p. 23, above.

[317] With study, with diligence and with love.

in Norfolk; he expects his cosen the king's chaplain[318] to be with him this week. Also, your cosen Marsham talks still of being admitted among you:[319] he will once more try to prevail with his father.

125 John Buxton to Robert Buxton [35/122]

Addressed: To Mr Robert Buxton at Stratton [*Strawless*].
2 September 1728

Dear Robert,

I have received your letter with the good account of yourself and as to the horses I hope you will soon hear of them if you have not already done it. The disappointment of going abroad can nowhere I think have been better born with them [?] where you have so good company at home. If you hear of any stray horses cryed, although the marks do not answer to yours, yet it is proper to send an enquiry for it is trick among those that take the strays to make mistake in order to keep them the longer when they are generally extravagantly payd for it.

Your freinds here continue pretty well. Betty [*Elizabeth*] is much mended, though the servants are yet bad. Your aunt Herne has had two fits of this feaver. The sudden alteration of weather is not so favourable to me but I must not complain since I feel a little inconvenience at most, and while I have the pleasure to see you and most of my children well I wish the continuance, and am your most affectionate,

Signed: John Buxton

Your mother sends her blessing and has sent up two shirts etc. by the servant who comes with my [*?word*]. Phill Phillips[320] is to be married tomorrow. As to your coming home you are at your own disposal and are to do as you like best.

[318] Thomas Herring, see note 181, p. 93, above.

[319] Referring to the admittance of Robert Marsham to Clare Hall, see note 143, p. 81, above.

[320] Jonas and Robert Phillips were Buxton's tenants. Philip was no doubt a son of one of these.

126 John Buxton to Robert Buxton [35/123]

Addressed: To Mr Robert Buxton at Stratton [*Strawless*]
Tuesday, 3 September 1728

Dear Robert,

This morning we had intelligence from Forncett[321] of your horses and I have taken the first oppertunity of restoring them to the owner. For security now it will be best to keep your mare a day two in the stable. The other, for want of company, will be less apt to stray, though a log for the[*m*] also may be a necessary precaution.

Your sister goes on in the way of recovering very fast but my aunt Herne after two days intermission has a severe return of her illness. The servants begin to be well again, the rest as you left us.

Mr D'Oyly who I heard of at Norwich and that he was to be with us this week, I have not heard of since. You need not on his account make any alteration in your present schemes. His visit will not be for above two or three days I suppose, if he comes at all.

The fat buck was this morning severely threatned: my gun was presented at him several times but I could not shoot without endangering two or three more so I belive he is fated to live till another season, and possibly our very good freinds for whom a part of him was intended may be in better health than to eat venison.

I am your most affectionate
Signed: John Buxton

My humble service to uncle and aunt Marsham and my cosens.

127 John Buxton to Robert Buxton [35/125]

Addressed: To Mr Buxton at Clare Hall in Cambridge
7 November 1728

Dear Robert,

I have the greatest satisfaction in hearing you continue well after having seen you so for a longer time together than I ever knew you could have your health in this place before; may that you are now in be as agreeable in this as <*word?*> in all other respects I believe it is.

[321] Forncett St Peter and Forncett St Mary: villages and parishes ten miles south-west of Norwich and three miles from Channonz.

I know not when I shall get to Snare Hill though I have a great desire to be there, for the workmen will do nothing at Shadwell while they know I am at this distance. My painter is now at work on the *bas relievos*[322] in the hall and does them very well.

It is good amusement for this season & I am much entertained with it. I met S[*i*]r Edm[*un*]d Bacon as I had appointed but the stupid woman of the house, if I may call her so who makes puddings so well, mistook my directions about the day and had provided nothing for diner. The dukes of Grafton & Newcastle came to Euston but not with S[*i*]r Rob[*er*]t [*Walpole*] to Houghton as in the newspapers.[323]

I had this a letter from my sister at Laxfeild and she says my mother is perfectly well; I think I may say the same of your friends here except my mother Gooch who is after the usual rate & for my self I think the pain of my side rather declines.

On the other side I have writ an order for the money, from, dear Robert, your most affectionate,

Signed: John Buxton

128 John Buxton to Robert Buxton [35/126]

Addressed: To Mr Robert Buxton at Clare Hall in Cambridge
Wednesday, 13 November 1728

Dear Robert,

Mr Layman gave me your letter by Mr Coopers sent. Your disorder is some cold you have lately taken: if the pain in your shoulder should continue it will be expedient to bleed 5 or 6 ounces; this will also be of service for your cough, though I shall hope all will go of without. Your mother & sisters continue

322 Basso rilievo, or bas-relief: projecting decoration. The painter was Thomas Bardwell (1704–67) of Bungay (Suffolk) who started in the 1720s as a decorative painter. The work for John Buxton is his earliest recorded. By 1732 he had a thriving business, writing in that year to Robert Buxton about the supply of lead and tiles, and the mixing of colours for painting external brickwork at Shadwell Lodge (CUL Buxton Papers, letter dated 31 May 1732). In 1738 Bardwell handed over the decorative painting to his younger brother Robert and developed his own career as a portraitist in oils. He was to paint Robert Buxton's portrait (see Plate 2) and a series of Norwich dignitaries from 1746. R. Jones, 'Thomas Bardwell (1704–1767)', *ODNB*; M. Kirby Talley, 'Thomas Bardwell of Bungay, artist and author, 1704–1767, with a checklist of works', *Walpole Society*, 46 (1976–8), pp. 91–163; Moore, *Family and Friends*, p. 112.

323 Charles FitzRoy (1683–1757), second Duke of Grafton, whose seat was Euston Hall (Suffolk). Thomas Pelham-Holles (1693–1768), fourth Duke of Newcastle, was then Secretary of State and later Prime Minister. See note 73, p. 20, above.

well; I have got a little cold myself. I believe that cold day we were out together when the wind was so at the east did neither of us good.

With all our wishes for your health concludes this from your most affectionate,

Signed: J[*ohn*] Buxton

I've writ in hast that Mr Layman may give it to the carrier from Diss.

129 John Buxton to Robert Buxton [35/127]

Addressed: To Mr Buxton at Clare Hall Cambridge
Channonz, 24 November 1728

Dear Robert,

Your mothers writing last week made me not do it then, I am now to thank you for your letter. The pleasure it gave me to find your complaints going of was allayed by the account in your last to your mother, where I perceive the disorder has not left you, but by its shifting its place I have hopes it will not stay long with you. I think you ought to avoid going into the cold air whilst this tendernes remains on your lungs. I have for some time my self felt an unusual disorder on that part, but by keeping within near a fortnight I am, thank God, very well again, but do not yet expose my self long together in the open air. I remember you formerly used a powder of Elecampane[324] on these occasions: why should you not try it again?

I know not when I shall get to Snare Hill, hearing nothing from the owners as I expect when it is fit to inhabit. As the season is now & is like to be perhaps for some time, I do not want it but [*?word*] shall be excessively dirty on the breaking of the frost. You were oblidged to Mr Carver[325] for the hare, and I think the more so as he is so little of a sportsman. I neither hear of nor see my neibour Mallom; his mother is dead & I suppose he taken up with the settling his affairs.

The latter end of this week your mother talks of sending you some of the good things from her kitchen by the Diss carrier. I do not forget what I promised you out of the park but I choose to defer it a little that you may with more

[324] Elecampane: a perennial composite plant (*Inula Helenium*), the horse-heal. Extracts from the bitter aromatic leaves and root were used as a tonic and stimulant.

[325] Philip Carver was vicar of Tibenham and Besthorpe. Son of Walter Carver, druggist of Wymondham, he was admitted sizar at the age of seventeen to Caius College, Cambridge in 1709. After graduating in 1713–4 he was ordained priest in Norwich in 1716 and held the Tibenham living until his death in 1759. Venn, part I, vol. I, p. 302.

pleasure partake of it: let me know therefore when you like to have the venison. Tom Bardwell[326] has been with me near 3 weeks, & has almost finished the pannels in the hall. He does this work extreemly to my liking, & I believe you will also be pleased when you see it. Enquire if Moresise or Collier's *Dictionary*[327] which is the same does not contain all that Lloyd & Hoffman have in theirs. The windows were just put up at Shadwell before this snow fell [*?word*] I hear for I have not been there since the day I met S[*i*]r E[*dmund*] Bacon. I hear from Laxfeild your friends continue well there, the same of those at Stratton & Norwich, and I wish for nothing more than to hear as much of you, for I am dear Robert your most affectionate,

Signed: John Buxton

I forgot to tell you we had letters from Playford & one from Lenny himself. They are well but a little angry that nobody from hence has writ to them since they left us. Our letters have twice miscarried to them. No news at all from Whitnesham yet.

/1688
43
———
1685/ [328]

130 John Buxton to Robert Buxton [35/128]

Addressed: To Mr Robert Buxton at Clare Hall in Cambridge
Channonz, 2 December 1728. /Received 4 December/

Dear Robert,

It was indeed a pleasure to receive so favourable an account of your illness, for this very severe weather had given me some uneasy apprehensions for you. May this find you quite free of the disorder & in condition to eat some of the venison I send by this carrier which, with my service, you are to present to Dr Wilcox. It was killed this day & I think is pretty good, & if the weather does not break will keep as long as you please, but this is left to your cook's discretion.

[326] The painter. See note 322, p. 146, above.

[327] Jeremy Collier (1650–1726) edited Louis Moréri's (1643–1680) *The Great Historical, Geographical, Genealogical and Poetical Dictionary* in several editions, published in 1701 for example, with an appendix in 1721 and a supplement in 1727. Nicholas Lloyd (1630–80) based a similar work upon the dictionaries of Charles Estienne (*c.* 1504–1564). An updated edition was published in 1686.

[328] This marginal note by John Buxton is unexplained.

Though the cold has been very intense here we have not had snow enough to keep the cattle from feeding on the grass. I find by the publick papers it has been otherwise in most parts of England. However, it is enough to keep me within doors except an hour or two about the middle of the day, for you know cold weather of all others is the most disagreeable to me. I have not been at Norwich this 5 or 6 weeks. I hear Dr Amyas[329] died there last week very suddainly, as did Miss Themelthorp,[330] one of the Norfolk great fortunes. She was apprehensive of having a red face, a thing her family has been subject to, & upon taking a mercurial purge to prevent it, threw the humour upon her vitals and dyed a martyr to her vanity. Mr Ferrier of Yarmouth,[331] the manager there for the court interest, was given over last Wednesday. If he is dead as I suppose he is, it falls out unluckily at this juncture for I think the Col[*one*]l Townshend[332] killed in the newspapers of the last & this post was a representative for that place.

329 Matthew Amyas M.D. (*c.* 1665–1728). Son of John Amyas of Hingham, he was admitted to Caius College, Cambridge, in 1681 and gained his M.D. in 1701. Venn, part I, vol. I, p. 27. Dr Amyas's memorial inscription in Hingham church records his death on 26 November 1729 aged 64 but John Buxton's letter indicates that he died a year earlier. The date is confirmed by Venn and an announcement in the *Norwich Gazette* of 11 January 1729 for the sale of the late Dr Amyas's 'Large and Commodious Dwelling-House, with a Beautiful Town Garden, well planted with the best Fruit Trees and Greens ... upon Tombland, in Norwich'. The house did not sell immediately for it was re-advertised on 14 March 1730 for sale or let.

330 Miss Sarah Themelthorpe, the only child of Charles Themelthorpe (d. 1723) of Worstead and his wife Sarah (d. 1733), daughter and co-heiress of Charles Windham. M. Sayer, writing of the Themelthorpes of Foulsham in 'Eynesford Families 1550–1700', *Norfolk Genealogy*, 4 (Norwich, 1971), p. 15, dates Sarah's death, aged seventeen, as 21 November 1727, but W. Rye, 'Worstead' in *The Monumental Inscriptions in the Hundred of Tunstead in the County of Norfolk* (Norwich, 1891), p. 173, copied the memorial inscription in Worstead church as 'MDCCXXVIII', a date consistent with John Buxton's report.

331 The Ferrier family of Yarmouth and Hemsby provided bailiffs, mayors and M.P.s for Yarmouth: Richard Ferrier (1671–1728) held posts in the period 1696–1713, and his son Richard (1695–1739) was mayor in 1724 and was appointed receiver-general for part of Norfolk in 1730.

332 Colonel Townshend was not the member for Yarmouth. The town was represented by William Townshend (1702–38) from 1723 to 1738, replacing Charles Townshend who was called to the house of lords during his father's lifetime in his father's barony. No references to the Townshend death have been found in either the *Norwich Mercury* or *Norwich Gazette* of around this date. John Buxton could possibly have been referring to the remarkable case of a colonel Townshend who was reported by Dr Cheyne (whom Buxton had consulted in Bath) to have had the power to enter a death-trance with all normal signs of life absent. Together with another physician and an apothecary, Cheyne witnessed the phenomenon although, on this last occasion, after recovering after half-an-hour, the colonel called his lawyer, made a will, and really died six hours later. Cheyne discussed the case in his *The English Malady or a Treatise of Nervous Diseases* (1733). See letters nos 19 and 33, pp. 45 and 57, above.

I believe Collier's *Dictionary* has all Hoffman & Lloyd & so you need make no further enquiry. It will be time enough to make your acknowledgements to Mr Carver. I fancy it will not be long ere Will Rant[333] will give us an oppertunity of doing it effectually for I hear he growes rather worse than better. The season has prevented all planting, only I found time just before the frost surprised us to set some oaks in the little meadow by the park as I had designed when you were here. I have heard nothing from Laxfeild since I writ last, but I have had a letter from Mr D'Oyly: he had defered till this time sending the apples he promised, & now upon sending to Diss today expecting to find them there they were told the carryers coud not travel this week. However, he writes a very good account of your brothers & says they make improvements beyond his expectation. This is better than all the apples in the orchard. Your little sister does no less at home & is at present our principal entertainment.

Am I to expect you before Xmas? If this weather continue, you are to do as you like best yourself & as you find most proper. I will if possible get to Snare Hill <If> if the weather breaks, otherwise I shall be here.

Your most affectionate,

Signed: John Buxton

You are desired to take care of the cloath the venison comes in.

131 John Buxton to Robert Buxton [35/129]

Addressed: To Mr Robert Buxton at Clare Hall in Cambridge
15 December 1728. Received 17 [*December*].

Dear Robert,

I received yours of the 13th and am glad to hear you are so well to think of seeing us this week. The horses shall be with you on Thursday as you desire, but you must be content to take such convenience and air as Channonz affords for the house at Snare Hill is not yet fit to be inhabited by those who have been used to warm rooms, for though they have done the glazing there, there is air enough yet within doors to put out a candle, as John Warns[334]

[333] William Rant (*c.* 1673–will proved 1732) of Dickleburgh. Educated in Wymondham and Norwich, he was admitted to Caius College, Cambridge, in 1691. Ordained priest in 1698 he was rector of Great Wacton and Bunwell 1698–1719, and of Carleton Rode 1719–30. Venn, part I, vol. III, p. 422.

[334] John Warn is named in the building accounts for Shadwell Lodge, being paid £34 7s. on account for the offices, and 18s. expenses at Lynn in connection with the purchase and carriage of materials. CUL Buxton Papers, 124/3.

informs me. Your freind you mention will be very welcom with you, therefore make no scruple of taking this liberty as often as you like.

Your mother designed writing now but the hopes of seeing you so soon makes her think it unnecessary. Your sister Betty [*Elizabeth*] is with Lady Ward at Norwich and we hope better for the change of air etc., and Lady Ward is so good to say she is not troublesome. I had a letter from the latter this day with little news only that Mrs Rant of Yelverton[335] dyed on Friday after a few days illnes. A report yesterday at Buckenham said Mr Rant[336] of Dickleburgh dyed on Thursday but upon sending thither today to enquire the truth I had an account he was not dead but very bad.

The season begins to make me wish with some impatience that Shadwell was habitable for the feilds and roads here were never more disagreeable. However, the good things the place affords makes some satisfaction for the inconveniencys, yet the hopes of a pleasanter winter aboad is my best relief.

I wish you a good journy and am, dear Robert, your most affectionate father,
Signed: John Buxton

132 John Buxton to Robert Buxton [35/130]

Addressed: To Mr Robert Buxton at Clare Hall in Cambridge
Monday, 16 December 1728

Dear Robert,

Your brother Jack having got an ague at Bury made your mother go thither and your horses come that way and perhaps will be with you a day sooner than designed. They will rest the more at Cambridge which will not be improper.

The weather is so very bad that I think you had need be well guarded against it. Suppose you keep the horses a day or two to wait for better. I should like it better than that you should venture out when it is so very sharp, or if it does not mend, send the horses back unless you find yourself so free of your cold as to be able to bear the weather. My fears for your welfare may make me too carefull so you must judge for yourself and do what you think proper. I shall be glad to see you well at Channonz.

Your most affectionate
Signed: John Buxton

A letter dated 18 December 1728 from Anne Buxton to Robert Buxton is written on the same sheet.

335 The Rant family had property in Yelverton but this Mrs Rant has not been identified.
336 See note 333, p. 150, above.

133 John Buxton to Robert Buxton [35/132]

Addressed: To Mr Buxton at Clare Hall in Cambridge
2 September 1729. Tuesday morn ½ hour past 6

Dear Robert,

I received your letter yesterday with much pleasure to find you bare your journy so well. This leaves us here much as you left us; we have yet had no account from Mrs Pigot[337] but your mother will I believe proceed in the journey. Mrs Nutthall came unexpected on Sunday evening: is good company with her agreeable singing.

I killed a pretty good deer yesterday towards evening; have sent you half by the carrier with as many partridges as Clem Serjant[338] could shoot: there is yet but a brace but he hopes to make them up a better number before he gets to Brettenham[339] where he is now going, as I am also my self, expecting to meet Mr Brettingham[340] there. I have thought it might be easier & less trouble to yourself if you give your venison in the hall all at once. Your perticular freinds will be as much oblidged & no room for others to take offence at their not being invited should you have it privately at your chambers, where you may also distinguish the former if you think fit, but this I leave to you to do as you think best & by this means, although if it is not customary to treat publickly, you in effect do it without breaking the rule.

The season promises to be very fine. I shall be glad it may continue, to make your journy pleasant & I shall accompany you with my good wishes, since I could not with convenience do it otherwise. I have had letters from both your brothers at Playford with good accounts of their health. Your mother will bring you two sent hither since you went, from Mr Partridge & Jarmy.[341]

[337] Mrs Lettice Pigott neé Lovett (*c.* 1651–1735), widow of Thomas Pigott (d. 1704), of Doddershall House, Quainton, Buckinghamshire. The Buxtons were related to Mrs Pigott through the Herne family. John Buxton's wife Anne's maternal grandmother was Sarah Herne, née Lovett, the daughter of Christopher Lovett, himself the son of colonel John Lovett. Sarah's sister Dorothy married John Herne. Lettice Lovett was Sarah's first cousin, being the daughter of the colonel's other son, Robert. The architect Edward Lovett Pearce was also related. His mother, Frances Lovett, was colonel John Lovett's sister. J. Burke, *Genealogical and Heraldic History of the Extinct and Dormant Baronetcies of England, Ireland and Scotland* (1977), pp. 323–6.

[338] Not identified.

[339] Brettenham: a parish and village neighbouring Rushford, four miles east of Thetford.

[340] Probably John Buckenham. See note 198, p. 104, above

[341] The Partridge family seat was Buckenham Tofts Hall, bought from the Vincent family who had built it in the later seventeenth century. The Partridges sold it *c.* 1736, settling at Hockham Hall.

It would not be amis if you carry about with you a little sketch book in octo or 4to doubled, to put plans of houses you think worth noting. If you make one of Dodershall[342] it will give me a better idea of the plan than any description, in which you may note the plan of gardens, offices, park &c. with the bearing. I leave this unsealed till I come to Shadwell, from your most affectionate,

Signed: J[*ohn*] Buxton

Dr Herring was well on Saturday. The buttons for your cloaths will come by the carrier, not with the venison but in a parcel by themselves from Norwich.

Shadwell parlour, 1 aclock.
Clem Serjant's horse strayed this morning so you have but a brace of partridges. Your mother desires that John may not come to Newmarket because she is not certain that it will be Saturday.

134 John Buxton to Robert Buxton [35/133]

Addressed: To Mr Buxton at Clare Hall
Channonz, 5 September 1729

Dear Robert,

Your letter afforded me a great deal of entertainment, but no part gave me so much pleasure as where you say you continue well, pray you have this to say as often as you write. The library makes amends for the thinnes of the colledge. There is not a great many designs in Gibbs[343] worth copying; I have tryed to mend one with good effect. I had always intended getting the d[*uke*] of Buckingham's works,[344] if it is the best edition it is not dear, but as I remember there is a castration the last editions either in the tragedy of Brutus or in the memoirs of K[*ing*] William.

Quare of this I have writ the towns in a paper which Sarah brings that seem to me the more direct, but whether the roads through these towns are practicable, I know not. You must get information of this of some carriers who come from those parts & what towns are best to bayt at, as also the inns in the towns.

342 Doddershall House was a timber-framed building of the sixteenth century with a new south front of some 120 feet in extent, with two wings, built by Thomas Pigott in 1689. The house would be again remodelled in 1789. G. Lipscomb, *History and Antiquities of the County of Buckingham*, I (1847), p. 411.

343 James Gibbs (1682–1754), *A Book of Architecture, containing Designs of Buildings and Ornaments* (1728).

344 *Miscellaneous Works* by George Villiers (1628–87), second Duke of Buckingham, collected by Tom Brown, was published in 1704–5 and had reached a third edition by 1715.

The plan 63 in Gibbs looks too full of windows, the rooms are too small & two of them lost by being throfares to the offices, the stairs but 3 foot wide: I like Shadwell better.[345]

I hope you received the venison safe & good: that part of it left here was so. I wish you a good journy & am your most affectionate,

Signed: J[*ohn*] B[*uxton*]

When you write from Dodershall let me know how I am to direct thither. If you make any excursion out of the road take Abram with you, he will be most proper.

135 Robert Buxton to John Buxton [34/110]

No address

Clare Hall, 7 September 1729. 7 a'clock morn.

Dear Sir,

I am ordered by my mother to tell you the [*?word*] my sisters got well to Cambridge yesterday about 3 a clock, & I hear this moment are so this morning. My sister thinks herself better than she was before she came out. I am to give you thanks for your kind letter, & am very glad to hear you continue so well. I must not defer my acknowledgement <due> for the venison, it proving the best I ever eat, & our cook indeed did justice to it by dressing it extreemly well. It was very acceptable to the sen[*iors*] in colledge (I should have told you before I had it all at once on Thursday in the hall, which was by far most convenient for me) & Dr Green,[346] I believe, eat of the party a 2nd & a 3rd time. The partridge I am also to thank you for, which I had made ready in my chamber.

The d[*uke*] [*of*] Buckingham's works[347] I brought home to my chambers, being almost assured you would have them, & since I find the castrations you mention at the end of the 2nd vol. of this edition I shall purchase them. This letter I have had just time to write out of them, imagining as well to give you

[345] See note 343, p. 153, above. Plan 63 in Gibbs is of a symmetrical seven-bay house, with two storeys over a basement. The central block is 45 feet by 37 feet (excluding the thickness of external walls) with two two-storey wings (containing the stables and domestic offices) connected to the central block with curving colonnades.

[346] Dr Robert Green (?-1730), was admitted sizar to Clare Hall in 1694 and graduated in 1699–70, gaining his D.D. in 1728. He was a fellow from 1703–1730. Ordained in London in 1705, he held livings in Bedfordshire and Huntingdonshire. He died in Tamworth, where he had been born. Venn, part I, vol. II, p. 257.

[347] See note 344, p. 153, above.

some pleasure in the reading, as myself advantage in the copying it. Whether it is a translation of the duke's from Latin or Greek I know not.

We have not yet come to a determination about the rout we are to take, but will inform ourselves according to your directions, which I will follow in what else you mention in your letter. As yet Gamblinghay, & 10 to Bedford, 18 miles from thence to Woburn seems to me the most direct way. Ampthill is L[*or*]d Fitzwilliam's.[348] He is now there with with [*sic*] a sen[*ior*] of his, *fellow* of this coll[*ege*] who went from hence a day or two after I came. We all beg our duty & service to you & fireside[?]. My mother's cold is better.

I am dear Sir, your most affect[*ionate*] son,

Signed: R[*obert*] Buxton.

Then follows a long transcript by Robert Buxton headed 'Letter of Epicurus to Meneceus', from the duke of Buckingham's work mentioned in the letter.

136 John Buxton to Robert Buxton [35/134]

Addressed: To Mr Buxton at Dodershall in Quainton near Winslow, Buckinghamshire, by Caxton bag[349]
Sunday 14 September 1729, at night from Channonz

Dear Robert,

I am to thank you for your agreable letter from Cambridge & for the pleasure you gave me by transcribing that of Epicurus; I shall expect a great deal more from the rest of the d[*uke*] of Buck[*ingham's*] works & am glad you met with them. I have yet received no letter since, have writ only one, directed at a venture but hope it will come safe to let you know we were then well, as this does now & your sister Tib has quite lost her cold. I shall defer sealing or directing this till I know whether I have a letter to morrow.

My mother Gooch & aunt Herne have their colds still & are after the usual

[348] William Fitzwilliam (1712–?), second son of Richard (*c.* 1677–1743), fifth Viscount Fitzwilliam of Merrion, co. Dublin, was admitted to Clare Hall in 1728–9. He matriculated in 1729, gained a B.A. in 1732–3, and an M.A. from Trinity College in 1735. Clare College, Cambridge, Index to Alumni. Richard, seventh Viscount of the Merrion line, left the Fitzwilliam library and funds for creating the Fitzwilliam Museum in Cambridge. Ampthill Park, the Fitzwilliam seat, had been built by the Ashburnhams in 1661, and bought from them in 1720 by Richard, Lord Fitzwilliam. The Irish line is distinct from the viscounts and earls Fitzwilliam of Milton (Northamptonshire) whose titles were also of Irish origin until the granting of English peerages in 1746.

[349] Caxton: a Cambridgeshire parish and village on the main London to York road, 12 miles west of Cambridge.

sort I told you to your mother in my last. I heared from your brothers at Playford that they had in that family been entirely free from sickness, & that Mr D'Oyly gave me hopes of better things from George than we all expected. I am to contradict what I said of Mr Sotherton:[350] he is not married. The season still promises fine & I make no doubt you take the advantage of it. I gave a caution about Oxford where I have heard the smallpox has been much, but you can have certain information of this. I never know the country more void of news, beside we had no letter last Saturday from Lady Ward, but it is notwithstanding exceeding pleasant. I have used my horse pretty freely & had no inconvenience from that exercise. My serv[*an*]ts who were ill are getting better, the lying the moat goes on very well: there is very much mud. The barn at Shadwell will be done as to the brickwork by Friday next but the plaisterers have not yet done the stairs. I will leave room to add somewhat if there's need to morrow & conclude with love & blessing to your mother & sisters from your most affectionate,

Signed: J[*ohn*] B[*uxton*]

Monday, 15 September. 1729
/received 21/

I add nothing but that all continue well & the post coming in so late I do not stay for yours but direct this as the 1st. I repeat my wishes for your health, my complements to Mrs Pigot &c.

137 John Buxton to Ann Buxton [35/135]

Addressed: To Mrs Buxton at Mrs Pigots at Dodershall, to be left at Mr Dagnals bookseller in Aylsbury Bucks. By Aylsbury bag by way of London.
/1729 Sept. 16 dated/
Tuesday, 16 September 1729, from Channonz

I received my dear wife's letter yesterday with very great pleasure though not time enough to return this by the same post. I have writ & sent two already but I fear they will be lost, being directed to &c. near Winslow by the Caxton bag which I find is not the proper direction, so you will not have the satisfaction so soon as I intended it of knowing your children & freinds here continue well. You left little Isabella with something of a cold, which she has now lost & is perfectly well & brisk. My mother Gooch & aunt Herne are much after the usual sort though both have their colds still. The servants keep in pretty good

350 See note 21, p. 40, above.

health, only the two husbandmen who are not yet recovered. Nanny is very good & oblidging to her little sister & they seem much pleased with entertaining one another.

We were all delighted to have so good an account of Mrs Pigot, especially those who have been of her acquaintance. You have had all the good fortune possible in your journy to render it pleasant, & I hope it will be continued to you till you arrive safe again here, & meet us all in good health. I writ you word in one of the letters I suppose is lost that the Mrs Williams mentioned in one of news papers who is said dyed of the small pox & was brought down to be buried near Ipswich was Mrs Meadowe.[351] She was first buried in London & then by her mothers desire taken up & brought to Witnesham. This I had from Georgy last week who also says he & his brother there are perfectly well. I had an account at the same time from Mr D'Oyly who sent his men on the usual errand that they both make good improvements in their learning, especially George who proceeds much beyond all our expectations of him.

I had a letter yesterday from Mr Lathbury[352] to tell me Jack, who is otherwise well, feels the old complaint in his knee, though he has not missed one day going to school for it. I shall give an account of it to S[*i*]r B[*enjamin Wrench*] to take his directions. I gave some hints in my letters of the small pox having been much at Oxford. I hope you'l make good enquiry concerning this if you go, & though I wish you all imaginable divertion, my fears for you all who are so dear to me make desire you to take care of your selves.

I am your most affectionate,

Signed: J[*ohn*] B[uxton]

138 John Buxton to Robert Buxton [35/135]

Included with letter 137
16 September 1729

Dear Robert,

I am extreem glad to find you & your sisters bear your journy so well & that your mother says nothing of her cold which by that I hope it is leaving her. I

351 Elizabeth Williams née Meadowe, who was buried at Witnesham on 4 April 1727. See note 27, p. 43, above.

352 Mr Joseph Lathbury (1690–1775). He was educated at Bury and Clare Hall, Cambridge and ordained in 1722. He was rector of Suffolk parishes from 1722 until his death and is listed in 1713 as the Lower Master at the Free Grammar School in Bury St Edmunds. S.H.A. Hervey, ed., *Biographical list of boys educated at King Edward VI Free Grammar School Bury St Edmunds from 1550 to 1900*, Suffolk Green Books XIII (Bury St Edmunds, 1908), p. 455; Venn, part I, vol. III, p. 49.

fancy you are in a very agreeable place: an assemblage of relations from different quarters of the world makes all entertaining to each other, for some time at least, though I fancy the mistress of it must make the most considerable part, by the account I have of her, who I imagine a person of good sense & breeding, of humanity & benevolence, & who by these good qualitys & her hospitality, makes a very venerable figure surrounded by her kindred.

I should be glad to have some beech mast for there is plenty in that county contrived to be sent: it is not yet ripe. You may mention my intentions of sending Mr Pearce[353] the designs &c. to his sister, but that I have a long time had that pain in my side which made it troublesome to set to that impist[?], but that I will do it soon.

My complements to the family, & to your sisters my best wishes & blessing of your most affectionate,

Signed: J[*ohn*] B[*uxton*]

I had writ you thanks for your letter from Cambridge in those I fear are lost. That of Epicurus gave great pleasure but more to know you are well.

139 John Buxton to Robert Buxton [35/136]

Addressed: To Mr Buxton at Mrs Pigots at Dodershall. To be left at Mr Dagnalls Boo[*k*]seller in Aylsbury Bucks. By Aylsbury bag & way of London. /1729 dated Sept. 20/
Thetford, Saturday, 20 September 1729

Dear Robert,

Though I writ to your mother last post it will not be unpleasant to you to know we all continue well, & this is the fourth letter I have sent, & the 2nd by London; the other directed to Winslow I suppose will be lost. If you have had as much rain in Buckinghamshire as lately we have here the roads will be made very bad but my horses being used to such will make the less difficulty of them. I came hither yesterday in the midst of the most violent storms of rain I ever saw but by seasonable putting in at the villages on the Harling road I escaped the worst & brought my self dry hither, though I was forced to dine on bread & cheese even at Capt. Draper's, where a little while since one might have found better entertainment. I stayed there till 4 a clock, when the heavens cleered, & the whole country became as pleasant as if no rain had

[353] The architect Edward Lovett Pearce. He seems to have been related to Mrs Pigott née Lovett, through his mother Frances Lovett. See note 337, p. 152, above.

fallen. I did but just look in at Shadwell, but found things in good disposition: the barn in great forwardness and the lean toos almost up.

It is now eight a clock & begins to rain most violently & as if it would continue. I would have stopped my letters here but they do not open the Attleburgh bag. I hope for the pleasure of my return to heare a good account of you; I have not yet received but one letter, another I expected this post. If the wet season should continue it will be much safest & easiest to come by the way of London.

I have had a letter from cozen Meadowe, some time after date. It is in a melancholy strain for the loss of Mis[*s*][354] & has also many expressions of thanks for her entertainment at Channonz. I propose being there to night if the weather gives me leave, otherwise must make this my quarters. Tell your mother little Isabella is perfectly well & brisk & Nanny agrees very well with her. My love & blessing is with you & best wishes from your most affectionate,

Signed: J[*ohn*] B[*uxton*]

Dr Herring's little son[355] is like & well though he had the worst sort. S[*i*]r Edw[*ar*]d Ward has a return of his ague or feaver.

140 John Buxton to Robert Buxton [35/137]

Addressed: To Mrs Buxton to be left at Mrs Richardsons Apothecary, the Black Boy over against the Watehouse in Holborn London. /1729 dated Sept. 29/
Monday, 29 September 1729, from Channonz

Dear Robert,

I have received two letters from you since I writ with very great satisfaction, (the last was the 3rd), to find you all continue well & are so well diverted, but the account you give me of your own health is a newer and greater pleasure than any you can meet with in your tour, & I pray for nothing more than its continuance. This leaves us here in perfect health except my mother Gooch, who has been much after the usual rate till within a day or two, & upon taking cold she is something worse. Your sister Isabella was never better in her life &

[354] Betsy Meadowe, see note 27, p. 43, above.

[355] This is presumably William Herring (1718–1774), although he could have had a younger brother. William was born in Norwich and educated at Clare Hall, where he was a fellow 1741–3. He was rector of the Norfolk villages Alburgh (1742–3) and Edgefield (1743–7). He became rector of Bolton Percy (Yorkshire) in 1747 and dean of St Asaph in 1751, posts he held until his death.

gives us all the most agreeable amusement we meet with. Nanny continues also well & there is so good a correspondence between them that I have scarce heard the least noise of difference between them: this will be very pleasing to your mother as it is to us here. My serv[*an*]ts who were ill are now pretty well again, only J. Downing mends but slowly.

This wet weather must have made the cross roads impracticable, so I conclude you take the way by London, it being fine now I direct this to meet you there, & hope it will meet you well. I suppose you make but short stay, the roads from thence into Norfolk are now become bad so that you must make very short stages & ought to make three days to New Market, but I will before I conclude the letter add at the end the most convenient rests in the journey.

Master Jermy has had the smallpox & is got up again, & so is Dr Herring's son.[356] He has beside this the good fortune to be presented to the living given him by Mr Marcon: Edgefield, a good £160 a year, the old incumbent being lately dead.[357] The smallpox continues much still at Norwich. I have not heard since my last from Playford; from Bury I have an account that Jack's old complaint came again but that he is now like to be well very soon having no other. I thank you for your complements on my birth day, you may live to find the pleasure one day of receiving such, from one as near to you. The rebus is easily found out to be our name & is ingenious. I shall be glad to hear Betty [*Elizabeth*] is well for in your mother's letter I think she was not so cleer in that point. Isabell now comes into my chamber, & would fain write, she talks a great deal, lives all day with her grandmother Buxton & I never saw my sister so fond or oblidging to any child in my life, but Isabella has peculiar charms, & people can't help being delighted with her.[358] I expect to hear this post of your rout[*e*]. Will New Market be so well to lodge at now in the time of the meeting, I think Chesterford will be most proper, & from thence to Barton Mills.

Love & blessing concludes this from your most affectionate,

Signed: J[*ohn*] Buxton

Suppose you lodge at Epping the first night which may with ease be done, or Hockeril, thence to Chesterford, thence to Barton Mills.[359] If you should

[356] See note 355, p. 159, above.

[357] Edgefield: a north Norfolk parish about 18 miles north-west of Norwich. Blomefield, IX, p. 386, states that William Herring was presented in 1729 by John Jermy, the first presentation by the Marcon family being in 1754, although it is also recorded that Thomas Marcon was Lord of the Manor in the 12th year of William III (1699–1700) and John Marcon in the 11th year of Queen Anne (1712–13).

[358] See note 191, p. 99, above.

[359] This itinerary envisaged a journey from London to Epping of about eighteen miles (or to

want any mony at London Mr Herring[360] will give you credit, The Golden Artichoke, Lombard Street.

141 John Buxton to Robert Buxton [35/138]

Addressed: To Mr Robert Buxton at Mr Marsham's house in Stratton [*Strawless*]
To be left at Mr Crosshold's in Norwich. /Nov. 1 1729/
Channonz, 31 October 1729

Dear Robert,

I must let you know we all continue well here though I have nothing els to write to you, besides my wishes that you may be so too. This fine weather has been so favourable that I hope you have lost your cold, & that you have not wanted divertion in a place I have been always sure of meeting with it.

Your most affectionate,
Signed: John Buxton

My complements as due.

142 John Buxton to Robert Buxton [35/139]

Addressed: To Mr Robert Buxton at Mr Marsham's house in Stratton in Norfolk
To be left at Mr Crosshold's in Norwich. /Nov. 5 1729/
Thetford, Tuesday night, 4 November 1729

Dear Robert,

I received yours on Saturday with much satisfaction & hope, notwithstanding the tempestuous weather, you continue well. You are above all things to endeavour to keep so & have free liberty to choose where you will abide till Shadwell can be made habitable. There is little more done there besides glazing the windows since you saw it; the barn they tell me will be covered the next week. I shall also get the lean toos tiled by the same time, having provided all the *necessaria*; no chimny peices are yet put up.

Your goods are at length come safe hither, all except the top part of the

Hockerill, Herts. near Bishops Stortford) then twenty-eight miles to Chesterford, followed by twenty-six miles to Barton Mills, some fifteen miles from Shadwell Lodge.

360 Probably a London merchant, related to Dr William Herring.

reading desk. I had fears for the whole for I did not till now learn any tidings of them: I shall give charge to make enquiry for what is missing.

I know not what to think of the Laxfeild journy now the weather is so very uncertain, for should the day prove wet which we are to fix for meeting at Harlston, how should we proceed. There will be no riding out of our pace in those roads to avoid a coming shower, & I have some fears that the air their may be equally offensive to you, especially if you should take cold. However, our resolutions must depend on your present state of health & if you are, as you say, grown so much hardier you will run no hazard in a journey to High Suffolk.[361] The small pox having been so much at Ipswich & the neibourhood there makes it not so proper to change into that air: why might you not for a week or two take up with your old quarters at Quidenham, & if by that means you can preserve your self well it will amply recompense the solitude. You may if you judge it proper stay another week where you are, I dare say you can find no where more agreeable company, if it is no inconvenience to the family. I will send the servant however on Friday & you may either keep him or send him home (for he will have business at Norwich) as you like best & I will write you more of thoughts then.

From your most affectionate,
Signed: John Buxton

Poor serjant Branthwayt:[362] how fast does that family fall of. I never can forget making my complements in the family you are with. Be perticular to my aunt.

143 John Buxton to Robert Buxton [35/140]

Addressed: to Mr Robert Buxton at Stratton [*Strawless*]
Friday, 7 November 1729

Dear Robert,

I received your letter by the post and am much pleased with the contents of it, as I find you are with the place you are in. Good air and good company with it are without question most powerfull promoters of health and I do not know there is better to be found anywhere than at Stratton.

I left Thetford on Wednesday, came home by Shadwell and saw your goods safe in your own room there, and John Warns[363] lodges in the house for their

361 A term descriptive of the claylands of central Suffolk.

362 This is seemingly a reference to Miles Branthwayt, barrister-at-law, but the meaning is unclear.

363 See note 334, p. 150, above.

protection. We continue well here and I think your mother is quite recovered of her cold. Your grandmother not worse than usual and little Isabella brisk. Some linning [*linen*] come by this bearer for you. I will next week send the servant and in the mean time consider of the Laxfeild journy. Your little Sarah had a letter last Wednesday from your aunt Han there. She told her in it that my brother was that day to go for Stratton and that she was half in the mind to go with him. I was glad to find she was so well as to think of taking such a journy. I have got a little cold but so small as not to prevent my going out this morning with your sister to course an hare found lying at Aslacton.

My blessing and best wishes for you are from that most affectionate

Signed: J[*ohn*] Buxton

All due complements.

144 John Buxton to Robert Buxton [35/142]

Addressed: To Mr Robert Buxton at Mr Marsham's house at Stratton [*Strawless*]. To be left at Mr Croshold's[364] in Norwich.
Channonz, Sunday, 16 November 1729

Dear Robert,

I took the inclosed last Friday as I went to Larlingford meeting. The waters were so much out and rising as to prevent my returning that night which was the reason it was not sent before, and also that you did not hear from me. Your sisters should have thought of this and writ to have told you we could not think of sending in such dismal weather.

We received your letter last Saturday but not on the Wednesday by the post as you mention. I heard at Thetford Captain Wright dyed that morning. He has made his youngest son executor with Mr Cocksedge[365] as attourny in Thetford and given the eldest an annuity only for life. This is Dame Sarjant's[366] news. She was very glad to get rid of your dog. He comes with this bearer to Norwich and is to be left at The Falcon. I hope he will arrive safe. I think he has had but little benefit of the boarding school besides slender diet.

These short days make but little progress in our work at Shadwell and the weather having been so bad has greatly interupted those abroad. They promise

[364] John Croshold was sheriff of Norwich in 1720, and mayor in 1724. His second wife was Mary, daughter of Thomas Marsham of Stratton Strawless. At one time Croshold lived at the Curat House in Gentleman's Walk, Norwich. Cozens-Hardy, p. 116.

[365] Not identified.

[366] Not identified.

the barn shall be covered this week if the weather permits. The lean-toos will not be long after, for the tiler is gone and he is a very expeditious person. Your mother will also this week look out for beds to be had in our neibourhood so I hope in a very little time there will be a being for you and a little family where if you continue to have your health it will be more than all the pleasures together I ever proposed to myself in building.

Your most affectionate
Signed: J[*ohn*] Buxton

All due complements.
Quidenham is let at Lady [*Day*] next to one Mr Leathes,[367] a member of the Commons and the ladies are to go to London.

145 John Buxton to Robert Buxton [35/143]

Addressed: To Mr Robert Buxton at Stratton [*Strawless*]
Channonz, Thursday, 18 November 1729

Dear Robert,

Your letter designed to be with us on Wednesday came but yesterday. I am glad you like the scheme I proposed for you, being a little time at Quidenham instead[?] of coming directly thither. I also approve and you may rest yourself at Wyndham[368] in the way. Mrs Bucknam[369] will have notice to prepare your lodging if you have a mind to go to Blickling before you leave Stratton. You may keep [word ?] a day or two longer.

Your mother goes tomorrow with one load of houshold goods to Shadwell. The wet weather here makes us wish that place habitable. So many little things go to the doing this that it has taken more time than I can have imagined. I had a letter this day from Laxfeild with a good account of our friends there and that they had some expectations of seeing you with me if the weather favoured. I fear this has been too bad to let us now think of performing that journy. The season being also so very sickly I'm not for running any hazard of taking colds, having hitherto pretty well escaped the epidemical one, but I think London feels most of it. The account from there come every post

[367] Cartaret Leathes M.P. (1698–1780) was the first son of John Mussendon of Hillsborough, County Down, by Jane, daughter of Adam Leathes. Their son inherited his uncle William's fortune in 1727, when he assumed the name Leathes. He was the member for Sudbury 1727–34 and 1741–47, and Harwich 1734–41. Sedgwick, II, pp. 201–2.

[368] Wymondham: a market town, nine and a half miles south-west of Norwich.

[369] Not identified.

worst than the last [word ?] is. There, so much of the diet, the necks of mutton and veal are sold at 10d. a pound.

I have no more to add but my humble service to my uncle and aunt Marsham and my cozens, from your most affectionate

Signed: J[*ohn*] Buxton

P.S. S[*i*]r Will[*ia*]m Holland was supplyed last year with spring or quickset from L[*or*]d Hobart's gardner.[370] Can you make enquiry if any more is to be had there?

Mrs Banton is certainly dead. I belive [*I*] did not mention this before. [*She*] has given the estate if her child dyes without issue, or before of age, to her husband's relations. I mean that which came from him. Mr Thurston and one Mr Dellick are guardians.[371]

The enclosed verses on Dr Bently[372] are very handsom. The other I suppose you have seen. I fancy they are borrowed for the[*y*] do not seem to be of a peice with the behaviour of the supposed author.

146 John Buxton to Robert Buxton [35/144]

Addressed: To Mr Rob[*er*]t Buxton at Mr Marsham's house in Stratton [*Strawless*]. To be left at Mr Crosshold's in Norwich.
Channonz, Thursday, 20 November 1729

Dear Robert,

The enclosed was writ on Tuesday with intention to send for you yesterday but the weather proved so bad I thought it was better to defer it, though your mother went to Shadwell as bad as it was, and I hear is well arrived there, in order to get the house ready.

Yours of the 18 [*th*] I just now read but do not send a sent [?] yet, for your mother sent me word last night that six of Charles Slappe's[373] servants came out with the smallpox altogether and are removed no further than to <Mr Baldwin's> the house over against Mr Baldwin's,[374] so you will not think of going to Mrs Bucknam's. I am now expecting Mr Rant[375] to take me up to go with him to a meeting at [*Long*] Stratton for I have a little cold and do not

370 Blickling Hall, Sir John Hobart's seat. See note 86, p. 62, above.
371 Not identified.
372 Not identified.
373 A Buxton tenant at Rushford. See Appendix C.
374 Not identified.
375 See note 333, p. 150, above.

venture on horseback. I make no doubt the time passes very agreeably but I fear you should should [*sic*] be too troublesom to your freinds who are so kind to you. Shadwell may in a week be fit to lodge in, the <wet> great rains <have> and my cold together have made me lay aside the Laxfeild journy.

With my complyments to all from your most affectionate

Signed: J[*ohn*] Buxton

Sarah is with your mother. The rest of your sisters are well and Isabella in good November company. I heard from Mr D'Oyly that your brothers were in health and that Georgy studyed. The high winds have blown down a barn at Rushford, that nearest Thetford.

147 John Buxton to Robert Buxton [35/145]

Addressed: To Mr Rob[*er*]t Buxton at Mr Marsham's house in Stratton [*Strawless*] Norfolk. To be left at Mr Crosshold's in Norwich.
Channonz, 21 November 1729

Dear Robert,

I writ to you yesterday to let you know your mother went to Shadwell on Wednesday and in her passage met with the account of Charles Slapp's servants having the smallpox, and that this was the reason I did not send for you. I know not what excuse to make for myself who am now the occation of your troubling your good freinds, but I am unwilling after so much rain to have you here, for the air must be affected with it. In a week or two Shadwell may be habitable.

Your cosen Marsham is about going to Cambridge I suppose. You may come with him to Thetford and stay there a fue days if you like it, till we are fixed and safe and warm at Shadwell. This I think of, that I would not by any means have you prevent your cosen's going his own time to Cambridge. I had not heard of Mr Crossholds[376] being ill. I hope this will find him better and all the rest of the family well, to whom you are to present my humble service from your most affectionate

Signed: John Buxton

Your grandmother Gooch is now so ill she is not able to be moved from the bed to the fire without the greatest difficulty. It is impossible I think that she should continue but a very little while. Your mother is not yet returned from Shadwell. I am to expect her tomorrow.

[376] See note 364, p. 163, above.

148 John Buxton to Robert Buxton [35/146]

Addressed: To Mr Rob[*er*]t Buxton at Mr Marsham's in Stratton [*Strawless*], Norfolk. To be left at Mr Crosshold's in Norwich.
[*No date. Probably 2 December 1729*]

Dear Robert,

I write this to let you know of the death of your grandmother Gooch who departed last night about 7 a clock and, having intimated a day or two before she dyed that she should like to be buried at Tibenham,[377] we are to persue her directions. Yesterday morning she was got up as usual though I thought she appeared altered, and after drinking a little chocolate was taken so ill that it was with some difficulty they were able to get her to bed again, where she continued in a quiet insensible posture as though asleep till the eternal sleep seized her.

I received yours at Norwich but without date. Attleburgh would <have> be your best place for baiting if you come to Shadwell but I fear your grandmother's death will put some stop to the preparations at that place. I cannot think there would be any danger at Bucknam's. It seems the distemper at C. Slap's was brought by a Norwich boy: they are all like to do well. There only Sarah Slap is dead. You shall hear further on Saturday.

From your most affectionate
Signed: J[*ohn*] Buxton

My humble service to all our kind agreeable freinds.

149 John Buxton to Robert Buxton [35/147]

Addressed: To Mr Rob[*er*]t Buxton at Mr Marsham's house in Stratton [*Strawless*], Norfolk. To be left at Mr Croshold's in Norwich.
Tuesday night, 2 December 1729

Dear Robert,

Though I have writ by the Buckenham post I shall repeat what I said least that should not come to hand, and let you know your grandmother Gooch dyed last night about 7 a clock and is to be buried privately at Tibenham. The rest of your freinds here are well and Betty [*Elizabeth*] much better since she went to Saxlingham, having a bad cold when she left us.

Attleburgh will be a convenient rest when you come to Shadwell but I am

377 Tibenham: the parish in which Channonz was located, 14 miles south-west of Norwich.

not sure the place will be so soon fit for us since this accident here may a little interrupt the preparations. I cannot think there is any danger lodging at Bucknam's. There will be more at Thetford where I hear the smallpox begins to increase.

With my humble service as due, from your most affectionate
Signed: J[*ohn*] Buxton

150 John Buxton to Robert Buxton [35/150]

Addressed: To Mr Robert Buxton
7 December 1729

Dear Robert,

This will let you know we continue pretty well though the heavines of the weather has somtimes affected me. Last Saturday no messenger went to Norwich so we had no intelligence. Your mother and aunt Herne were both much concerned at your grandmother's death. It is hard to part with old freinds though it is happy for them to be released from their trouble. She has given you £20 for mourning, as much to myself and your mother, and to Sarah, Nancy [*Anne*] and Isabella £500 each, my aunt Herne sole executrix. I am perfectly well satisfied with the disposition she has made for it is the same thing whether kindnesses are done to me or my children. Nanny Mapes has a small legacy of two guineas, and Mis[*s*] Molly Jacob one, being goddaughters; Mrs Wheatly two guineas and a child of Richardson's one.[378] This beside 40s. to the poor of Tibenham, Earsham and Thuxton, and 20s. to Ditchingham,[379] is all she has given from us. She was certainly a very kind parent and a good freind and though she was not always happy in a way of things, yet had always a good intention.

The weather makes the remove to Shadwell very slow but we are every day doing something towards a being there.

I am your most affectionate
Signed: J[*ohn*] B[*uxton*]

You need not speak of what is given to your sisters, only that those three have legacys in general.[380] Your last I received had no date.

[378] Not identified.

[379] Thuxton: a parish on the river Yare, 13 miles west of Norwich; Ditchingham: a parish and village on the river Waveney, 13 miles south-east of Norwich.

[380] The provisions of the will are noteworthy for the absence of any reference to John Buxton's sons, beyond the £20 for Robert Buxton.

151 John Buxton to Robert Buxton [35/152]

Addressed: To Mr Rob[*er*]t Buxton at Mr Marsham's in Stratton [*Strawless*], Norfolk. To be left at Alderman Croshold's, Norwich.
Friday night, Channonz, 12 December 1729

Dear Robert,

A little busines in one of my farms, and the fine weather, together invited me out <to> today on horsback and I find myself much better for it though this, and the consequence of it – a treaty about a little timber – has kept me till now from writing to thank you for your last, and to desire you'l do the same for me to my cosen Marsham for his, since I do not trouble him now with an epistle.

I heard last Tuesday from Laxfield that my sister Han does not get of[*f*] her cold so soon nor so well as they had hopes she would when I heard before from there.

Lord Bacon's[381] works are advertized in the London *Ev*[*ening*?] *Post* to be published as on the 8th inst. I suppose you will write about them to your bookseller and also concerning Thomas's [?] *Hist*[*ory*][382] if you determine that for your present to your coll[*ege*].

Confinement and want of excersise has been very disagreeable but, thank God, I have escaped so well the common illnes that I ought not to complain to this when I add that you have also been free. I bless the great disposer of all things and I am your most affectionate

Signed: J[*ohn*] B[*uxton*]

152 John Buxton to Robert Buxton [35/154]

Addressed: To Mr Rob[*er*]t Buxton. /You have £3 by Abram/
Wednesday, 17 December 1729

Dear Robert,

I went yesterday with your mother and sister Nanny to Shadwell where I left them to make provision against your coming thither, and you are expected on Friday. Your mother will take such care of airing the beds &c. that I hope you'l take no cold in the removal. It will be best that you dine at Attleburgh, so get the longest part of your journy over. From thence you come to Hargham and to Ecclesford[383] and so hither by the Harling towns or fields as you like.

[381] Presumably a new edition of Francis Bacon's (1561–1626) works.

[382] Not identified.

[383] Ecclesford: the parish and village of Eccles on the river Thet, on the road from Thetford, 20 miles south-west of Norwich.

The season has been favourable for planting and I have made some progress in that agreeable work, though the roads makes the transporting trees from hence somewhat difficult.

Your brother Jack is come home in perfect health and with great alacrity in his countenance. Tomorrow I send for your brother from Playford and shall enclose your letter to George which I dare say he will take very kindly from you as he ought. Shall I tell you it gives me the greatest pleasure in the world to see these early beginnings of friendship between brothers. I hope he will never be wanting to pay you that regard and affection you so well deserve from him. Abram brings you the money you desired, half in silver which perhaps is most convenient.

I have not heard since last Tuesday from Laxfield. My sister was then but ill with her cold. Your freinds here continue well and desire their complements to to [*sic*] all those at Stratton. Be perticular in mine to my uncle and aunt and my cosens with repeated thanks for their favours, from your most affectionate

Signed: John Buxton

Appendices

APPENDIX A

A Catalogue of Books[1]

1	[*Elisha*] Coles, Latin Dictionary	London	*[Eighteen editions, 1677–1772]*
2	C[*aii*] Julii Cæsaris Commentarii, a S[*amuel*] Clark[*e*]	Londini[2]	1720
3	Introduction to Latin, by J. Clark	London	1721
4	Latin Common Prayer Book	Londini	1685
5	[*Abel*] Boyer's Royal Dictionary abridged	London	1708
6	Grammaire de [*Claude*] Mauger	London	1714
7	Grammaire de [*Abel*] Boyer	London	1721
8	Le Nouveau Testament	a Amsterdam	1710
9	Les Aventures de Télémaque, [*by François de Salignac de la Mothe Fenelon*]	a Londres	1708
13	Œuvres de Moliere, 4 vols	a Utrecht	1713
15	Œuvres de Racine, 2 vols	a Amsterdam	1709
17	Les Curiosites de Paris, 2 vols	a Paris	1719
19	La Geographie de Robe [?], 2 vols	a la Haye[3]	1704
20	[*Geographia Classica*] The Geography of the Ancients, [*by Herman Moll*]	London	1712
21	The [*New*] Description [*and State*] of England, with maps, [*by Robert Morden and Herman Moll*]	London	1701
22	Advice to a Son, [*by Francis Osborn*]	Oxford	1656
23	The Bible	London	1692
24	The Common Prayer Book	London	1722
25	Don Quixote, vol. 2nd	London	1706
26	Remarks on Italy, by Mr [*Joseph*] Addison	London	1718
27	Fables, by Mr [*John*] Dryden	London	1721
30	Les Commedies de Terence, p[*a*]r M. de Ducier, 3 vols	a Rotterdam	1717

[1] CUL Buxton Papers, 37/30. The list is in more than one hand, with the first clear change after entry 79. It is not dated. The book publication dates (not necessarily those of the first editions) are as given in the original document. They suggest that the list could not have been started before 1723 and could have been completed in 1728. Gaps in the numbering of items are not explained. The citations are presented as in the original document with editorial additions to clarify the identity of the books.

[2] Londini, Londres = London.

[3] La Haye = The Hague (Netherlands).

31	[*Publii*] Terentii Opera, a T. Farnabio [*Thomas Farnaby*]	Londini	1651
32	[*Patrick*] Gordon's Geographical Grammar	London	1702
33	Amusements serieux et comiques, [*by Charles Dufresny*]	a La Haye	1719
34	Incognita; or, Love & Duty Reconciled, nov[*el*] by Mr [*William*] Congreve	London	1713
35	Instructions for Youth, by several hands	London	1722
36	The Polite Gentleman, translated from French	London	1700
37	Gramatica Latina Compendium	Londini	1723
38	Athenian Sport, [*by J. Dunton*]	London	1707
41	Les Œuvres de Rousseau, 3 vols	a Paris	1714
42	Description de Versailles & de Marly	a Paris	1701
43	British Curiosities [*in art and nature, by Samuel Illidge*]	London	1721
44	Antiquities of London & Westminster, [*by Nathan Bailey*]	London	1722
45	Remarks on London, by W. Stowe	London	1722
46	Greek Grammar, by E[*dward*] Leedes	Londini	1720
47	Encomium More [*Erasmus*], translated by S[*i*]r R[*oger*] L'Estrange	London	1722
48	Tully's [*Marcus Tullius Cicero*] Offices, translated by S[*i*]r Ro[*ger*] L'Estrange	London	1680
51	Histoire des Revolutions Romaines, p[*a*]r l'Abbe [*de*] Vertot. 3 vols	a Paris	1720
52	P[*ublii*] Ovid Nas[*onis*], Metamorphoseon in usum Delphini	Oxonii[4]	1696
53	ΤΗΣ ΚΑΙΝΗΣΔΙΑΘΗΚΗΣ, &c	ΚΑΝΤΑΒΡΙΓ[5]	αχέε
54	Lexicon [*Græco-Latinum*], [*George*] Passoris [*Pasor*]	Londini	1644
55	P[*ublii*] Virgilii Maronis Opera ad usum Delphini	Londini	1696
56	A Journey from Aleppo to Jerusalem [*at Easter, AD 1697*], by Henry Maundrell	Oxford	1703
62	The Dramatick Works of Mr [*John*] Dryden in 6 vols	London	1717
64	The Dramatick Works of Mr [*Nicholas*] Rowe, in 2 vols	London	1720
65	Poems & Songs, by Tho[*mas*] Flatman	London	1674
67	Ovid's Metamorphoses, translated by severall hands 2 vols	London	1720
68	Tully's Offices, translated by Nic[*holas*] Grimald	[*London*]	1583
69	P[*ublii*] Virgilii Maronis Opera, Pauli Manutii [*annotationes*]	Le Ouvardiæ [?][6]	1614
70	An Essay on Health, translated from Len. [*Luigi*] Cornaro	Londo[*n*]	1722
71	Introduction to the History of [*the Principal Kingdoms and States of*] Europe, by Sam[*uel*] Puffendorf	London	1706
72	Miscellanea, 1st & 2nd part, by S[*i*]r William Temple, 4th vol.	London	1705

[4] Oxonii = Oxford.

[5] Cambridge.

[6] Le Ouvardiæ [?] = possibly Louvain (Belgium).

73	Miscellanea, 3rd part, by the same [*Temple*], 3rd vol.	London	1701
74	[*An*] Introduction to the History of England, by the same [*Temple*]	London	1695
75	Posthumous Works of Mr John Lock[*e*]	London	1720
79	Œuvres de Nicolas Boileau-Despreaux, 4tre vols	a la Haye	1722
80	Q[*uinti*] Horatii Flacci Opera in usum Delphini	Londini	1699
81	Q[*uinti*] Horatii Flacci Poemata, annot. Johannis Bond, cum D[*ecimus*] Junii Juvenalis et Auli Persii Flacci Satyræ, annot. Tho. Farnabii	Amstelod[*ami*][7]	1648
91	M[*arci*] Tullii Ciceronis Opera, 10 vol.	Amstelod[*ami*]	1659
92	C[*aius*] Sallustius Crispus, cum Vet[erum] Histor[*icum*] Fragmentis	Amstelod[*ami*]	1667
93	Luciani Samosatensis, Dialogi Selecti, Græcé Latiné		
94	M[*arci*] Annæi Lucani Pharsalia, Hugo Grotii et T. Farnabii not.	Amstelod[*ami*]	1665
95	Desid[*erius*] Erasmi, Colloquia	Amstelod[*ami*]	1650
96	Cl[*audii*] Claudiani, Poemata	Amstelod[*ami*]	1630
97	Poems upon severall Occasions, by Edmund Waller Esqr.	London	1712
98	Don Quixote, vol. 3rd, by Don Alonso Fernandez de Avellaneda	London	1705
99	Eacharer's Gazeteer &c.	London	1692
101	The Antiquities of Greece, by John Potter D.D., 2 vols	London	1722
104	Caractères de Théophraste Traduits et les Mœurs de ce Siecle, p[*a*]r M. [*Jean*] de La Bruyere, 3 vols	a Amsterdam	1720
105	Epigrammatum Delectus &c. in usum Scho [*læ*] Etonensis	Londini	1699
106	Biblia Sacra cum Testamento novo	Amsterod[*ami*]	1631
107	The Italian Tutor or a [*new and most*] compleat Italian Grammar, by G[*iovanni*] Torriano	London	1690
108	Epicteti Enchiridion & Cabetis Tabula Græcé & Latiné	Amstelodami	1670
110	T[*iti*] Livii Patavani Histor[iæi] Decad. quæ inpersnnt, tom. 2	Londini	1702
111	Xenophontis de Cyri Institutioni, lib[*er*] octo., Græ[*cé*] Lat[*iné*]	Londini	1720
112	The New Italian Grammar, Signor [*Giovanni*] Veneroni, Eng. Uvedale	London	1711
113	Theatrum Scholasticum in quo &c., Joh[*ann*] He[*inrich*] Alsted	Herbornæ Nassouiorum[8]	1610
114	Epitome Theatri Orteliani [*Abraham Ortelius*]	Antwerpia[9]	1589

7 Amstelodami = Amsterdam.

8 Herbornæ Nassauiorum = Herborn (Germany).

9 Antwerpia = Antwerp (Belgium).

115	Colloquia & Dictio[*naliolum*] Octo Linguarum &c., [*by Noël de Berlemont*]	Amstelodami	1622
116	The Anatomy of the Human Body, abridg[*e*]d by Jam[*es*] Keill M.D.	London	1710
117	Of Education [*especially*] of young Gentlemen, in 2 parts,by Mr [*Obadiah*] Walker	Theatri Oxford	1677
118	Satires of Juvenal & Persius, trans. by [*John*] Dryden & others	London	1713
119	A Treatise of Geography, with a set of maps, by Edw[*ar*]d Wells	London	1717
120	Essay on [*concerning*] Human Understanding, by John Locke Gent.	London	1706
121	Latin & English Dictionary, by Francis Gouldman	Cambridge	1678
122	Thesaurus Græcé Linguæ, Gulielmo [*William*] Robertson	Cantabrigiæ[10]	1676
123	Hudibras, by Samuel Butler	London	1704
125	Petrone Latin et François avec la Cont're Critique de Petrone, 2 tom.		1713
128	Essais de Michel Seign[*éu*]r de Montaigne	a Bruxelles[11]	1659
129	C[*aii*] Suetonii Tranquillii Opera omnia	Oxonii	1676
130	L[*ucius*] A[*nnæus*] Florus Not[*is*] Salmasii Variorum, & L[*ucius*] Ampelius	Amstelodami	1674
131	M[*arci*] Accî Plauti Comœdiæ superst[*ites*] & Fragi Phil. Parei No. 8	Francofurti[12]	1641
132	Isocrates Orat[*iones*]et Epist[*ulæ*], Lat. interpret. H[*ieronymi*] Wolfii	Rothomagi[13]	1662
133	Q[*uinti*] Horatii Flacci Opera	Cantabrigiæ	1701
134	P[*ublii*] Terentii Afri Comœdiæ	Cantabrigiæ	1701
135	P[*ublii*] Virgilii Maronis Opera omnia	Cantabrigiæ	1712
136	Phalaridis Agrigentinorum Tyranni Epist. Græ[*cé*] & Lat[*iné*]	Basileæ[14]	1558
137	Gondibert, an Heroick Poem, by Sir Wil[*lia*]m D'Avenant	London	1651
138	Methodus legendi Hist[*orias*] Civiles et Ecclesiasticas, a Deg[*ory*] Whear	Oxon[*ii*]	1662
139	Hist[*oriæ*] Romanæ Epistomæ ex mus[*æa*], Nic. Blanckardi	Lug[*duni*] Batau[*orum*][15]	1649

10 Cantabrigiæ = Cambridge.

11 Bruxelles = Brussels (Belgium).

12 Francofurti = Frankfurt (Germany).

13 Rothomagi = Rouen (France).

14 Basileæ = Basel (Switzerland).

15 Lugduni Batauorum = Leiden (Netherlands).

140	L[*ucius*] An[*næi*] Senecæ Philosoph[*orum*] Senten[*tiæ*] Morales, Thiol.[?] G. Sylvani	Londini	1696
141	Novum Testamentum Græ[cé] & Lat[iné], inter. The[*odore*] Beza	[*Geneva*]	1566
142	Novum Testamentum	Amstelodami	1670
143	Desid[*erii*] Erasmi Colloquia	Amstelodami	1668
144	L'Annæi Senecæ Tragædiæ, no. 8, Tho[*mæ*] Farnabii	Amstelod[*ami*]	1678
145	Greek Common Prayer	Cambridge	1665
151	History of the Civil War in England, by Edw[*ar*]d [*Hyde*],1st Earl of Clarendon, in 6 vols	Oxford	1707
152	Euclidis Element[*orum*], lib[*ri*] 15, Christo[*p*]horo Clavio	Francofurti	1607
153	Elements of Euclid, trans. from the French of [*C.G. Milliet*] de Chales	Oxford	1700
154	Abridge[*ment*] of S[*i*]r Walt[*er*] Raleigh's History of the World	London	1698
155	Q[*uinti*] Horatii Flacci Poemata, annot. Jo[*annes*] Bond	Amsterod[*ami*]	1670
156	Hugo Grotius De Veritate Religionis Christ[*ianæ*]	Lug[*duni*] Batau[*orum*]	1633
157	Dr [*Gilbert*] Burnet's Travels	Amsterdam	1687
158	Essais &c., by Sir Francis Bacon	London	1606
159	Des[*iderii*] Erasmi de Verb[*orum*] ac Rer. Copia, lib. 2	Londini	1668
160	Connection of the Old & New Testaments p't's by Humph[*rey*] Prideaux	London	1716
161	Memoirs of the 100 years before the Revolution in 1688, by Ja[*mes*] Wellwood M.D.	London	1700
162	C[*aii*] Jul[*ii*] Cæsaris quæ extant, Thiol. Arn[*oldi*] Montani	Lug[*duni*] Batau[*orum*]	1651
163	C. [*Publii*] Cornelius Tacitus	Amstelodami	1649
	et C[*aius*] Suetonius Tranquillus	Amstelodami	1650
164	Abridge[*ment*] of the 3rd vol. of Dr Burnet's Hist[*ory*] of the Reform[*ation*]	London	1719
165	M[*arcus*] T[*ulli*] Ciceronis Epist[*ulæ ad*] Fam[*iliares*], lib. 16	Lugduni [*Batauorum*]	1545
166	Abridge[*ment*] of the 2 1st vols of Dr Burnet's Hist[*ory*] of the Reform[*ation*]	London	1683
167	[*The*] Works of Francis Osborn Esqr.	London	1673
168	Adag[*iorum*] Des[*ideri*] Erasmi Epitome	Amstelod[*ami*]	1663
169	[*Lexicon Tetraglotton,*] An Eng[*lish*] French It[*alian*] Span[*ish*] Dictionary, by Ja[*mes*] Howell Esqr.	London	1660
170	La Bibia	1562	
172	Hugonis Grotii de Jure Belli ac Pacis, lib. 3 in 2 vol.	Amstelædami	1720
173	Selectæ Demosthenis Orationes, Græ[*cé*] & Lat[*iné*]	Londini	1726

174	Abridge[*ment*] of Mr [*John*]Lock[*e*]'s Essay on Hum[*an*] Understanding, by Dr [*John*] Wynne	London	1721
176	Traité du Poëme Epique, par le R[*ené*] P[*ere*] Le Bossu, 2 tom.	a la Haye	1714
177	The Whole Art of the Stage, trans. from the French of Mr [*François Abbé d'Aubignac*] Hedelin	London	1684
178	Dict. Royal Franc. Ang. & Ang. Franc., 2 vol. par Mr [*Abel*] Boyer	Amst[*elodami*]	1727
185	Œuvres de Mr [*Charles de Saint Denis*] de Saint-Evremond, 7 tom.	a Amsterdam	1726
186	Græcæ Grammatices Rudimenta, [*by Richard Busby*]	Londini	1671
196	Histoire L'Angleterre par Mr [*Paul*] Rapin de Thoyras, 10 vol.	a La Haye	1724
197	A Coll[*ection*] of English Proverbs by J[*ohn*] R[*ay*]	Cambridge	1670
198	Euclidis Elementorum lib. prior. 6 11 & 12, ex Vers. Lat. F[*ederico*] Comandino	Oxoniæ	1723
199	Biblia or Summ[*a*]ry of the Old & New Testament	London	1727
200	An Account of the Horrid Conspiracy of the Rye House, [*by Thomas Percival*]	London	1696
201	Q[*uintus*] Horatius Flaccus Notis et Emend[*ationes*], Rich[*ardi*] Bentleii	Amstelæd[*ami*]	1728
204	T[*iti*] Livii Histor[*iarum*] qu[*o*]d extat, 3 vol., cum C[*ar*]. Sigonii &J[*ohannes*] F[*redericus*] Gro[*vonius*], no. 8	Amstelod[*ami*]	1679
206	Gli Auvenimenti di Telemaco 2 vol. trad. dal Franc. p[*a*]r B. L. Moretti	Leiden	1719
208	Dizionario Italiano, per F. Altieri, 2 vol.	London	1726
209	D[*ecimus*] Junni Juvenalis et A[*uli*] Persii Flacci Sat[*yræ*]	Lugd[*uni*] Bat[*auorum*]	1648
210	Paradise Lost, a poem in 12 books by John Milton	London	1725
211	The Principles of the Philosophy [*of the expansive and contractive forces*] &c., by Rob[*er*]t Green M.A.	Cambridge	1727
212	Mathematical Defin. Explic. Propos. &c., by Rich[*ar*]d Laughton D.D.	Cambridge	1727
213	[*Le*] Cuisinier François &c., par [*François Pierre*] le Sr. de la Varenne	a Lyon	1685
214	Racc[*olta*] di Lettere scritte dal S. Card[*inal Guido*] Bentivoglio	Cambrigi[*a*]	1727
224	Œuvres D'Horace Lat[*in*] et en Franç[*ais*] avec des Remarques [*Critiques et Historique*] par Mr [*André*] Dacier, 10 vols	Amsterdam	1727
225	The Craftsman, a Critique on the Times, vol. 1st	London	1727
226	Christof[*ori*] Helvici, Theatr[*um*] Hist[*oricum*] et Chron[*ologicum*], cur[?] J[*ohan*] B[*althasar*] Schuppio	Marpurgi Cattorum[16]	1638

[16] Marpurgi Cattorum = Marburg (Germany).

227	Dictionarium Hist[*oricum*] Geog[*raphicum*] Poeti[*icum*], Car[*olo*] Stephano	Geneva	1627
228	J[*ohannis*] Sleidani de 4 Monarchiis, lib. 3	Cantabrig[i*a*]	1686
229	Several Pieces of Mr J[*ohn*] Locke	London	1720
230	Works of J[*ohn*] Oldham, vol. 1st	London	1722
231	Instructions to a Son, by Archibald [*Campbell*], Marg. [*Master*] of Argyle	London	1689
232	A Voyage into Tartary, by M. Heliog[*enes*] de L'Epy	London	1689
233	Jac[*ques*] Rohault's Physica, Lat. vers., S[*amuel*] Clark[*e*] S. T. P	Londini	1718
234	De Rebus Gestis Lud[*ouici*] 11 & Phil[*ippi*] Cominæi Comment[*arii*]	Argentinæ[17]	1545
235	[*Entretiens sur*] La Pluralité des Mondes, p[*a*]r M. [*Bernard*] de Fontenelle	a Londres	1707
236	Dialogues des Morts, par le meme [*Fontenelle*]	a Amsterdam	
238	D[*ionysii*] Petavii [*Denis Petau*] [*Aurelianensis*] Rationarium Temporum, ad A. D. 1709 continuatu. tom. 2	Lugd[*uni*] Batau[*orum*]	1710
239	A[*n Analytick*] Treatise of Conick Sections, by the Marg. [*Marquis*] de L'Hospital, Eng'd	London	1723
240	Les Voyages de Cyrus &c., par M. [*Andrew Michael*] Ramsay, 2 tom.	a Paris	1727
241	Reflections upon Learning &c., by Mr [*Thomas*] Baker of St John's [*College*] Cam[*bridge*]	London	1727

[17] Argentinæ = Strasbourg (France).

APPENDIX B

A calculation of John Buxton's personal fortune *c*.1710[1]

A valuation of what lands and moneys I have been possest of since I married.

	By descent etc I was worth		I am now worth
	£		£
All Tibenham estate			
Channonz	250		250
Taylor	55		55
Westhaugh	30		30
Bargate	30		30
Manor of Barwell	60		60
Manor of Channonz	15		15
Manor of Aslacton	8		8
Manor of Renshall	40		40
Rushford	270		270
Loddon farm	80		97
Mannor there	10		10
Ersham estate	168		250
Manor Dubbles	5	New purchase at Tibenham	25
Hempnall	38		38
Stratton	48	Aslacton bushes	5
Totals	1007		1183

This at 20 years purchase makes	20,140–0–0	At 20 years purchase
Rec'd of my father Gooch with my		23,660–0–0
wife for portion	3,000–0–0	I paid my sister
and more at his death	1,000–0–0	3,000–0–0
	24,140–0–0	26,660
		24,140
		2,520

[1] CUL Buxton Papers, 37/10.

APPENDIX C

John Buxton's tenants and their rents[1]

Estate account 1710. Income from manors, rents and incidentals:

'Of my own' £1005–11–0
'Of my father' £ 223–00–0

Tenants:	Property	rent £/a
Jonas Phillips	Channonz farm	130
Robert Phillips	The Grange	86
Robert Taylor	Casons in Tibenham	55
John Sewel	Cargate in Tibenham	30
Francis Buxton	Westhaugh lands	30
Charles Slapp	Rushford: farm, cottages and Harling farm	270
Page	Loddon farm	172
George Barber	Earsham	25
Anthony Freston	Earsham	30 then
Thomas Squire		15
William Page	Loddon: Stubb's farm	72
John Wall	Stratton	48
John Roberts	Hempnall	38

[1] CUL Buxton Papers, 124/4 'John Buxton Account Book 1710'.

APPENDIX D

John Buxton's Rent Roll, 1729

A rental of the several rents due to me [*John Buxton*] at Lady Day last for the half year with the arrears to that time.[1]

Tenants names	Rent with arrears[2, 3]
Robert Tayler	30 00 00
William Kemp	26 10 00
John Scutchion	32 10 00
James Blazer	18 00 00
John Briting	15 00 00
more due at Mich. 1728	15 00 00
John Kerridge	10 00 00
Henry Willis	12 00 00
James Lincoln	15 00 00
John Smith	07 00 00
more arrear	07 00 00
John Walpole	04 10 00
Rudledge	02 00 00
more arrears	02 00 00
John Jarmyn	02 00 00
Widow Chapman	01 12 06
Edward Blomfeild	00 12 06
more arrears	01 05 00
Shipley	00 10 00
John Stribbin	40 00 00
Thomas Betts	27 00 00
John Bensley	19 00 00
more arrears one year	38 00 00

1 CUL Buxton Papers, 124/7. The rental is dated 25 March 1729 and is at the back of a book largely concerned with the accounts of Robert John Buxton for the years 1782–89.

2 Other columns in the account list dates and receipts, cash, taxes and quit rents. The tax column is headed 'at 3s in the £', but some of the entries are not consistent with this rate.

3 The annual rental calculated from this table is £1,173 10s.

John Bateman	60	00	00
George Smith	63	10	00
more arrears	63	10	00
more Lady last	63	10	00
Robert Beals	25	00	00
Richard Gent	175	00	00
more one years arrears	350	00	00

APPENDIX E

Country House Visiting

Itinerary of John Buxton's Tour 8–18 May 1720[1]

Huntingdon 8th May
Stilton
Wansford Laid

9th
Burley.[2] Lord Exeter's seat. Most magnificent old house, fine ceilings of Verrio's[3] and a few capital pictures viz *Seneca in the bath*, *The Salutation of the Virgin*, and some of Snider's[4] fowl pieces and some carvings of Gibbons.[5]

Stamford. Burley on the Hill.[6] Lord Winchelsea's, a hansom plain house situ-

[1] CUL Buxton Papers, 122/64.

[2] The great gothic mansion, Burghley House (Cambridgeshire), was begun in 1556 by William Cecil (1520–98), from 1588–72 principal secretary to Queen Elizabeth I. The house was completed about 1587. From 1680 the private and state rooms were remodelled by John Cecil (succ. 1688–d. 1700), fifth Earl of Exeter, in the fashionable baroque style. R. Fedden and J. Kenworthy-Brown, *The Country House Guide* (1979), pp. 91–4.

[3] Antonio Verrio (1639–1707), a Neapolitan painter who settled in England in the early 1670s. He became Court painter in 1684 and after 1688 worked chiefly at Chatsworth and Burghley, where he worked for ten years on the walls and ceilings of the Great Apartment. P. and L. Murray, *A Dictionary of Art and Artists* (Harmondsworth, 1968), p. 431; Fedden, pp. 92–3.

[4] Frans Snyders (1579–1657) was a pupil of Peter Bruegel the Younger. He settled in Antwerp and worked with Rubens on the still-life and animal parts of his pictures. In his own right he painted many hunting scenes and large still-life subjects. Murray, p. 389.

[5] Grinling Gibbons (1648–1721) was appointed Master Carver to the Crown by Charles II. He worked in wood and stone and was strongly influenced by Dutch still-life and flower painters. Accounts survive for payments received for work at Burghley in 1683 and 1685. G. Beard, *Craftsmen and Interior Decoration in England 1660–1820* (1986), p. 260.

[6] Burley-on-the-Hill (Rutland) was built 1694–1708 by Daniel Finch (1647–1730), second Earl of Nottingham and sixth Earl of Winchilsea. He spent about £50,000 on the purchase of the property and more than £30,000 building the house. H.J. Habakkuk, 'Daniel Finch, 2nd Earl of Nottingham: His House and Estate', in J.H. Plumb ed., *Studies in Social History* (1955), pp. 139–178. The house was built on a plateau facing south over the Catmose Vale. To the north, quadrant arms link the main block to two seven-bay pavilions facing each other. From them

ated on an eminence from whence there's a very extensive prospect. A remarkable court with a very fine colonade. Three capital pctures viz a Madona, our Saviour in his infancy, the third unknown.
Grantham.

10[*th*]
Belvoir Castle.[7] Duke of Rutland's. One of the highest situations in England from whence there's a most extensive view and rather unentertaining a very old castle in which there's a most admirable collection of pictures: the Dutch proverbs; a perspective of an Antwerp church; a Madona; Adam and Eve; Venus and the [word?] Herod when presented with the Baptist's head by Herodius' daughter.

Newark. A neat built town with a pretty market place and handsome church.

11[*th*]
Lord Rob[*er*]t Sutton's.[8] An elegant furnished house and the river Trent running at its front and from whence to Nottingham a most delightful ride on a fine verdant mead by the Trent's side, and a prospect from the opposite side of a fine hanging hill covered thick with shrubs.

Nottingham. A handsome and perhaps best situated of any in England. remarkable for its castle built by Cavendish, Duke of Newcastle.[9] A most

them closed colonnades inscribe two vast arcs, joined to yet another pair of pavilions. J. Lees-Milne, *English Country Houses. Baroque 1685–1715* (1970), pp. 112–8.

[7] Belvoir Castle (Leicestershire) crowns a limestone outcrop in the Vale of Belvoir. At the time of the visit it was a seventeenth-century house, the seat of John Manners (1676–1721) second Duke of Rutland. A major rebuilding scheme started in 1801 by John Henry Manners (1778–1857) the fifth Duke, transformed the house into the form known today. Fedden, p. 63–6.

[8] Sir Robert Sutton, second Baron Lexington of Averham (1661–1723). The Suttons' seat at Averham was destroyed by the parliamentarian army during the siege of Newark. By the early eighteenth century they had three properties in Nottinghamshire. Sir Robert was born at Averham Lodge but his house at Kelham was the one seen by John Buxton. His daughter and heiress Bridget married John Manners, third Duke of Rutland, and rebuilt the house in 1729–31. This house burned down in 1857, and was replaced by a large new mansion designed by George Gilbert Scott. M. Girouard, *The Victorian Country House* (New Haven and London, 1979), pp. 224–35.

[9] William Cavendish, first Duke of Nottingham (d. 1676), bought the site of Nottingham's medieval castle in 1663 and from 1674 began to build a palace that in its use of baroque references was unique in England at the time. It was completed in 1679 at a cost of £14,000 and John Vanbrugh altered the interiors in 1719. The building was burned down during the Reform Bill riots in 1831 and rebuilt 1876–8 as a municipal museum of art. Pevsner, *Nottinghamshire*, pp. 225–8.

noble situation, from whence there's one of the most enriched prospects as can be conceived, remarkable for King C[*harles*] setting up his standard.

12[*th*]
Tyton [?].[10] Sir Robert Clifton. A most romantick charming situation unassisted by [*word?*].

Derby. A well situated floroshing town, the first which set up silk mills in England.[11]

Ashdown. A peak town surrounded by immense hills. Okover[12] a seat of Okover Esq: very pleasant situation. There there's a cap[*ital*] picture the subject the Holy family.

Dovedale. A most solemn awfull scene. The river Dove running with a melancholy murmur between two prodigious perpendicular rocks.

16[*th*]
Matlock. A most interesting place.

17[*th*]
The river Derwent running with a most agreeable murmuring at the foot of a rock covered with shrubs. A most delightfull wood on the opposite side. Most prodigious rocks and fruitfull vales. A bath and wells much frequented.[13]

[10] 'Tyton' is probably Clifton Hall, Clifton near Nottingham (Nottinghamshire), the house of Sir Robert Clifton (1690–1762), who succeeded as fifth baronet in 1731. The large Tudor mansion included work by Robert Smythson (d. 1634) and was altered and extended for Sir Gervase Clifton by John Carr (1723–1807) in 1778–97. Pevsner, *Nottinghamshire*, pp. 270–2; Colvin, pp. 224–5 and 904; M. Girouard, *Robert Smythson and the Architecture of the Elizabethan Era* (1966), pp. 197–8; B. Wragg, *The Life and Works of John Carr of York*, ed. G. Worsley (York, 2000), p. 129; Sedgwick, I, p. 560.

[11] Defoe described Derby as a town of gentry rather than trade yet he noticed Thomas Lombe's (1685–1739) silk mill, powered by a water wheel, established in 1719 and possibly the first factory operation in Britain. Defoe, *Tour*, p. 239.

[12] Okeover Hall (Staffordshire), close to the river Dove on the Derbyshire border. The seat of the Okeover family, of Elizabethan or Jacobean origin, was sacked by the Jacobite army as it travelled south in 1745. Leak Okeover then rebuilt the house. The surviving house of three ranges round a courtyard open to the north is partly of the early eighteenth century and partly of 1953–60. Pevsner, *Staffordshire*, pp. 215–6.

[13] Matlock (Derbyshire) was a group of hamlets. At Matlock Bath a lead-lined oak bath was made in 1698. This was replaced by a stone construction before 1725. Pevsner, *Derbyshire*, pp. 272–3.

18[*th*]
Chatsworth, the duke of Devonshire's seat.[14] A grand light building of Sir Chris[*topher*] Wren's situated on the brow of hill, the Derwent running at the bottom. The tops naturally barren but now adorned at great expence and care with fine woods of Scotch firs. The gardens pleasant, remarkable for their cascades and fountains. The apartments grand and well furnished. A great many carvings of Gibbons.

[*Then follows a list of places with no dates or comments*]

Manchester	Wentworth	Harwood Bridge
Rochdale	Rugby	Naisbrough
Repindon	Heath	Ripon
Huddersfield	Wakefield	Burrough Bridge
Barnsley	Leeds	York[15]

[14] Chatsworth (Derbyshire), the seat of William Cavendish (1673–1729) second Duke of Devonshire. Set in what was still desolate Peak country at the time of John Buxton's visit, although newly planted woods were beginning to soften the inhospitable rock, Chatsworth was then a relatively new house. It was built by the first duke of Devonshire between 1685 and 1707 to replace the family's Elizabethan mansion, although this predecessor determined the plan of four fronts around a courtyard. John Buxton's attribution of the house to Wren is incorrect. The architects were William Talman (1650–1719) who worked there 1685–96 and Thomas Archer (*c.* 1668–1743). Lees-Milne, *Country Houses:* Baroque, pp. 70–84; Colvin, pp. 76–77 and 948–53.

[15] The journey from Chatsworth in Derbyshire seemingly continued northwards into

APPENDIX F

Robert Buxton's journey to Oxford, September 1729[1]

Introduction

This brief journal covers a three-week period in the late summer of 1729. At the end of August nineteen-year-old Robert Buxton set out from the family home at Channonz for Cambridge. He dined with his father at Brettenham, fifteen miles into his journey, and then continued to Barton Mills, where he stayed overnight, arriving in Cambridge in the early afternoon of the next day. One week later he left Cambridge and rode some sixty miles to Buckinghamshire, where he met his mother and sisters at Mrs Pigott's Doddershall Hall.[2]

In response perhaps to his father's exhortation to carry a sketchbook in which to record the details of houses of interest,[3] Robert Buxton made notes about the soils, and the man-made landscape, with Camden's great survey *Britannia* in mind, and he listed the country houses that he passed, and described those that he visited. He spent two days in Oxford, a little over thirty miles from Doddershall, visiting colleges and museums and dining with friends.[4] He could write approvingly of medieval buildings but he was especially enthusiastic about the new, in stark contrast to the conservative John Byng, travelling later in the eighteenth century, who wrote: 'I do abominate seeing modern houses, and modern furniture, or entering within the vortex of public places'.[5] And there was much new for Robert to see: Blenheim Palace, the gardens at Stowe, Christ Church Oxford, and the Sheldonian Theatre, in addition to country houses in the latest fashion such as Wotton, were all fresh, indeed some were still under construction.

1 CUL Buxton Papers, 127/6.

2 An excellent account of Buckinghamshire's political and social worlds in Mrs Pigott's time, based upon the letters of the Verney family of Claydon House, is given by Susan E. Whyman, *Sociability and Power in Late Stuart England. The Cultural Worlds of the Verneys 1660–1720* (Oxford, 1999).

3 See letter no.133, p. 153, above.

4 Robert Buxton's statements of distance are unreliable.

5 C. Bruyn Andrews ed., *The Torrington Diaries*, II (1935), p. 39.

Robert Buxton set out for home on 29 September, and the urge or need to keep a journal evaporated. But in a letter of the same date Robert Buxton sent his father an account of the great new gardens at Stowe, thereby completing the record of his tour.

The Journal

Saturday, 30 August 1729

Set out from Channonz. Dined with my father at Bretenham Green Man. Left him and came on to Barton Mills to lodge. Observed at the inn there a neat sort of pavement in the yard, of little round stones gathered in the field at 2d. per bushel and laid by a man at Mildenhal[*l*] for 1s. 6d. per day.

Sunday, 31 August

Got to Cambridge from Barton Mills by 2 a clock.

Monday, 8 September

Set out from Cambridge by 10. At Comberton 4 miles from thence the base of a hansome stone cross. A raised strait road, seeming to be a Roman causeway, runs across from near a large wood of my Lord Bedford's towards Bourn where an old large house of Captain Haggers.[6] A very stiff clay from Cambridge to Gamblingay, then alters to a very light soil of reddish sands. Got to Potton 12 m. by ½ an hour after 1. Open country with a few enclosures. Elm trees chiefly. Baited at the George in Potton, the best inn there. The daubing at Gamblinghay, 2 m. short of Potton, of a redder colour than that in Norfolk and more of sand in it. 10 out of Potton at ½ past four. Through Biggleswade and Shefford, a mile on the right hand of which is a new small built house of Lord Torrington's, the name Southold [*Southill*].[7] Arrived ½ past 7 at Clophill, a small town a mile north of which is Haynes a seat of my

[6] Bourn Hall (Cambridgeshire), a red-brick U-shaped house, was built *c.* 1602 by John Hagar. The house was remodelled in the early nineteenth century by John and John Adey Repton. Burke's and Savills, p. 7.

[7] The Southill (Bedfordshire) estate had been bought by Admiral George Byng (1663–1733), first lord of the admiralty 1727–33, who was created the first baron Southill and viscount Torrington in 1721. J. Hattendorf, 'Byng, George, first Viscount Torrington (1663–1733)', *ODNB*. The small country house seen by Robert Buxton was enlarged, probably by Isaac Ware, around 1750. The 4,300 acre estate was sold in 1795 to Samuel Whitbread (1720–96), founder of the brewery. His son engaged Henry Holland to rebuild the house 1795–1800. A.E. Richardson *et al*, *Southill, a Regency House* (1951).

Lord Carteret's,[8] and a mile and a ½ south is Wrest Park, Duke of Kent's.[9] The soil between Potton and Clophill sometimes light and at others somewhat heavy. The country breaks into agreable risings, having been very flat in Cambridgeshire. Elm trees are the chief also here. Lodged at the Flying Horse at Clophill, an ale house which had good accommodation. N.B. A rind of slate amongst the veins of sand you meet with between Biggleswade and Shefford. Also between Gam[*blin*]gay and Potton you see on the right Sir George Downing's, a new house [*Gamblingay Park*].[10]

Tuesday, 9 September

Set out from Clophill at 8. The country changed to a sort of heath and the road exceedingly heavy sand 2 miles to Amphill, on the right hand of which before you enter the town you see into part of a park belonging to a seat of my Lord Alesbury, now it seems about selling.[11] On the right hand as you go just out from Amphill from you see a park of a house belonging to Lord Fitzwilliam's. A little further you have a prospect of the house which seems old and large and here, though the whole road between Ampthill a[*nd*] Woburn 5 miles is heath or warren and very sandy, it affords on each side very distant and delightful views of a fine country though most distant on the right. As you enter Woburn you see on the left a great deal of tall wood in groves in which the Abbey belonging to the Duke of Bedford.[12] That place seems agre-

[8] Haynes Park (Bedfordshire) was a large square mansion, originally Earl Grenville's and then Lord Cartaret's, with a red-brick west range of 13 bays of *c.* 1720. The house was extended in 1790. Pevsner, *Bedfordshire*, p. 96.

[9] Wrest Park (Bedfordshire), the Grey family seat, was described by Horace Walpole as 'a wretched low bad house built round a small court'. The house was rebuilt on a new site by Earl de Grey in 1834–9 to escape damp mists and 'the cloud of gnats which used to eat us up'. 'Horace Walpole's Journals of Visits to Country Seat, etc.', ed. Paget Toynbee, *Walpole* Society, 16 (1927–8); J. Collett-White, 'Inventories of Bedfordshire Country Houses, 1714–1830', *Publications of the Bedfordshire Historical Record Society*, 74 (1995), pp. 243–51.

[10] Gamblingay Park (Cambridgeshire) was built 1712–13 for Sir George Downing third baronet (1684?-1749). The house had a Baroque facade of three storeys and four pilasters with a cornice crowned with urns. Two single-storeyed wings projected to form a courtyard. The house was demolished in 1776. Burke's and Savills, p. 15.

[11] Houghton House (Bedfordshire), said to have been started *c.* 1615, for Mary, Countess of Pembroke. On her death *c.* 1630 the property passed to Thomas Bruce, first Earl of Elgin, whose son was first Earl of Ailesbury. In 1738 the duke of Bedford bought the house and his son the marquis of Tavistock was there in the 1760s. The house was dismantled in 1794. Pevsner, *Bedfordshire*, p. 40.

[12] The suppressed Cistercian abbey at Woburn (Bedfordshire) was granted in 1547 to John, Lord Russell, later first Earl of Bedford. The house became the principal family seat in 1625, when the house was rebuilt on the old quadrangular plan. John Russell, (1710–71) the fourth

ably situated. In the town of Woburn a new house or two well built. The road from thence to Leighton [*Buzzard*] 4 miles. After a mile of the same as before changes to heavy soil which continues for a mile only, when you go by the side of a great wood. Having left that and the clay you come again into a prodigious sand and disagreable road and continues so to Leig[*h*]ton, the views not so agreable as at Ampthill. Got thither by noon. A fine spire there but more curious small stone market cross, very antique with 5 arches and 5 figures in stone over them. Dined at the Swan in Leighton. Set out from thence with Mrs Lee's coachman for a guide. By 3 in our way to Dodershall Hall[13] nothing very remarkable. A seat of Lord Limerick's near Leighton.[14] The road hilly through an entire champaigne country[15] and the fields a very strong soil, some fine pasture and others plowed. From the highest places you have agreable summer views especially upon the rich vale lying round the town of Alesbury, bounded by Chiltern Hills which seem exceedingly high and run a great way. They show in some part of that a whiteness which I guess to be chalk and from which Camden[16] says they take their name. There is a hard white stone they dig in the fields through which we came, with which they mend the worst part of their roads and I saw 2 or 3 churches I imagined to be built with the same. 3 miles before we came out of Dodershall we descended for some time into the vale of Alesbury which is all a great level of the richest land. You go not far off Winchenden, Lord Wharton's,[17] which makes part of the beauty of the prospect. Arrived well at Dodershall, Mrs Pigot's, a litle after 6.

duke, engaged Henry Flitcroft to remodel the house in the mid eighteenth century and Henry Holland rebuilt the south wing in 1787. R. Fedden and J. Kenworthy-Brown, *The Country House Guide*, (1979), pp. 344–6.

13 Doddershall House (Buckinghamshire). See note 342, p. 153, above.

14 The earldom of Limerick having expired with the death in 1715 without issue of the second earl, Thomas Dongan, this title appears to refer to James Hamilton (*c.* 1691–1758) created Viscount Limerick in 1719 and earl of Clanbrassill in 1756. He married Lady Harriet Bentinck, daughter of the first earl of Portland, in 1728. The titles expired in 1798. *Burke's Peerage*, 106th edition, II (1999), p. 1709; Ingamells, p. 452.

15 Champagne or champion country was an unenclosed landscape of open fields without hedges. O. Rackham, *History of the Countryside* (1986), p. 5.

16 William Camden (1551–1623), historian and pioneer of archaeological research, published his nationwide survey *Britannia* in 1586.

17 Thomas Wharton (1648–1715), first Marquis of Wharton, remodelled and enlarged an old house at Upper Winchendon (Buckinghamshire), surviving fragments suggesting a date of *c.* 1700. The extensive gardens were widely known. The house was demolished in 1758. Pevsner, *Buckinghamshire*, pp. 706–7.

Wednesday, 10 September

Went to the races at Alesbury, a mile north of the town, in coaches, 1 of 6 horses.

Thursday, 11 September

Ditto

Friday, 12 September

Went in the morn[*ing*] to Wotten, a seat of Mr Greenville's,[18] a young gentleman now upon his travels, about 3 miles from Doddershall. The situation not good but very dirty. So much done there as computed to have cost [£]30,000. The tapistry in some of the rooms fine, the wainscotting now out of fashion. The gardens small but altered to the present taste; the offices but small in two wings as in Buckingham House but not joined by a corridore, the passage being underground. A water at the bottom but not equally grand to that at Col[*onel*] Townshends at Rainham, Norf[*olk*].[19] A picture of the Wharton family of Vandike's in Watton and not many more good ones.

Saturday, 13 September

Went in the morn[*ing*] to Lee House,[20] a mile from Dodershall, to see the gardens which are pretty. The house very old and indifferent. 2 or 3 small pictures in a bedchamber with which I was much pleased. Nothing more remarkable.

N.B. You see Blenheim[21] at about 14 miles distance from some part of Lee gardens.

[18] Wotton House (Buckinghamshire) was built 1704–14, by an unknown architect, for Richard Grenville (1678–1728). With its central block connected to two independent pavilions by quadrant walls it was modelled on Buckingham House (London), of 1702–5 by William Winde or William Talman, immediately one of the most imitated houses in England. Pevsner, *Buckinghamshire*, pp. 764–7. Robert Buxton refers to Richard Grenville's son, also Richard (1711–79), who had recently inherited the estate and left Eton in 1729 for a Grand Tour, staying abroad for more than four years. Ingamells, p. 429. The builder's wife, Hester Temple, inherited the Stowe estate, fourteen miles away, in 1749. Wotton then became an alternative residence for the Grenville family that became the marquesses and dukes of Buckingham and Chandos. Fedden and Kenworthy-Brown, pp. 348–9.

[19] Raynham Hall (Norfolk), the seat of the Townshend family.

[20] Presumably a house in Shipton Lee, like Doddershall a hamlet in the parish of Quainton (Buckinghamshire). The Dormer family had a manor house there, demolished in the eighteenth century. Pevsner, *Buckinghamshire*, p. 609.

[21] Blenheim Palace (Oxfordshire). A grand baroque palace built to celebrate the victory at Blenheim of John Churchill (1650–1722), first Duke of Marlborough, over the French and

Tuesday, 16 September

Set out at 10 for Oxford, 12 miles. The country not very agreable. Dirty till we came near Oxford, it then rained and was not able to look about me. Left Col[*onel*] Farrel's Shotover,[22] a new built little place 5 miles short of Oxford, on the right hand. Came to the Angel Inn in Oxford by ¼ after one in the afternoon. Saw the colledges and chapels of Queen's and All Souls, the chapel of the latter exceeding fine.[23] After that went to the theatre, a fine room in which are the pictures of the architect Mr C[*hristopher*] Wren, the founder archbishop Sheldon, and D[*uke*] of Ormond.[24] The manner of the roof curious: the timber all supported by screws. Went from thence to New Coll[*ege*] into the garden and chapel which is something in the manner of King's Coll[*ege*] chapel in Cambridge but nothing near so magnificent.[25] Supped with Mr Pigott (son of Pigott of Shropshire)[26] at Wadham Coll[*ege*], handsomely entertained.

N.B. Miss Pearce,[27] my mother and sisters were our company. Half way on

Bavarians. Built from 1705 to 1725 by Sir John Vanbrugh, with Nicholas Hawksmoor first as his assistant and then from 1722 in charge of the completion of the house. J. Lees-Milne, *English Country Houses. Baroque 1685–1715* (1970), pp. 166–83.

[22] Shotover Park (Oxfordshire) was built from *c.* 1714 to 1718 by James Tyrell who gained the estate in 1701. A tall, narrow house of seven bays with three storeys on the west front and four storeys on the garden side. A formal garden laid out from *c.* 1718 to the 1730s is a rare survival today. Pevsner, *Oxfordshire*, pp. 763–5.

[23] All Souls was founded in 1438 and a new screen was added to its fifteenth-century chapel by Sir James Thornhill in 1713–16. G. Tyack, *Oxford, an architectural guide* (Oxford, 1998), p. 57.

[24] The Sheldonian Theatre was designed as the ceremonial centre of the university. It was one of the first buildings in England to be modelled directly on a classical structure, the U-shaped theatre of Marcellus in Rome, illustrated in the third volume of Serlio's *Architettura* (1540). Tyack, pp. 123–7. Wren's ingenious design for the trussed roof, which without internal columns was intended to imitate an antique theatre open to the sky, was well known to visitors to Oxford. D. Yeomans, *The Architect and the Carpenter* (1992), pp. 27–28.

[25] New College, founded in 1379, served as a model for collegiate architecture in Oxford and elsewhere. Tyack, pp. 39–47. Robert Buxton compared the chapel unfavourably with that of King's College, Cambridge, which took a century to complete from the start of building *c.* 1450.

[26] John Pigott, second son of Robert Pigott of Chetwynd (Shropshire), entered Wadham College and matriculated in 1724 at the age of eighteen. He succeeded to the Pigott's Buckinghamshire property on the death in 1735 of the Buxtons' hostess Mrs Lettice Pigott. Her late husband Thomas (d. 1704) was the last of the Buckinghamshire line of the family. Foster, p. 1116; *The Victoria History of the Counties of England: Buckinghamshire,* IV (1925), p. 96. Robert Buxton's satisfaction with his entertainment at Wadham is consistent with an early-eighteenth-century note of an alleged visitor to Oxford: 'Wad. C. is no less famed for liquor than learning; here 'tis at your option to be a Sot or Scholar, Pot and Book are both Exercised'. Quoted by G. Midgley, *University Life in Eighteenth-Century Oxford* (New Haven and London, 1996), p. 61.

[27] Probably the sister of the architect Edward Lovett Pearce. A cousin of the Pigott's, she

the right we saw Branthall [*Boarstall*], an old castle of the Aubernys [*Auberys*].[28]

Wednesday, 17 September

Went in the morn[*ing*] to Christ Church. Peckwater Court very hansome, one side not yet finished.[29] The hall and kitchen in the old court very good. In the quire a very neat monument, I forget the name of the gentleman who was young. Returned by All Saints church, a very hansome new building after the manner of the new churches at London.[30] Very neat in the inside, the ceiling very fine fretwork by Italians. Dined this day with Dr Hewin.[31] In the afternoon saw the museum: a great many curiositys there. A collection after the manner of the Royal Society. Some small paintings that appear confused to the eye, reflected in a cylinder forms regular pictures.[32] A fine collection of the marbles that seem to describe landscapes, buildings etc. Went this evening to the George at Woodstock where we laid. Good lodging.

shared a maternal grandfather with Mrs Lettice Pigott. E. McParland, *Public Architecture in Ireland 1680–1760* (New Haven and London, 2001), p. 177, refers to a 'short-lived' Mary Pearce. See note 83, p. 23, above.

[28] Boarstall (Buckinghamshire) came to the Aubery family by marriage after 1680; the owner in 1729 was Sir John Aubery (1680–1743), third baronet. The property had allegedly never been sold since the time of Edward the Confessor. By the early nineteenth century only a fourteenth-century gatehouse remained of Boarstall House, garrisoned by royalists in the Civil War, changing hands several times until finally controlled by parliamentarians in 1646. The village and its church were destroyed. *Burke's Peerage and Baronetage*, 106th edn (1999), p. 141; S. Porter, *Destruction in the English Civil Wars* (Stroud, 1997), p. 134.

[29] Peckwater quadrangle in Christ Church was part of the largest classical building scheme in Oxford, begun in the seventeenth-century. It was designed in 1707–14 by Dean Henry Aldrich and three sides were complete by 1711. The fourth side was not built until 1761. Tyack, pp. 142–3.

[30] All Saints Church, now the library of Lincoln College, was classically inspired to the designs of Dean Henry Aldrich, and built 1700–10 after the tower of the medieval church had collapsed. Tyack, pp. 145–8.

[31] Not identified.

[32] The old Ashmolean museum, of 1679–83, open to the public from the start, displayed the collection of scientific and other curiosities of Elias Ashmole (1617–92). Robert Buxton saw an anamorphoscope, a device employing a cylindrical mirror by which a distorted picture was made to appear normal. J. Baltrusaitis, *Anamorphic Art* (Cambridge, 1977), pp. 131–58. The old museum was replaced in the 1840s by a new building designed by Charles Robert Cockerell (1788–1863). The original building now houses the Museum of the History of Science. Tyack, pp. 127–9.

Thursday, 18 September

Walked at 8 to view Blenheim through the triumphal gate leading out of Woodstock town into the park, which is walled round. This grand gate is built after the Roman manner, finished by Sarah, the Duchess Dowager of Marlborough, to the memory of the duke her husband.[33] It has one large arch for carriages and 2 small ones on each side, and it has the finest effect possible, and coming out of it you see Blenheim to the best advantage with the bridge, the lake lately enlarged, and the new erected pillar at ½ a mile distance from the house.

Tuesday, 23 September

Went in the afternoon to see Winchendon, lately Duke Wharton's, purchased by the trustees of money left by the D[*uke*] of Marlborough to buy estate for the present Marquiss of Blandford.[34] The park agreable though situate in a very deep dirt full of many sorts of trees of some growth, and broken into hills and vales. Half a fine walk of elm trees run through it from the back front of the house, in length a mile and a quarter. The gardens pleasant, the ironwork in them very good, an elm curtain walk 300 yards long, the finest ewe hedge I ever saw, some good statues in stone. The house plaister work, few good pictures left and stript of all its other furniture; 3 or 4 fine inlaid tables. Cloisters of limes before the house have a pretty effect. A good prospect from the house being situate pretty high.

Monday, 29 September

Set out between 8 and 9 from Doddershall, Alesbury 5 miles, Wendover 3, and Great Missenden 3. Dined there, the country a strong clay till Wendover then alters to a chalk rising up the Chilterns. Alesbury but an indifferent town, one large church and town house designed by Sir J[*ohn*] Vanbrugh in a pretty

[33] See note 21, p. 192, above. The triumphal arch leading into the park from the western end of Woodstock town was built by Nicholas Hawksmoor in 1723. Vanbrugh's bridge crossed three canals created from the small river Glyme. A larger lake was established later in the eighteenth century by Lancelot Brown. The fluted column of victory bearing the effigy of the first duke was raised by the architect Henry Herbert, Earl of Pembroke. Lees-Milne, *Country Houses: Baroque*, pp. 170–4.

[34] See note 17, p. 191, above.

[35] Aylesbury Town, now County Hall, was begun in 1722. Plans were submitted by Thomas Harris and Mr Brandon in 1720 and judged by Sir John Vanbrugh. The design by Harris was accepted and it is not known if Vanbrugh altered them. Work was suspended between 1724 and 1737 for lack of funds but clearly enough had been built in the first two years to attract Robert Buxton's attention. Pevsner, *Buckinghamshire*, p. 153.

good stile.[35] Just out of Alesbury left a house of Lady Dashwood's;[36] on the left in [*Great*] Missenden a large house built with flint of Fleetwood Esq.[37] The country is broken by the Chiltern Hills which are set thick with great groves of beech which make agreable prospects. The views are more distant into a fine country as you come near Beaconsfield, 6 miles, within a miles of which you go by Mrs Waller.[38] Lodged at the King's Head. Ewe tree near this inn 30 ft high.

The journal, written in a small notebook, ends here. In a letter dated Monday 29 September 1729 to his father,[39] written from Doddershall, Robert Buxton describes a visit he made to Stowe. He continued the letter from London, outlining the plans for the family's journey home.

Dear Sir,

I begin this from this place with an intent to finish it at London where we hope to be on Wednesday. I writ last Thursday a line or two to let you know we have fixed upon going that way and that we continued well as, thank God, we all do still. We went that day to see Lord Cobham's gardens at Stowe.[40] They excel any I have yet seen and indeed can't be imagined as beautiful as they are. They are not exceeding large but laid out in the most agreable manner and I may say almost filled with small (in comparison I mean with those at Rome etc. from whence they seem to be taken) edifices of different

[36] Lady Dashwood's house has not been identified. West Wycombe, the creation of Sir Francis Dashwood (1708–71), was not near Aylesbury. Pevsner, *Buckinghamshire*, pp. 727–41.

[37] Missenden Abbey was suppressed in 1538 and adapted as a residence. William Fleetwood bought the property in 1574 and the first major conversion work was done *c.* 1600. The Fleetwoods sold in 1787. Pevsner, *Buckinghamshire*, pp. 351–5.

[38] The Waller family moved from Kent to Buckinghamshire *c.* 1500 and for most of the seventeenth and eighteenth centuries owned three estates close to Beaconsfield: Hall Barn, Wilton Park, and Gregories, their main seat. Hall Barn was a house of the second half of the seventeenth century; Gregories a grand baroque mansion by Thomas Milner, enlarged in the late eighteenth century and burned down in 1813; Wilton Park was an old house remodelled in the later eighteenth century and again in 1803–5. The last-named house was close to the road Robert Buxton would have taken. Pevsner, *Buckinghamshire*, pp. 168, 171 and 176.

[39] CUL Buxton Papers, 105/86. Written on the same sheet is a letter from Anne Buxton to her husband and a second letter from Robert Buxton, completed in London.

[40] The gardens at Stowe (Buckinghamshire) were laid out for Sir Richard Temple, later Viscount Cobham (1669?-1749). Buildings by Sir John Vanbrugh, within a garden designed by Charles Bridgeman, were completed in the period 1715–24. After Vanbrugh's death in 1726, William Kent and James Gibbs designed more buildings. The gardens were repeatedly extended and remodelled for half a century. G. Worsley, *Classical Architecture in Britain. The Heroic Age* (New Haven and London, 1995), pp. 215–6.

kinds: temples, oblisks, pavilions etc. They were all designed and executed by Sir John Vanbrugh except 2 which are now just finished by Gibbs and are published amongst his designs for pavilions, as he calls them, in gardens.[41] The materials the greatest part of them are built with is stone. They are most of 'em in too good a taste not to appear to be copys in small of publick buildings in Italy that have been or still remain there. What pleased me most was a pyramid of stone exactly in the manner of the great ones in Egypt, 63 foot perpendicular height, 40 square and a room within 20 cube. An inscription in Latin upon the outside tells us 'Lord Cobham dedicates this pyramid as sacred to the memory of Sir J. Vanbrugh who designed this as many other edifices in these gardens.' The effect this building has is as agreable as 'tis hard to be described, something exceedingly ancient and religious in its look with great strength and beauty.

Miss Pearce was so kind to go along with us and was assistant to us in pointing out many beautys in this place we might have otherwise overlooked. We could not help wishing you with us when she told us Captain Pearce said they were the finest he had seen in Europe.[42] The owner whom we saw creeping at middle age in a manner [*?word*] could but just walk, sensibly affected me. The fatal damage [*?word*] great debauches in youth, which not fine gardens [*?word*] after recover. But how well is it ordered that we all have it in our power to be happy, that is by following temperance, which is virtue.

There came hither last Friday Lady Conway and her two daughters.[43] The former is a widow and seems an agreeable woman. No relation of Mrs Pigot, I believe their stay won't be very long. We will procure some beech mast though it is not so plentifull in the Chiltern Hills in this county this year as it used to be. I have also mentioned to Miss Pearce what you ordered me concerning the designs you intend sending the captain.[44]

London. Wednesday night 1 October 1729

We arrived here safe this afternoon between 3 and 4, having found the roads very good, and no other molestation. The greatest pleasure we have had since

[41] James Gibbs (1682–1754), *A book of architecture, containing designs of buildings and ornaments* (1728).

[42] Captain Pearce was the architect Edward Lovett Pearce. He visited Italy in 1723–4. Ingamells, p. 750. See note 83, p. 23, above.

[43] Lady Conway, daughter of Richard Grenville of Wotton Underwood, (Buckinghamshire), was the second wife of Sir John Conway (d. 1721), second and last baronet of Bodrythan. There were no sons of the marriage. See note 18, p. 192, above. J. Burke and J.B. Burke, *A Genealogical and Heraldic History of the Extinct and Dormant Baronetcies of England, Ireland and Scotland*, sec. edn (1844), p. 127.

[44] See letter no. 138, p. 158, for John Buxton's request.

we came was your kind letter of last Monday, received an hour after we had been here. We are glad to hear you all continue so well, and my mother hopes to find my grandmother better. We are all very well, and my sister my mother says is now a good deal better than at the beginning of the journey, though at once for a little while she was worse than she used to be. We are all much delighted at the good account of my dear sister Isabella as well of her health as her changing disposition.

This is Thursday evening and my mother bids me tell you she intends setting out tomorrow, not purposing to make less than four days of the journey. I had laid out Chesterford[45] for the lodging place the 2nd night having account of its being two easy stages from hence and knowing of good accommodation there. The first place we have not yet fixed upon. I have room to say no more than with wishes for a happy meeting to us all. I am, dear Sir, your most obedient and affectionate son,

Signed: R. Buxton

[45] Chesterford (Essex), a village on the main road from London to Cambridge, on the Cambridgeshire border, some forty-five miles from London. Robert Buxton expected the party to travel twenty to twenty-five miles a day.

APPENDIX G

Robert Marsham's Tour Through England in 1730

Introduction

Robert Marsham, Robert Buxton's cousin and contemporary at Clare Hall, with three companions, journeyed through England and Wales in the summer of 1730.[1] They travelled north-west, taking in grand houses such as Woburn, Blenheim and Chatsworth, and marvelling at the 'mountainous' Peak District, so different from lowland England from whence they came. Robert Marsham and his companion Henry Partridge wrote letters to Robert Buxton describing the places they visited. The letters are reproduced below.

Robert Marsham to Robert Buxton [106/6]

Addressed: To Mr Robert Buxton Esq at Channonz near New Buckenham in Norfolk
By London post
Stafford. 24 July 1730

Dear Buxton,

As you were better to me than your promise in writing a very agreeable letter to me since our disagreeable parting I will not stay till I come to Norfolk before I thank you for it, and as I have little to say, I will give you an account of our journey hither.

[1] For Robert Marsham see note 143, p. 81, above. Henry Partridge (1711–1793) was the son of Henry Partridge of Buckenham House (Norfolk). He was admitted fellow commoner at Clare Hall in 1728. He pursued a legal career, being called to the bar in 1731. Venn, part I, vol. III, p. 315. The younger Molesworth was seemingly Hender Molesworth (1709–1733), second son of Sir John Molesworth (1668–1723) third baronet of Pencarrow (Cornwall). He was admitted fellow commoner at Clare Hall in 1728 and the Middle Temple in the same year. The senior Molesworth of the party could have been Hender's elder brother John (1705–66), who succeeded his father as fourth baronet. Venn, part I, vol. III, p. 197; *Burke's Peerage and Baronetage*, 106th edn (1999), p. 1956.

Partridge and the two Molesworths are with me. Partridge and young Molesworth and I met senior Molesworth at Buckingham in his jorney from London and we from Cam[*bridge*] on Sunday last, but we did not come there till [word?] in the morning having lost our way. We saw duke of Kent's gardens at Wrest[2] as we went to Bucking[*ham*] and had a view of duke of Bedford's house at Woobarn [*Woburn*][3] as we past by. The pavilion in duke of Kent's garden is vastly pretty; the gardens 110 acres as the gardener says and good agreeable having some good canals in them. The Monday we saw Lord Cobham's house and gardens[4] and went that night to Oxford where we did not arrive till near 10 at night. Wednesday in the afternoon we left that seminary of learning and journeyed to Woodstock: saw Blenheim.[5] I shall say nothing of these 3 last places because I am assured you know much more of them than I do. Only tell you that the first did more than answer my expectation and the 2 latter did not come up to it.

We went that night to a town 6 miles beyond Blenheim where we were forced in by the night coming upon us before we expected and found but 2 beds in the house and such fare as you never have met with, nor I hope ever will, but we must take travelers' luck. The next day we went on for Warwick but I must tell you that the farther part of Oxfordshire is the finest prospect I ever saw. We saw into part of Glocestershire and Worcestershire and the mountains so high that we could see the top of them above the clouds that skimmed along the valley. We dined at Warwick and saw the castle[6] which is a charming old house being 6 rooms in a string and all very well furnished. The hall was 66 by 36, the parlor 48 by 26. The other 4 rooms made up in all 240 feet if I paid [*attention*] right.

Then we rode on for Coventry but by the way we saw a fine new house of Lord Lee's.[7] It is 185 by 63, the principal floor up some steps. The rooms 15

[2] See note 9, p. 190, above.

[3] See note 12, p. 190, above.

[4] See note 40, p. 196, above.

[5] See note 21, p. 192, above.

[6] In 1604 James I granted Warwick Castle, then in a state of disrepair, to Fulke Greville (created Lord Brooke in 1621), and he began the conversion of the castle into a country residence. When the fourth Lord Brooke succeeded in 1658 the buildings again needed repair and from 1669 to 1678 he created a grand state apartment, the doors in the sequence of rooms being aligned in an *enfilade* in the latest French fashion. G. Tyack, *Warwickshire Country Houses* (Chichester, 1994), pp. 200–8.

[7] Lord Lee was George Henry Lee (1690–1743), second earl of Lichfield, son of Sir Edward Henry Lee (d. 1716), fifth baronet of Quarendon (Buckinghamshire), who was created viscount Quarendon and earl of Lichfield in 1674. The title expired with the death of the third earl in 1776. George Lee built Ditchley House (Oxfordshire) in 1720–26 with work on the interior

[*feet high*], the chamber 14, the attick 10. 15 windows in front built of stone and the front light and pretty. The hall and 2 rooms on each side the hall is about 50 x 28 if I paid right and goes up two storys but very poorly furnished the whole house. Thence we went to Coventry which was not far and came there by 9, and this morning, after having seen the church[8] (as all people do when they are in a new town) and then the cross, we left it by 6 a clock and rid through a very delightfull country, except the shineyness of the roads, 20 miles to Litchfield where we dined and also saw the cathedral,[9] and thence to Ingstring (if I spell right) Lord Chetwynd's house,[10] and saw the gardens which are vastly charming and would have been much more so if we had not seen Lord Cobham's. But these have beauties his have not, that is a grove of the finest oaks I have ever seen, not excepting Raynham. They are about 50 acres and kept very neat. There is not a gravel walk in the whole gardens. The pavilion in them is very handsom and so large that my lord lodges there sometimes.

Thence we came to Stafford though it was late, first from whence this comes to you and desire you to excuse the long and dire account I have made. Tomorrow morning we intend to set out early for Chester. I don't know the day I shall return to Cam[*bridge*] nor then the day I shall leave it for Norfolk, so I will not give you the trouble of coming to Shadwell to meet me, I shall see

continuing until the 1750s. The architect was James Gibbs (1682–1754). Robert Marsham saw a new large house, the full extent of the central block and office pavilions being nearly 350 feet. His disappointment with the interior reflected its unfinished state. C. Hussey, *English Country Houses. Early Georgian 1715–1760* (1955), pp. 66–71; Colvin. p. 693.

8 Robert Marsham refers to St Michael's church, not then a cathedral. The city's original cathedral had fallen into decay after the suppression of its parent Benedictine community in 1539 and the transfer of the see to Lichfield. St Michael's was designated a cathedral in 1918 when the diocese of Coventry was recreated. It was destroyed during an air raid in 1940. Pevsner, *Warwickshire*, pp. 250–2.

9 A see was established at Lichfield in the seventh century and a succession of buildings culminated in a gothic cathedral begun in 1195. The cathedral was severely damaged during the Civil War and the spire collapsed in 1646. Marsham saw the cathedral as restored in the 1660s. Its modern form is the result of work by James Wyatt (1746–1813) in 1788–95, Sydney Smirke (1798–1877) in 1842–6, and the restoration of 1857–1901 by Sir George Gilbert Scott (1811–78) and his son John Oldrid Scott (1841–1913). Pevsner, *Staffordshire*, pp. 174–89.

10 Ingestre Hall (Staffordshire), the seat of Walter Chetwynd (1678–1736), created viscount Chetwynd of Bearhaven, Co. Kerry, in 1717. The house, noted for its very grand entrance front, was built in 1613 by Sir Walter Chetwynd (d. 1638) on the site of an earlier manor house. The house became the seat of a cadet branch of the Talbots (Chetwyn-Talbots from 1784, when created earls Talbot), created earl of Shrewsbury in 1856. The house was altered by John Nash (1752–1835) in 1808–10 for the second earl Talbot, and rebuilt after a fire in 1882. Pevsner, *Staffordshire*, pp. 154–7.

you with infinite pleasure at Stratton [*Strawless*], at Shadwell or Channonz soon after.

Dear Sir, yours R[*obert*] M[*arsham*]
excuse [*word?*]

My humble service to all you know. This scheeme is seen at Lord's [*sentence incomplete*]
The people with me send service to you.

Henry Partridge to Robert Buxton [106/7]

Addressed: To Mr R. Buxton at Channonz near New Buckenham in Norfolk
Clare Hall. 2 August 1730

Dear Sir,

I return your many thanks for the favour of yours which I found here last night at my return home. We were all much more pleased than tired with our journey which has been extremely to our satisfaction. As Mr Marsham wrote to you from Stafford I shall say nothing of what adventures we met with before that time and shall give you a short but lamė account of what we have seen since.

I suppose he gave you our opinions of Lord Cobham's and Lord Chetwynd's gardens. We reached Chester yesterday was sennight: it is a large old-fashioned town and has this remarkable in it that you go up one pair of stairs to the shops before which there is a covered gallery which the upper part of the houses jut over. Here you may walk the whole length of the streets free from rain or sun but this contrivance darkens the houses which have all a narrow front to the street but go a great way in depth. In this town the neighbouring gentlemen have houses which they come to in the winter like London, and here there are plays, assemblys &c. as in London.

From hence we took a trip into Flintshire and saw a fine spring there called Holywell[11] which the superstitious people here imagine to have as much virtue in curing distempers as the famous pool of Bethesda, which they attribute to the miraculous influence of St Winifrede. Here we dined, had a Welsh

[11] The spring at Holywell (Flintshire) owed its supposedly curative powers to a legend of the seventh century concerning the death of a local maiden Winefride at the hands of a chieftain whose advances she had rejected. D. Defoe, *A Tour through the whole Island of Great Britain*, ed. P.N. Furbank, W.R. Owens and A.J. Coulson (New Haven and London, 1991), p. 199. Holywell was likened by Partridge to the Pool of Bethesda in Jerusalem, where the sick waited for the moving of the waters so they could be healed. John, ch. 5, v. 2–4.

harp playing to us and drank health to all our friends in England. I went down a lead mine in Wales, 70 yards deep. Our way home was through Derbyshire where we saw some of what they call the wonders of the peak.[12]

Chatsworth is a charming place and the more so in that it stands in the most desert mountainous country that ever was. I could have no idea of such mountains had I not seen them myself. The clouds are upon the tops of them. Chatsworth is a noble house: no doubt but you have seen it in *Vitruvius Britannicus.*[13] The cielings are most of them painted. The chappel is the most compleat thing I ever saw in that way. The gardens are 133 acres cut out of a solid rock and in them great plenty of curious waterworks. One fountain throws water 100 feet high. There is a cascade by which the water rolls down a hill, 99 feet perpendicular, by 23 falls in 212 yards in length. But as for the particulars of this place and Lord Exeter's at Burleigh House by Stamford I cannot pretend to give you an account in a letter but must defer them till I am so happy as to have the performance of your promise to spend some time with us at Cambridge which I hope will be very soon, and which I shall now begin to expect every day.

All friends send their complements by this from your humble servant

Signed: H. Partridge

Marsham goes through to Stratton in a day so cannot dine with you. Pray excuse this scrawl for I fear I shall not save the post.

[12] The term 'wonders of the peak' was inspired first by Thomas Hobbes' (1588–1679) Latin poem *De Mirabilibus Pecci: Concerning the Wonders of the Peak,* published in 1636 and, secondly, by Charles Cotton's (1630–1687) poem *Wonders of the Peak,* published in 1681. The latter was the first successful guide book to the region and described seven curiosities, including caverns, wells and Chatsworth House.

[13] C. Campbell, *Vitruvius Britannicus,* I (1715), pls 72–6; II (1725), pls 67–8.

Index

Note: Page references in *italics* indicate illustrations. References of the form '131 (n.272)' indicate a footnote on page 131. Reference '117 & n.232' indicates a reference to text and a footnote on that page. Books and authors mentioned in letters have been indexed but not the books listed in Appendix A.